THE SEDUCTION THEORY
IN ITS SECOND CENTURY

Committee of Psychoanalytic Psychotherapeutic Publications and Organizations

Monograph I

Arnold D. Richards, M.D.

Book Series Editor

THE SEDUCTION THEORY

In Its Second Century

Trauma, Fantasy, and Reality Today

Edited with an
Introduction and Postscript by

Michael I. Good, M.D.

International Universities Press, Inc.
Madison, Connecticut

Library of Congress Cataloging-in-Publication Data

The seduction theory in its second century : trauma, fantasy, and reality today / edited with an introduction and postscript by Michael I. Good.
     p. cm.—(Committee of Psychoanalytic Psychotherapeutic Publications and Organizations ; monograph 1)
  Includes bibliographical references and index.
  ISBN 0-8236-6035-4
  1. Seduction–Psychological aspects—Congresses. 2. Psychoanalysis—Congresses. 3. Sexually abused children—Mental health—Congresses. 4. Child sexual abuse—Congresses. 5. Fantasy—Congresses. 6. Freud, Sigmund, 1856–1939—Congresses. I. Good, Michael I. II. Series.

BF637.S36S433 2006
150.19′5—dc22

                                        2003067629

Manufactured in the United States of America

Contents

Series Editor's Foreword   ix
     Arnold D. Richards, M.D.
Preface and Acknowledgments   xiii
Contributors   xvii

Editor's Introduction
The Roots of the Seduction Theory:
     A Perspective from Genesis to Scientia Sexualis   3
     Michael I. Good, M.D.

Part I
What Is the Seduction Hypothesis?
Why Are We Talking About It Today?

Introduction
Chair: *Owen Renik, M.D.*   43

1. The Seductions of History: Sexual Trauma in Freud's
   Theory and Historiography   45
   George J. Makari, M.D.
2. The Ambiguity of Seduction in the Development of
   Freud's Thinking   65
   Jay Greenberg, Ph.D.

Discussion of "What Is the Seduction Hypothesis? Why Are
   We Talking About It Today?"   77
   Helen C. Meyers, M.D.
On Literal Misreadings and Reconstructed Truths   85
   Henry F. Smith, M.D.

General Discussion and Audience Questions   97

Part II
Analysts at Work with Patients
Whose Lives Are Characterized by
the Traumas of Everyday Life

Introduction
Chair: *Arnold M. Cooper, M.D.*   111

3. Trauma and Pathogenesis   117
   Jacob A. Arlow, M.D.
4. Psychological Trauma of Everyday Life   129
   Scott Dowling, M.D.
5. What Happened Matters, and What Really Happened
   Really Matters   141
   Marylou Lionells, Ph.D.
6. Traumas of Everyday Life: A Self Psychological
   Perspective on the Neuroses   157
   Anna Ornstein, M.D.

Discussion: Analysts at Work with Patients Whose Lives Are
    Characterized by the Traumas of Everyday Life   173
        Robert Michels, M.D.

General Discussion   181

Part III
Analysts at Work with Severely Traumatized Patients

Introduction: The Analytic Aims in the Treatment
of Severely Traumatized Patients
Chair: *Leon Hoffman, M.D.*   191

7. Living the Experience of Childhood Seduction: A Brief
    Account of an Unusual Psychoanalysis   199
        Peter Fonagy, Ph.D.
8. A View of Severely Traumatized Patients—Soul
    Murder Victims   213
        Leonard Shengold, M.D.

Discussion of Papers by Fonagy and Shengold   227
        Glen O. Gabbard, M.D.

General Discussion   237

Part IV
Concluding Papers

Introduction
Chair: *Arnold Rothstein, M.D.*   243

9. Freud and the Seduction Hypothesis   245
        Steven J. Ellman, Ph.D.
10. The Seduction Hypothesis Axis: What's External, What's
    Internal, and What's in Between?   263
        Stephen A. Mitchell, Ph.D.

Postscript

The Seduction Theory: A Leitmotif in the Evolution of
    Psychoanalytic Theory, But Is It a Testable Hypothesis?   281
       Michael I. Good, M.D.

Name Index   305
Subject Index   311

Series Editor's Foreword

Arnold D. Richards, M.D.

The history of psychoanalysis is in part a history of splits, but this collection of papers and discussions, and the symposium at which they were initially presented, represent a different dynamic, one of coming together rather than coming apart.

Let me try to offer some historical context. In 1912, Freud wrote to his student, Lou Andreas-Salomé, "We found ourselves obligated to break off all contact between Adler's splinter group and our own, and even our medical guests are asked to choose between one or the other" (Pfeiffer, 1966, p. 8). On April 29, 1941, the New York Psychoanalytic Institute voted to demote Karen Horney from training analyst status to lecturer. She, along with Clara Thompson and three others, walked out of the meeting and subsequently resigned from the society (Hale, 1995, pp. 143–144). The story goes, perhaps true, perhaps apocryphal, that she and her group left the building and marched down West 86th Street singing, "Go Down, Moses, Let My People Go!" Horney and her group founded the American Association for the Advancement of Psychoanalysis (AAAP) later on in 1941, but that group came apart. In 1943 Clara Thompson, Eric Fromm, and others left the

AAAP to start the William Alanson White (WAW) Institute. In 1953, Thompson, Horney, Fromm, and others were threatened with expulsion from the American Psychoanalytic Association (APsaA) for training in unauthorized institutes (the AAAP, the WAW, and the Flower and Fifth Avenue Institute), and at one point the APsaA attempted to have the WAW enjoined from using the term *psychoanalysis* in its name or literature (Hale, 1995, pp. 219–220; Mosher & Richards, 2004).

In the decades that followed, the APsaA maintained a policy of excluding nonphysicians from training and non-APsaA institutions from membership in the International Psychoanalytical Association (IPA). In 1987, as a result of a lawsuit, the APsaA reversed its policy on training, and four institutes (now affiliated with each other as the Independent Psychoanalytic Societies [IPS]) were admitted to the IPA. This brings us to 1998, when this symposium was held. It was the first meeting jointly sponsored by the APsaA, the IPS, and the WAW Institute. Indeed a ''coming together,'' it was, I believe, the first time in the history of psychoanalysis that psychoanalysts and psychoanalytic organizations of these diverse orientations—Freudian, Sullivanian, classical, interpersonal, and self psychological—had collaborated in the planning of a substantive scientific meeting. It is also noteworthy that the impetus for this conference came from psychoanalytic journals rather than psychoanalytic organizations.

At the symposium I was pleased to offer a welcome not only from myself as Editor of the *Journal of the American Psychoanalytic Association* but also on behalf of Jay Greenberg as Editor of *Contemporary Psychoanalysis;* Owen Renik as Editor of *The Psychoanalytic Quarterly;* and Arnold Cooper as North American Editor of *The International Journal of Psycho-Analysis,* all of whom participated in the program and contributed to this volume, as well as Albert Solnit as Editor of *The Psychoanalytic Study of the Child,* who could not join us. These editors represented the five journals linked together on the Psychoanalytic Electronic Publishing (PEP) CD-ROM, a scientific enterprise that has already significantly affected the level of intertheoretical scientific discourse in psychoanalysis. The premise of the symposium was that science and search engines transcend our organizational divisions. The journals and the participants do not stand on common theoretical ground. We have Freudian, relational, interpersonal, and self psychological contributors, but we share a common cause—the advancing of psychoanalytic scholarship regardless of organizational or theoretical commitments.

Our model for scholarship is one in which we look for solid ground in the delineation of the historical development of core concepts. The first panel, which was chaired by Owen Renik of the San Francisco Psychoanalytic Institute, provides the opportunity to view history through prisms provided for us by two colleagues trained in two psychoanalytic traditions: Jay Greenberg of the William Alanson White Institute and George Makari of the Columbia Center for Psychoanalytic Training and Research, whose founding member, Sándor Radó, was also part of a coming apart—a split from the New York Psychoanalytic Institute in 1942, one year after Horney and Thompson resigned. Helen Meyers of the Columbia Center for Psychoanalytic Training and Research and Harry Smith of the Psychoanalytic Institute of New England, East, discuss the presenters' papers. In the second panel, chaired by Arnold Cooper of the Columbia Center, we look to the clinical situation for further definitional clarification and conceptual relevance. The papers are by Jacob Arlow of the New York Psychoanalytic Institute, Scott Dowling of the Cleveland Psychoanalytic Institute, Marylou Lionells of the William Alanson White Institute, and Anna Ornstein of the Psychoanalytic Institute of New England, East. Robert Michels of the Columbia Center discusses the papers. History is important, but of even greater importance is what this has to do with what each of us does in our office. The third panel, chaired by Leon Hoffman of the New York Psychoanalytic Institute, brings us further along on this clinical exploration, with papers by Peter Fonagy of the British Psycho-Analytical Society and Leonard Shengold of the New York Psychoanalytic Institute, with a discussion by Glen Gabbard of the Houston/Galveston Psychoanalytic Institute. Finally, in the fourth and concluding panel, chaired by Arnold Rothstein of the New York Psychoanalytic Institute, we explore the similarities and differences in theory and technique which derive from our topic and which reflect our diverse traditions. The summarizing discussions are by Steven Ellman of the Psychoanalytic Institute for Training and Research and the late Stephen Mitchell of the William Alanson White Institute. Our aim is to achieve an atmosphere of ''freedom and open exchange.'' I think we all agree that it is such an atmosphere which will assure the vitality of our common psychoanalytic enterprise.

Several closing notes: First, I want to thank the organizing committee, Arnold Rothstein, Arnold Cooper, Carolyn Ellman, Lawrence Friedman, Glen Gabbard, Jay Greenberg, Leon Hoffman, Ruth Imber, Muriel Laskin, Laurie Levinson, Nadine Levinson, Marylou Lionells, George Makari, Owen Renik, Judith Schachter, Henry Smith, Albert Solnit, Barbara Stimmell, and Phyllis Tyson; and our conference organizers, Lawrence Schwartz Partners, who manned the phones, maintained the database, produced the badges, and took care of the many other tasks that need to be addressed in order to make such meetings happen. I also want to thank the audience for attending the symposium. There were over 570 people, not counting those who registered at the door, from six different countries, including Norway, Mexico, and all across the United States. It was a diverse professional group—psychoanalysts, psychologists, social workers, and other mental health professionals and academicians.

Let the discourse begin!

REFERENCES

Hale, N. G. (1995), *The Rise and Crisis of Psychoanalysis in the United States: Freud and the Americans, 1917–1985 (Volume II).* New York: Oxford University Press.

Mosher, P. W., Richards, A. D. (2004), The history of membership certification in the American Psychoanalytic Association: Old demons, new debates. (unpublished manuscript).

Pfeiffer, E., Ed. (1966), *Sigmund Freud and Lou Andreas-Salomé Letters.* tr. W. & E. Robson-Scott. New York: W. W. Norton.

Preface and Acknowledgments

A scientific symposium, "The Seduction Hypothesis One Hundred Years Later: Trauma, Fantasy, and Reality Today," was held in New York City on February 28 through March 2, 1998. It was sponsored by the six journals of the Psychoanalytic Electronic Publishing (PEP) CD-ROM project (*Contemporary Psychoanalysis, The International Journal of Psycho-Analysis, The International Review of Psycho-Analysis, Journal of the American Psychoanalytic Association [JAPA], The Psychoanalytic Quarterly,* and *The Psychoanalytic Study of the Child*), the American Psychoanalytic Association, the British Psychoanalytical Institute, the William Alanson White Institute, and the Independent Psychoanalytic Societies, with support from the American Psychoanalytic Foundation, International Universities Press, and the Psychoanalytic Connection. The event, the result of a *JAPA* initiative to bring psychoanalytic perspectives to both a broader professional audience and to the general public, was chaired by *JAPA* editor Arnold Richards, with Arnold Rothstein as program chair.

The topic of the seduction theory has had a renaissance. During the time that I was in psychiatric training in the early 1970s at the Massachusetts Mental Health Center in Boston and in psychoanalytic training starting later that decade at the Psychoanalytic Institute of New England, East, the ferment brought about by more recent reconsiderations of the seduction hypothesis had not yet begun in earnest. Inferences about early seduction or abuse were less on many clinicians' minds then than is the case today. In my experience at that time, however, teachers and supervisors with a psychoanalytic perspective did not automatically doubt patients' reports of sexual molestation or simply call it "fantasy." While some analysts tended to overemphasize what was believed to be the patient's fantasy, and did not clearly distinguish between fantasy and psychic reality (Meissner, 2000), a number of them were quite ready either to suspect unfortunate and untoward sexual or abusive experience through reconstructive inference, even without patients reporting or recalling such experience, or to take the patient's report of sexual molestation or incest at face value. In addition, in my experience during child psychiatric training, the visible reality of environmental factors impinging upon unfolding development took on an immediacy that brought into relief the issues of nature and nurture, including trauma and constitutional factors. Various types of child psychic trauma, including seduction, were a part of the landscape for those evaluating and treating children and adolescents, even if the psychiatric, psychological, and psychoanalytic literature on seduction and abuse was less plentiful in decades past than it has become. Even so, ambiguity about what is actual and what is fantasy—based on the productions of both children and the adults in their lives—is a challenge now as it was then, in ways that reflect the origins of psychoanalysis. In that sense, psychoanalysis is a means of seeking to understand the (at times convoluted) vicissitudes of individual experience (e.g., Good, 1994a,b).

Since the early 1980s, psychoanalysis has refocused to a considerable degree on seduction and trauma. It is as if we have been gearing up for the centenary of Freud's initial effort to come to grips with the issues of psychic reality and actuality. From the perspective of the seduction hypothesis, the evolution of psychoanalysis over the past century to the point at which we currently understand trauma, fantasy, and reality in psychoanalytic terms is the focus of this volume.

There are many who have contributed directly and indirectly to this volume. I wish to express particular thanks to Arnold Richards for his energetic and integrative capacity in bringing together both people and ideas and for his support and confidence in my pursuing this editing project; to the contributors for their superlative clinical and scholarly work and their cooperation in submitting their manuscripts for editing; to Lawrence and Tamar Schwarz for original copies of manuscripts and discussion typescripts; and to the editorial staff of International Universities Press for their generous spirit and assiduous copy editing necessary to getting this volume to press. I am particularly appreciative of Margaret Emery, Ph.D., Editor-in-Chief of International Universities Press, for her enthusiasm, generosity, and support. I am also grateful to the innumerable individuals, including teachers, supervisors, colleagues, and patients, who have taught me over the years and continue to do so. Last but not least, my wife and daughters have offered enduring patience and sustenance during the time demanded by this endeavor. To them all I express my continuing gratitude.

Appreciation is also due to *The International Journal of Psycho-Analysis* for permission to reprint the paper by George Makari, M.D., "The Seductions of History: Sexual Trauma in Freud's Theory and Historiography" (1998; 79:857–869), which appears here with only slight changes, and the paper by Peter Fonagy, Ph.D., "Living the Experience of Childhood Seduction: A Brief Account of an Unusual Psychoanalysis," which was included in an article coauthored by Mary Target entitled "Playing with Reality: III. The Persistence of Dual Psychic Reality in Borderline Patients"(2000; 81:853–873); *Contemporary Psychoanalysis,* which published the paper by Jay Greenberg entitled "The Ambiguity of Seduction in the Development of Freud's Thinking" (2001: 37:417–426); the *Canadian Journal of Psychoanalysis* for permission to reprint sections quoted from James McLaughlin's 1996 paper "Through the Patient's Looking-Glass: Reflections Upon the Analyst's Self-Inquiry" (4:205–229); Simon & Schuster Adult Publishing Group for permission to reprint portions quoted from Primo Levi's *The Drowned and the Saved* (translated from the Italian into English by Raymond Rosenthal, copyright 1988); and to Yale University Press for permission to reproduce sections from Leonard Shengold's *Soul Murder Revisited: Thoughts about Therapy, Hate, Love, and Memory* (1999) in his paper entitled "A View of Severely Trauma-tized Patients—Soul Murder Victims." Appreciation and acknowledg-ment of copyright permission also go to the Artists Rights Society (ARS) in New York and Société des Auteurs Dans les Art Graphique et Plastique (ADAGP), Paris, on behalf of the estate of Marc Chagall (1887–1985) for permission to reproduce his painting *Le Paradis,* and to Réunion des Musées Nationaux/Art Resource, New York, for pro-viding a high resolution digital copy of the photograph by Gérard Blot. The original painting is found in the Musée National Message Biblique Marc Chagall, Nice. For this volume, the painting is reproduced as representing the "first seduction" and its aftermath.

REFERENCES

Good, M. I. (1994a), The reconstruction of early childhood trauma: Fantasy, reality, and verification. *J. Amer. Psychoanal. Assn.,* 42:79–101.
——— (1994b), Differential constructions of trauma in cases of suspected child sexual molestation. *The Psychoanalytic Study of the Child,* 49:434–464. New Haven, CT: Yale University Press.
Meissner, W. W. (2000), Reflections on psychic reality. *Internat. J. Psycho-Anal.,* 81:1117–1138.

Contributors

Jacob A. Arlow, M.D., is Training Analyst Emeritus, New York Psychoanalytic Institute; Clinical Professor of Psychiatry, New York University College of Medicine; Past President, American Psychoanalytic Association; former Editor-in-Chief, *The Psychoanalytic Quarterly*. He has written numerous books and articles on the theory and practice of psychoanalysis. He is on the editorial board of *Neuro-Psychoanalysis*.

Arnold M. Cooper, M.D., is Training and Supervising Analyst, Columbia University Center for Psychoanalytic Training and Research; Professor of Psychiatry, Cornell University Medical College; Past President, American Psychoanalytic Association; Past Vice President and North American Secretary, International Psychoanalytical Association; former North American Editor, *The International Journal of Psycho-Analysis*; former Deputy Editor, *The American Journal of Psychiatry*.

Scott Dowling, M.D., is Training and Supervising Analyst, Cleveland Psychoanalytic Society and Institute; Associate Clinical Professor of Child Psychiatry, Case Western Reserve University; Coeditor, *The Psychoanalytic Study of the Child;* author of numerous articles on infant development and adult and child psychoanalysis.

Steven J. Ellman, Ph.D., is President, the Independent Psychoanalytic Societies of the U.S.A.; Past President and Training Analyst, Institute for Psychoanalytic Training and Research (IPTAR); Professor and Supervisor, New York University Postdoctoral Program in Psychoanalysis; and editor or co-editor of a number of books on psychoanalysis and related areas.

Peter Fonagy, Ph.D., is Training and Supervising Analyst, British Psycho-Analytical Society; Freud Memorial Professor of Psychoanalysis and Director of the Sub-Department of Clinical Health Psychology, University College London; Director of Research, Anna Freud Centre, London; Director, Child and Family Center, Menninger Foundation; Vice President, International Psychoanalytical Association; past Chair, Standing Committee on Research; member, Executive Council, World Association of Infant Mental Health. He is on the editorial boards of a number of journals, including the *The International Journal of Psycho-Analysis, Psychological Issues,* and the *Bulletin of the Menninger Clinic*; and has authored or edited numerous psychoanalytic books.

Glen O. Gabbard, M.D., is Professor of Psychiatry, Baylor College of Medicine; Training and Supervising Analyst, Houston/Galveston Psychoanalytic Institute; Joint Editor-in-Chief and North American Editor, *The International Journal of Psycho-Analysis*; former Associate Editor, *Journal of the American Psychoanalytic Association;* former editorial board member, *Psychoanalytic Inquiry, Psychoanalytic Dialogues* and *The Psychoanalytic Quarterly*; and is author or editor of many volumes on psychiatry and psychoanalysis.

Michael I. Good, M.D., is a Faculty Member, Psychoanalytic Institute of New England, East; Associate Clinical Professor of Psychiatry, Harvard Medical School. He has published psychoanalytic articles on the seduction theory, sexual trauma, differential constructions of trauma, memory and suggestibility, and screen reconstruction. His paper "False Memories, Negative Affects, and Psychic Reality: The Role of Extra-Clinical Data in Psychoanalysis" (with Max Day and Eve Rowell) was awarded the Cesare Sacerdoti Prize for 1999 at the Congress of the International Psychoanalytical Association, Santiago, Chile.

Jay Greenberg, Ph.D., is Training and Supervising Analyst, William Alanson White Institute; Faculty and Supervisor, New York University Postdoctoral Program in Psychoanalysis and Psychotherapy; member, North American Editorial Board, *The International Journal of Psycho-Analysis;* Former Editor, *Contemporary Psychoanalysis*; and author or co-author of psychoanalytic books.

Leon Hoffman, M.D., is Training and Supervising Analyst, New York Psychoanalytic Institute; Codirector, Bernard L. Pacella, M.D., Parent–Child Center, New York Psychoanalytic Society; Chair, Committee on Public Information of the American Psychoanalytic Association; Instructor, Mount Sinai School of Medicine; and is an Associate Editor of the *Journal of the American Psychoanalytic Association.*

Marylou Lionells, Ph.D., is Training and Supervising Analyst, and former Director, William Alanson White institute; Faculty member, Colorado Center for Psychoanalytic Studies, the Northwest Center for Psychoanalysis, and the Minneapolis Institute for Psychoanalysis; and co-editor of the *Handbook of Interpersonal Psychoanalysis.*

George J. Makari, M.D., is Director, Institute for the History of Psychiatry; Associate Professor of Psychiatry, Weill Medical College, Cornell University; Faculty, Center for Psychoanalytic Training and Research, Columbia University; and is on the editorial boards of *The International Journal of Psycho-Analysis, American Imago,* and the *Journal of the History of the Behavioral Sciences.* He is in private practice in New York City.

Helen C. Meyers, M.D., is Clinical Professor of Psychiatry, Columbia University, Department of Psychiatry; Training and Supervising

Analyst, Columbia Psychoanalytic Center for Training and Research; Vice President, International Psychoanalytical Association; and is on the editorial boards of the *Journal of the American Psychoanalytic Association* and the *Journal of Clinical Psychoanalysis.*

Robert Michels, M.D., is Walsh McDermott University Professor of Medicine, Cornell University; University Professor of Psychiatry, Weill Medical College of Cornell University; Training Analyst and member, Executive Committee, Columbia University Center for Psychoanalytic Training and Research. He is or has been a member of several editorial boards, including *The American Journal of Psychiatry, The New England Journal of Medicine, Journal of the American Psychoanalytic Association, Psychiatry, The International Journal of Psycho-Analysis, The Psychoanalytic Quarterly, The American Journal of Drug and Alcohol Abuse,* and *The Journal of Psychotherapy Practice and Research.*

Stephen A. Mitchell, Ph.D., was Director and Supervising Analyst, William Alanson White Institute. He was a Faculty member there and at the New York University Postdoctoral Program in Psychoanalysis. A founding editor of *Psychoanalytic Dialogues,* he was author of *Relational Concepts in Psychoanalysis: An Integration, Relationality: From Attachment to Intersubjectivity* and *Freud and Beyond: A History of Modern Psychoanalytic Thought* (with Margaret Black), coauthor of *Object Relations in Psychoanalytic Theory* (with Jay Greenberg), and author of numerous articles on relational concepts and object relations in psychoanalysis. Dr. Mitchell died suddenly and unexpectedly on December 21, 2000.

Anna Ornstein, M.D., is Supervising Analyst, Cincinnati Psychoanalytic Institute, Professor Emerita of Child Psychiatry, University of Cincinnati; Lecturer on Psychiatry, Harvard Medical School; Faculty member, Psychoanalytic Institute of New England, East; Clinical Associate Professor, Smith College School for Social Work; Codirector, International Center for the Study of Psychoanalytic Self-Psychology; and is on the editorial boards of *Psychoanalytic Inquiry* and several other journals.

Owen Renik, M.D., is Training and Supervising Analyst, San Francisco Psychoanalytic Institute; Associate Clinical Professor, Department of Psychiatry, University of California, San Francisco; former Editor-in-Chief, *The Psychoanalytic Quarterly;* Coeditor of *Psychoanalytic Inquiry;* Consulting Editor, *The Journal of Applied Psychoanalysis;* former Chair, Program Committee of the American Psychoanalytic Association.

Arnold D. Richards, M.D., is Training and Supervising Analyst, New York Psychoanalytic Institute; former Editor, *Journal of the American Psychoanalytic Association*, and co-editor of numerous psychoanalytic books.

Arnold Rothstein, M.D., is Training and Supervising Analyst, New York Psychoanalytic Institute; Clinical Professor of Psychiatry, Mt. Sinai Medical School; former Editor, Workshop Series of the American Psychoanalytic Association, and author or co-author of many books on psychoanalytic subjects.

Leonard Shengold, M.D., is Training Analyst and former Director, Downstate (later N.Y.U.) Psychoanalytic Institute; Clinical Professor of Psychiatry, New York University School of Medicine, and author of numerous psychoanalytic books.

Henry F. Smith, M.D., is Training and Supervising Analyst, Psychoanalytic Institute of New England, East; member, Boston Psychoanalytic Society and Institute; Faculty member, Massachusetts Institute for Psychoanalysis; Editor-in-Chief, *The Psychoanalytic Quarterly;* former Associate Editor, *Journal of the American Psychoanalytic Association.*

Editor's Introduction

The Roots of the Seduction Theory: A Perspective from Genesis to Scientia Sexualis

Michael I. Good, M.D.

> And the eyes of them both were opened, and they knew that they were naked. . . .
> And the woman said, The serpent beguiled me, and I did eat [Genesis 3:7, 13].

> "It sounds like a scientific fairy tale." And this, after one has demonstrated to them the solution of a more-than-thousand-year-old problem, a *caput Nili* [source of the Nile] [Freud, quoted in Masson, 1985, p. 184].

Freud's seduction hypothesis[1] was first communicated in his correspondence with Wilhelm Fliess (Masson, 1985, pp. 141, 144 [October

---

[1] As delineated by Blass and Simon (1994), between the years 1892 and 1898 Freud maintained four etiological theories of neurosis involving seduction, all of which different authors at different times have referred to as *the* "seduction theory." Freud himself did not use the term *seduction theory*, which Blass and Simon attribute to Kris in 1954. Kris actually had also referred

3

8 and 15, 1895]) and was subsequently published in 1896. He enunciated the proposition and his excitement about it as follows:

> I therefore put forward the thesis that at the bottom of every case of
> hysteria there are *one or more occurrences of premature sexual experi-
> ence*, occurrences which belong to the earliest years of childhood but
> which can be reproduced through the work of psycho-analysis in spite
> of the intervening decades. I believe that this is an important finding, the
> discovery of a *caput Nili* in neuropathology [Freud, 1896c, p. 203; see
> also 1896a,b; Masson, 1985, p. 184 (April 26, 1896)].

The seduction theory constitutes a nodal point in human intellectual history. However, it did not arise entirely ex nihilo. Precursors in
its chronicle extend back more than a millennium. This introduction
is intended to serve as an overview of the multifaceted prehistory of
Freud's seduction thesis, which, as this volume illustrates, still rever-
berates within psychoanalysis. Although the history of psychoanalysis
has been described in a number of works (e.g., Jones, 1953; Andersson, 1962; Stewart, 1967; Ellenberger, 1970; Levin, 1978; Fine, 1979;
Gelfand and Kerr, 1992; May, 1999; Geyskens, 2001), this introduction focuses more specifically on the evolution of ideas and issues
leading to the seduction hypothesis itself. Although not the only strand
in the history of psychoanalysis, the seduction thesis was seminal in
its development.

PARADISE INTERRUPTED

One of the earliest representations of seduction and its traumatic aftermath can be found at least as far back as the sixth century B.C.E. in the

---

to the "seduction hypothesis" (1950a,b). These variations in the seduction hypothesis reflect
how Freud's ideas were evolving and how he was struggling with confusing and emotionally
charged data. On the one hand, it could be said that the "hypothesis" never actually became a
"theory" in the sense of a formulation that was to some degree verified. In a sense, it was an
educated, creative speculation about a deterministic, universal proposition regarding the cause
of hysteria. The facts of seduction constituted clinical observations that Freud initially made
into clinical generalizations (e.g., Waelder, 1962). On the other hand, as expressed by Laplanche
and Pontalis (1973), "To speak of a *theory* of seduction is to do more than simply acknowledge
that these sexual scenes have an outstanding aetiological function as compared with other traumas: For Freud, this preponderance became the basic assumption of a highly detailed attempt
to explain the origins of the mechanism of repression" (p. 405). In that vein, Freud sought to
justify theoretically the connection he had discovered among sexuality, trauma, and defense
(Laplanche and Pontalis, 1968).

story of Genesis (*Holy Bible*; Armstrong, 1996). Taken as myth, the story of Adam and Eve in the Garden of Eden condenses a great deal about primal themes in the collective human psyche. Myths are largely the residues of fantasies of whole peoples and represent the conflicts and strivings of early humankind (Freud, 1908; Abraham, 1909; Hacker, 1964). Thus, in Lévi-Strauss's words, they concern "the unconscious nature of collective phenomena" (Leach, 1970, p. 59). The story of Genesis can be viewed as expressing a primal fantasy about our origins and early developmental experience. The pivotal human event in that story is a seduction. Consequently, seduction may be seen as playing a major role in the psychic residue of early experience. Given the sorrow and pain that Adam and Eve came to bear in being banished from Paradise, Genesis may also be viewed as an allegory about the origin of neurosis.

It therefore is conceivable that Freud would have made use of the Biblical seduction story, at least in its metaphoric sense, in his concerted investigation of the etiology of neurosis. In his autobiographical study (1925), Freud wrote: "My deep engrossment in the Bible story (almost as soon as I had learnt the art of reading) had, as I recognized much later, an enduring effect upon the direction of my interest" (p. 8). Freud was well versed in the Old Testament and steeped in knowledge of the antiquities, including those of Greece and Egypt (Fine, 1979). In particular, he identified with the Biblical characters of Joseph (the interpreter of dreams) and Moses, whom he wrote about in "The Moses of Michelangelo" (1914b) and *Moses and Monotheism* (1939) (Shengold, 1979; McGrath, 1986; Gay, 1988, pp. 314–317; Blum, 1991). In all his published writings, however, Freud referred to "Paradise" only sparingly (Ginsburg and Ginsburg, 1992). In his letter of July 12, 1883, to his fiancée, Martha Bernays, he mentioned John Milton's writings (Freud, 1883a), and in his letter to her on August 28, 1883, he quoted directly from Milton's *Paradise Lost* (Freud, 1883b). He also listed *Paradise Lost* as the first of two "favourite books" (1907, p. 235). And in his letter of December 17, 1911, to Jung (McGuire, 1974), he noted the interpretive possibility that the story of Eden distorts an original myth through reversal—as can happen in dreams. Rather than being created from Adam, Eve is his mother. And rather than the woman giving the man an agent of fruitfulness (pomegranate), the story reverses a familiar old marriage rite in which the man gives the woman a fruit to eat. In its unreversed version, as Freud saw it, the story more clearly concerns the well-known motif of mother incest with guilt and punishment.

Freud ultimately contemplated his own "Paradise Lost" through his self-analysis. This endeavor included a disguised autobiographical screen memory, the reconstruction of which involved the fantasized defloration of a younger niece (1899, p. 311) that paralleled the story of Adam and Eve (Lehmann, 1966; Ginsburg and Ginsburg, 1992).

THE UTERUS, THE NERVOUS SYSTEM, AND EARLY IMPRINTS OF SHOCK

Subsequent to the writing of the Bible, the prescientific exposition of the notion that sexuality and seduction are related to neurosis is obscure. However, the idea that a breach of a taboo is related to functional disorders has a long history, and, as in the Garden of Eden, not infrequently involved forbidden foods. Remedies and healing techniques for these disorders have included confession, exorcism, condoned gratification of frustration, and versions of hypnotism, which have been practiced for centuries (Ellenberger, 1970). As nomenclature and notions of causation evolved, one type of ancient disorder came to be known as *hysteria*. It became a prototype for creative explanation of disturbance in mind and body. Something akin to hysteria was identified 4000 years ago in ancient Egypt (Veith, 1965; cf. King, 1993).[2] Even then, the uterus was assumed to cause disturbance, an idea accepted by the Greeks, whose term for this condition has continued into modern times. While Hippocrates (c. 460–c. 377 B.C.E.) believed that in hysteria the uterus migrated through the body (a mechanism for conversion symptoms), the Greco-Roman physician Claudius Galen (c. 129–c. 210) presaged more modern discharge theories. He hypothesized that the uterus did not literally wander but rather that symptoms were the consequence of a substance (analogous to semen) that an unmarried or widowed woman could not dispel from her uterus due to her celibacy and that affected various body parts. This notion

---

[2] Briquet went so far as to state that hysteria has been known since the dawn of civilization ("L'hystérie est connue depuis qu'il existe une civilisation" [1859, p. 1]).

was analogous to the ancient humoral theory of diseases that predominated in the West well into the seventeenth and eighteenth centuries (Drinka, 1984). Freud, moreover, like the imaginative Berlin physician Wilhelm Fliess (1858–1928), maintained a version of this theory when he repeatedly argued that endogenous "sexual toxins" played a key role in the physiology of the neuroses (Levin, 1978, pp. 184–191; Eissler, 2001, pp. 48–64).

The Galenic tradition, however, was opposed by the French physician Charles Lepois, more commonly known as Carolus Piso (1563–1633), in a book published in 1618. He claimed unequivocally that hysteria could affect both men and women, an observation tentatively made by Galen and by the Greek physician Aretaeus of Cappadocia (c. 30–90). The British physicians Thomas Willis (1622–1675) and Thomas Sydenham (1624–1689) also opposed the Galenic view and considered hysteria to be due to a disorder of the nerves and brain. They originated the concept of "nervous disease" and thus marked the emergence of the "modern view" in the study and classification of nervous conditions (López Piñero, 1963, pp. 2–4; Veith, 1965).

Pertinent to clinical developments in the nineteenth century, in 1649 René Descartes (1596–1650) described in *Les Passions de l'Âme*, his last and most important psychological contribution, how traumatic events could affect behavior well after those events were forgotten (Perry and Laurence, 1984; Wozniak, 1992):

> It is not difficult, for example, to think that some people's unusual aversions, which make them unable to tolerate the smell of roses or the presence of a cat or similar things, come only from having been badly shocked by some such objects at the beginning of life, or from having sympathetically felt the sensation of their mother who was shocked by them while pregnant. . . . The smell of roses may have given a child a severe headache when he was still in the cradle, or a cat may have frightened him badly, without anyone having been aware of it and without him having had any memory of it afterwards, though the idea of the Aversion he had then for the roses or the cat may remain imprinted in his brain to the end of his life [Descartes, 1649, p. 91].

Descartes thus anticipated by some 240 years the work of Charcot, Janet, Breuer, and Freud on unconscious fixed ideas or repression.

THE ENLIGHTENMENT AND ANIMAL MAGNETISM

Beginning with the Enlightenment, evolving ideas about the relationship between seduction and psychopathology resulted from advances in three areas: the medical use of hypnosis, wider recognition of psychic trauma, and scientific attempts to understand hysteria. The notion that sexual factors play a dynamic role in neurosis stemmed from ideas and inquiries extending back more than 200 years. With the evolution of hypnotism came a gradual recognition of the role of sexual and traumatic factors in hysteria. As described by Ellenberger (1970) in his encyclopedic work, *The Discovery of the Unconscious: The History and Evolution of Dynamic Psychiatry*, efforts toward the development of scientific theory and therapy for the manifestations of mental conditions emerged in about 1775 with Franz Anton Mesmer (1734–1815) and evolved over the succeeding 100 years through the time of Jean-Martin Charcot (1825–1893) at the Hôpital du Salpétrière. Hypnosis has been linked to sex and seduction at least since its origins as mesmerism. Mesmer's work reflected the thinking of the Enlightenment, the emergence of dynamic psychiatry, and the decline of exorcism with its ties to religious belief. In turn, the technique of hypnosis was a central feature in Charcot's attempts to understand hysteria and subsequently also played a pivotal role in Pierre Janet's (1859–1947) and Sigmund Freud's (1856–1939) studies of psychopathology and the unconscious. In addition to the role of hypnosis, a crucial step in understanding the cause of neurosis was the recognition of the role of psychic shock, which came into focus as a result of train accidents following the growth of railways across Europe beginning in the mid-nineteenth century (Drinka, 1984, pp. 112, 114).

Prior to Mesmer there had been little in the way of coherent theory and method for treating neurotic conditions in the Western world other than the nonmedical practice of exorcism. Indeed, the German philosopher Arthur Schopenhauer (1788–1860) noted that "Animal Magnetism is the most momentous (*inhaltsschwer*) discovery ever made, even if, for the time being, it brings more enigmas than it solves" (quoted in Ellenberger, 1970, p. 159). Others since then, certainly including Freud, have attempted to solve versions of this enigma.

Mesmer, who completed his medical studies in Vienna in 1766, developed what he considered to be a scientific (although pseudoscientific by today's standards) theory and approach to *animal magnetism* (his own term for his discovery) that appeared to have diagnostic and therapeutic value. His practice thrived, but not without controversy. In 1777 he treated a blind young pianist, Maria-Theresa von Paradies, using magnetic therapy that partially restored her sight. However, rumors spread that the young woman had developed an excessively strong attachment to Mesmer, and a commission investigating his methods concluded that animal magnetism was a public menace. Thereupon he was enjoined to stop what was considered a fraudulent practice (Tatar, 1978, p. 11). Consequently, Mesmer decided to leave Vienna. Arriving in Paris in 1778, Mesmer had posited the existence of an invisible fluid that surrounded and permeated all bodies, analogous to the "fluid" or "ether" medium through which planets attracted one another by gravity, another kind of extraordinary and invisible force whereby two bodies act upon each other. Indeed, vitalistic theories of the day considered health to be a state of fluidic or ethereal harmony between the individual microcosm and the celestial macrocosm (Darnton, 1968, p. 14).

Mesmeric (hypnotic) sleep could be induced by having the subject stare at a fixed or slightly moving point, known as the technique of fascination, a method already known to the ancient Egyptians and to the German humanistic mystic, Heinrich Cornelius Agrippa (1486–1535) (Ellenberger, 1970, p. 114), who studied medicine and law, and among his activities, defended women accused of witchcraft, many of whom had signs of hysteria. Mesmer maintained that sickness resulted from an "obstacle" to the flow of this magnetic fluid in the body, which could be remedied by "mesmerizing" or massaging the body's "poles" and inducing a "crisis" of epilepticlike convulsions or somnambulistic trances that supposedly restored equilibrium and health (Darnton, 1968, p. 4; Tatar, 1978).

RAPPORT, SEXUAL EXCITATION, AND SEDUCTION

It was Mesmer who identified the need for rapport between magnetizer and patient (Ellenberger, 1970, p. 102; Crabtree, 1993, especially pp.

89–105). Remarkably, the French noun *rapport* means *contact* or *connection*, and in the plural it means *intercourse*. The mesmerists would sit with the patient's knees enclosed between their own and run their fingers all over the patient's body. As part of establishing rapport, they sought to locate the poles of small magnets that comprised the great magnet of the body as a whole, concentrating on the body's "equator" at the hypochondria on the sides of the upper abdomen just below the ribs. As noted by Darnton (1968, p. 4), this practice stimulated gossip about "sexual magnetism." One can readily imagine the erotically stimulating effect such magically medical "laying-on of the hands" had on the patients being mesmerized.

Rapport came to be recognized as the central phenomenon in magnetism, with an influence that extended beyond the actual séance. Elaborating on rapport as a concept, Armand-Marie-Jacques de Chastenet, the Marquis de Puységur (1751–1825), considered it to be a psychological phenomenon that was the channel for what was, in effect, its psychotherapeutic action. Puységur recognized that the curative agent was not a physical fluid but rather the magnetizer's will, or suggestive influence (Ellenberger, 1970, pp. 70–74, 102; Good, 1996). His emphasis on the mysteries of psychological elements served to replace animal magnetism with personal magnetism. He also replaced physical contact with verbal commands (Tatar, 1978, pp. 29–30).

Soon the reciprocal influence between the patient and the magnetizer was included within the concept of rapport. The effects of mutual suggestion developing between magnetizer and magnetized included such feats as reading with eyes covered, discerning others' thoughts, finding lost objects, and even predicting the future (Ellenberger, 1970, p. 117). Of note is the fact that early magnetizers warned of the danger inherent in the powerful interpersonal attraction issuing from this rapport (p. 76). Indeed, Mesmer and others had thought of the mesmeric process as involving a physical fluid that circulated not only in the body of the magnetized but also between the patient and the magnetizer. These speculations were later replaced by theories involving nervous energy or the repartition of zones of excitation or inhibition in the brain.

In these regards, sexual theories involving mesmerism were enunciated from the beginning (Ellenberger, 1970, p. 119). Joseph Phillipe

François Deleuze (1753–1835) and other early mesmerists experimented with posthypnotic suggestion, which was discovered as early as 1787 (p. 113). They described complications that resulted from too frequent or too prolonged magnetic sessions. Subjects tended to become addicted to mesmerism or dependent on their own magnetizer. This dependency often took on sexual overtones (p. 119).

Because of the ensuing sexual controversy, in 1784 a commission of inquiry headed by Benjamin Franklin (an expert on electricity, which had links to magnetism) was appointed by Louis XVI to investigate the validity of the medical claims of animal magnetism. Other luminaries on the commission were the chemist Antoine-Laurent de Lavoisier, the astronomer Jean-Sylvain Bailly, and the physician Joseph-Ignace Guillotin. A secret appendix to the Report of the Commissioners noted that "crises" undergone by magnetized women were often of an obviously sexual nature. This confidential document described in vivid detail how magnetizers and female patients would make physical contact and how this could arouse women sexually, a temptation to mesmerist physicians stemming from the strong emotional bond to their physician that these women formed (Tatar, 1978). As a result of this report and a vigorous antimagnetist campaign by the French government, Mesmer's reputation in France waned, and he returned to Vienna. Even subsequently, writing in 1819, A. Lombard saw dangers in the practice of animal magnetism, including a threat to the "virtue" of young women who submitted to the ministrations of magnetizers (Crabtree, 1988). The issues of what we now call erotic transference and countertransference clearly were identified.

Nevertheless, as Tatar (1978) pointed out, "Because mesmerism serves as the principal link connecting primitive rites of exorcism with modern psychoanalysis, Mesmer himself has assumed the role of a transitional figure in the development of therapeutic procedures for functional disorders" (p. 3). There is a nearly direct line of influence stemming from Mesmer and Puységur through Bernheim and Charcot to Freud. Moreover, although the terms *mesmerism* and *animal magnetism* are used today primarily in a metaphoric sense, they retain distinct erotic overtones that are comparatively absent in the related term *hypnotism.*

The dependency and sexual overtones associated with hypnosis were rediscovered by Charcot, who gave an account of such a case involving a woman who had been hypnotized five times within three weeks. She became preoccupied with her hypnotist and ran away from her home to live with him until her husband took her back, whereupon she developed severe hysterical symptoms necessitating hospitalization (Ellenberger, 1970, p. 119).

Theodor Meynert (1833–1892), a psychiatrist and brain anatomist in whose clinic Freud served, was opposed to hypnotism because the attitude of many women toward the male hypnotist was permeated with strong sexual overtones, and sexual emotions also were observed in hypnotized men (Ellenberger, 1970, p. 119). Interestingly, Hippolyte Bernheim (1840–1919) of the Nancy school (p. 85) emphasized the fact that pseudomemories can be suggested under hypnosis, following which the patient believes that he or she saw or did something according to the hypnotist's suggestion (p. 118). It is noteworthy that as time passed, Bernheim used hypnotism less and less because he found that the effects were equally attainable by suggestion in the waking state, a procedure that the Nancy school termed *psychotherapeutics*. Freud (1888b), it should be added, wrote the preface to the translation of Bernheim's book on suggestion (1888b).

Freud had seen a public demonstration by "Hansen the 'magnetist' " (1925, p. 16), knew of Josef Breuer's (1842–1925) use of hypnosis with Anna O., and began using it himself even before his journey to Paris in 1885. By December 1887, he was hypnotizing most of his patients (Stewart, 1967, p. 37). Ultimately, Freud was ambivalent about hypnosis and abandoned it. Yet he also felt he had found something "positively seductive in working with hypnotism," which could yield the "highly flattering . . . reputation of being a miracle-worker" (1925, p. 17). He realized, however, that "even the most brilliant results were liable to be suddenly wiped away if my personal relation with the patient became disturbed" and that "the personal emotional relation between doctor and patient was after all stronger than the whole cathartic process." He elaborated:

> [O]ne day I had an experience which showed me in the crudest light what I had long suspected. It related to one of my most acquiescent patients, with whom hypnotism had enabled me to bring about the most marvellous results, and whom I was engaged in relieving of her suffering by tracing back her attacks of pain to their origins. As she woke up on

one occasion, she threw her arms around my neck. The unexpected entrance of a servant relieved us from a painful discussion, but from that time onwards there was a tacit understanding between us that the hypnotic treatment should be discontinued. . . . I felt that I had now grasped the nature of the mysterious element that was at work behind hypnotism [1925, p. 27].

Breuer, in contrast, broke off treatment with Anna O. in the context of her erotic attachment to him and hysterical pregnancy during her extended "talking cure," a phenomenon Freud came to recognize as transference and countertransference (Schlessinger et al., 1967; Rosenbaum and Muroff, 1984).

A pattern of seductive influence recognized at least since the time of the mesmerists was replayed in Breuer's and Freud's experiences. Freud added the comment that he was "modest enough" not to ascribe the patient's impetuous behavior to his own "irresistible personal attraction." Instead he pursued other explanations, shifting his focus from hypnotic catharsis to a pursuit of repressed secrets and hidden meanings (Barron et al., 1991; Ellenberger, 1966). Freud, however, was not the first to give up hypnotism and to investigate secrets as a cause of neurosis.

SECRETS AND PSYCHIC TRAUMA

Freud was absorbing the influence of a number of distinguished clinical researchers during the 1880s, in addition to that of Breuer. He received a traveling fellowship and went to Paris to study under Jean-Martin Charcot from October 3, 1885, until February 28, 1886 (Chertok, 1970), after which he spent about a month in Berlin, including time with the neurologist Hermann Oppenheim (1858–1919) and the pediatrician Adolf Baginsky (1843–1918), before returning to Vienna. Then he traveled to Nancy in 1889 to see the hypnotic work of Ambroise Auguste Liébault (1823–1904) and Bernheim, who emphasized the suggestive element in hypnosis that Charcot had generally neglected. These men, particularly Charcot and Bernheim, had an influence well acknowledged by Freud.

Less well recognized, however, is the role of Moritz Benedikt (1835–1920), a Viennese neurologist who investigated hysteria and its causes (1894). Benedikt may have had more influence upon Freud than is generally recognized, an observation made by Eva Lesky (1965; see review by Eissler [1966]) and developed by Ellenberger (1970, 1973). Not only did Benedikt and Freud know each other, but Benedikt also knew Charcot, visited him annually, and wrote the letter of introduction that Freud presented when he arrived to study with Charcot (Ellenberger, 1973; Eissler, 1966).

As described by Ellenberger (1973) and summarized by Micale (1993), Benedikt was one of the most original scientific thinkers of the late nineteenth century and was a major influence on Freud. Yet he remained a maverick throughout his medical career (Levin, 1978, p. 49), and his work has been largely unrecognized. From the mid-1860s to the early 1890s, Benedikt wrote about clinical observations, causes, and treatments of hysteria and other neuroses based on his work with patients at the Vienna Polyclinic, where he became chief physician. As early as 1868, he maintained that hysteria often is due to a functional disorder of the *libido,* a term he used repeatedly (Ellenberger, 1973; Sulloway, 1979). Benedikt supported the idea of psychic causes for these disorders at a time when theories based on hereditarian, neurological, and gynecological concepts prevailed. He emphasized the pathogenic role of thwarted love, repressed ambition, functional sexual disturbances, and a "secret life" of fantasies and frustrated, often sexual, desires. Even a decade before Charcot's work, Benedikt contended that males could have hysteria. Abandoning the use of hypnosis in the treatment of hysterical patients, he employed nonhypnotic verbal psychotherapies, particularly the cathartic release of concealed sexual and emotional secrets. Ellenberger concluded that no medical texts, including those of Janet, are closer to the *Studies on Hysteria* than Benedikt's works, which were scattered in unorthodox publications over a period of almost three decades.

CHARCOT'S SCHOOL AND THE PUZZLE OF HYSTERIA

Freud commented (1888b, p. 41) that in earlier centuries hysterics had been burned at the stake or exorcised, while in more enlightened times they had only been subjected to the curse of ridicule. Up to the time of Charcot, hysterics had been the bêtes noires of medicine, their states considered by many to be simulation and exaggeration unworthy of clinical observation and study. Charcot's recognition that hysteria had traumatic and psychological factors among its causes had a profound influence on Freud's thinking (Miller et al., 1969). Charcot built upon the work of Pierre (Paul) Briquet (1796–1881), who is considered to have written the first systematic and objective study of hysteria, the 724-page *Traité Clinique et Thérapeutique de l'Hystérie*, published in 1859 after ten years of preparation involving the study of over 400 hysterical patients (Sulloway, 1979, p. 41). Briquet did not believe hysteria to be due to an organic lesion or to unsatisfied sexual urges, and he related many cases to intense emotional and adverse environmental factors, including extreme dread or grief, rape, and habitual maltreatment or abuse of children by their parents or wives by their husbands (Briquet, 1859; Crocq and DeVerbizier, 1989; van der Kolk, McFarlane, and Weisaeth, 1996, p. 49).

Charcot thought of hysteria as a neurosis of the brain precipitated by psychic trauma in hereditarily predisposed persons (Wozniak, 1992). Having studied the differences between organic and hysterical paralyses, Charcot recognized the connection between posttraumatic and hysterical paralytic symptoms. Through the probable influence of Charles Richet (1850–1935), a physiologist who rediscovered Puységur's work, in 1878 Charcot began using hypnosis to study hysteria (Ellenberger, 1970, p. 90; Levin, 1978, pp. 50, 266–267). Although he continued to seek out a lesion associated with hysteria, he also demonstrated the role of psychological factors, since he could induce and relieve symptoms with hypnosis alone. In fact, by hypnotic means he could reproduce not only hysterical symptoms but also posttraumatic phenomena resembling the paralyses that sometimes occurred in railway accidents ("train brain" or "railway spine" [Drinka, 1984]). In contrast to organic paralyses due to a lesion of the nervous system, Charcot considered hysterical, posttraumatic, and hypnotic paralysis to have similar features. Some patients' arms became paralyzed even without hypnotic suggestion after they were slapped on the back or extremities. Charcot considered this phenomenon to demonstrate the mechanism of posttraumatic paralysis. He theorized that trauma induced a type of hypnoid phenomenon analogous to hypnotism that caused an autosuggestive state (Ellenberger, 1970, p. 91; 1965).

Likewise, Paul Richer (1849–1933), a disciple of Charcot who in 1881 wrote a 976-page book on grand hysteria (*Études Cliniques sur l'Hystéro-épilepsie ou Grand Hystérie*), considered hysterical crises to be reenactments of psychic trauma previously experienced by the patient (Ellenberger, 1970, p. 143; Gauld, 1992). Charcot's observations suggested the existence of unconscious *idées fixes* at the core of some neuroses, a concept that exerted considerable influence on both Freud and Janet, as well as Breuer (Freud, 1892–1894, p. 141; 1893a; Wozniak, 1992). Freud concluded that Charcot's explanation of the mechanism of hysteria led to ''a theory of neurosis which coincided with the mediaeval view—when once they had replaced the 'demon' of clerical phantasy by a psychological formula'' (1893a, p. 22). As Sulloway (1979) put it, ''Charcot was the first to understand the hitherto hidden *mechanism* of hysterical phenomena, and he did so, moreover, in proto-Freudian terms'' (p. 34). Thus, a link was made between hypnotic or suggestive conditions, trauma, and certain psychopathologic states.

During his travels, as mentioned previously, Freud also met Hermann Oppenheim, a Berlin neurologist who, starting in 1888, published papers and then a book on cases of trauma. Oppenheim introduced the more general term *traumatic neurosis* (in contrast to Charcot's *traumatic hysteria*) (Freud, 1886; Drinka, 1984, pp. 109, 112, 117–119, 322). Charcot was just making his link between hypnosis and traumatic hysteria at that time, and Oppenheim and he differed on how encompassing the effects of trauma could be (Freud, 1893a, p. 21). In the ''Neuro-Psychoses of Defense'' (1894), Freud wrote that ''Breuer and I are coming closer to Oppenheim's and Strümpell's well-known definition of hysteria, and are diverging from Janet . . .'' (p. 51, including footnotes on Oppenheim's and Strümpell's views). However, two to three years later, in a letter to Fliess on December 6, 1896, Freud dissociated himself from Oppenheim's view that an hysterical attack is an ''intensified expression of emotion'' (Freud, 1954, p. 180, n. 1; cf. Masson, 1985, p. 213).

Generally considered to be the ''first stone'' in the construction of psychoanalysis (Ellenberger, 1970, p. 486), the ''Preliminary Communication'' (Breuer and Freud, 1893–1895) extended Charcot's concept of traumatic hysteria to hysteria in general, which sometimes involved symbolic disguise as a result of a psychic trauma that had been excluded from consciousness. The theory could be considered a combination of Benedikt's concept of the pathogenic secret and Janet's method of returning subconscious fixed ideas to consciousness (Ellenberger, 1970, p. 486, citing Mandl, 1893). Indeed, Breuer and Freud footnoted Benedikt:

> In this preliminary communication it is not possible for us to distinguish what is new in it from what has been said by other authors such as Moebius and Strümpell who have held similar views on hysteria to ours. We have found the nearest approach to what we have to say on the theoretical and therapeutic sides of the question in some remarks, published from time to time, by Benedikt. These we shall deal with elsewhere [1893–1895, pp. 7–8, n. 3]

However, other than a later footnote citing some "interesting observations and comments by Benedikt" (p. 210, n. 1) that refers to his 1894 book, *Hypnotismus und Suggestion*, they mentioned no more of Benedikt's ideas.

In the sketches for the "Preliminary Communication" (Breuer and Freud, 1893–1895, p. 150), Freud mentioned the importance of the "sexual life" in psychic trauma but did not develop that idea at the time, perhaps only making a concession to clinical lore (Levin, 1978, p. 125). Greater attention to sexual life came only with the development of the defense theory (Freud, 1894) and the notion of repression guarding against typically sexual memories.

"CHAINS OF MEMORY" AND THE LINK TO SEXUAL SPECIFICITY

It was recognized that not all cases of hysteria were due to trauma, however, and the cause of common, so-called nontraumatic hysteria remained a puzzle (Freud, 1893b). Meanwhile, with an echo of Galen, the idea that hysteria came from frustrated yet secret sexual desires was never fully abandoned and remained part of the lore about hysteria (Ellenberger, 1970, p. 143). Although Briquet had denied the sexual theory of hysteria, Charcot recognized that sexual factors played a significant role in the life of his female patients who had hysteria, even if he did not consider hysteria itself to be a sexual neurosis. He identified points or zones that could set off hysterical attacks. The locations of these points had sexual implications that Charcot was aware of even though it remained part of his informal teachings and not his lectures. Charcot listened to historical details that eventually came to be assembled and conceptualized as psychoanalysis. He even reported intrusions into sleep from nightmares repeating traumatic memories (Havens, 1973).

Initially, however, Freud had minimized any link between sexuality and hysteria, consistent with a belief in Charcot's hereditarian emphasis. Freud wrote:

> As regards what is often asserted to be the preponderant influence of abnormalities in the sexual sphere upon the development of hysteria, it must be said that its importance is as a rule over-estimated. In the first place, hysteria is found in sexually immature girls and boys, just as, too, the neurosis with all its characteristics also occurs in the male sex . . . [and] in women with a complete lack of genitalia . . . [sic] [1888a, pp. 50–51].

Here Freud was focusing primarily on physical factors, such as immature or hypoplastic genitalia. But he added, "It must, however, be admitted that conditions related *functionally* to sexual life play a great part in the aetiology of hysteria (as of all neuroses), and they do so on account of the high psychical significance of this function especially in the female sex" (p. 51). Written in 1888, this formulation appears to be Freud's earliest link between sexuality and the cause of hysteria, and it specifically notes the psychical importance of sexuality. Freud even went on to identify trauma as a "frequent incidental cause of hysterical illness" (p. 51) with "conscious or unconscious ideas" (p. 57) having a role in the excitations that he considered partly physical and partly psychical. However, as McGrath observed (1986, p. 166), since this sexual link was made within the framework of Charcot's hereditarian point of view, it has not been sufficiently appreciated as a precursor of Freud's subsequent formulation. Only later did Freud take an environmentalist view of the cause of hysteria in contrast to the hereditarian emphasis of Charcot, Janet, and others (Freud, 1896a, p. 143; Macmillan, 1992; see also Gilman [1993] on fin-de-siècle medical literature making a racist association of Jews with sexual crimes).

Regarding sexual specificity, Freud claimed (1896a) that ''[s]exual disorders have always been admitted among the causes of nervous illness, but they have been subordinated to heredity and co-ordinated with the other *agents provocateurs*; their aetiological influence has been restricted to a limited number of observed cases'' (p. 149). The term *agents provocateurs* refers to nonhereditary, concurrent, incidental causes (Freud, 1893a, p. 21; 1896a, p. 155; 1896c, p. 191). Charcot and Breuer had reservations about positing exclusively sexual causes in hysteria, and Freud himself initially had doubts or reservations of his own (see also Bonomi [1994] on Freud's original ''aversion'' to sexual etiology):

> When I began to analyse the second patient, Frau Emmy von N., the expectation of a sexual neurosis being the basis of hysteria was fairly remote from my mind. I had come fresh from the school of Charcot, and I regarded the linking of hysteria with the topic of sexuality as a sort of insult—just as the women patients themselves do [1893–1895, pp. 259–260].

In the discussion of the report on Katharina in the case histories of the *Studies on Hysteria* (Breuer and Freud, 1893–1895), Freud moved to conclude, ''In every analysis of a case of hysteria based on sexual traumas we find that impressions from the pre-sexual period which produced no effect on the child attain traumatic power at a later date as memories, when the girl or married woman has acquired an understanding of sexual life'' (p. 133). Here Freud not only had not yet considered the idea of childhood sexuality in the etiology of neurosis but also implied that some cases of hysteria are *not* due to sexual trauma (Eissler, 2001, p. 91). Nevertheless, effects from childhood were entertained. At the same time, Breuer was affirming that ''[t]he sexual instinct is undoubtedly the most powerful source of persisting increases of excitation (and consequently of neuroses)'' (Breuer and Freud, 1893–1895, p. 200) and is ''one of the major components of hysteria'' (p. 244), even if ''the non-sexual affects of fright, anxiety, and anger lead to the development of hysterical phenomena'' (p. 246). Still, lest his readers (or perhaps Freud himself) possibly misunderstand his position, he clarified, ''But it is perhaps worth while insisting again that the sexual factor is by far the most important and the most productive of pathological results'' (pp. 246–247). Breuer gave clinical examples. One was a 12-year-old boy with a history of night terrors who developed difficulty swallowing, vomiting, headache, and withdrawn behavior attributable to a man's attempting to seduce the boy into performing fellatio on him in a public washroom (p. 212). Another case involved a 17-year-old woman who developed hysterical symptoms after a cat jumped onto her shoulder on a dark staircase (compare Descartes' example described above). Further history revealed that a few days before, a young man had attacked her, apparently with sexual intent, on the same dark staircase, and she had escaped from him only with difficulty and not without psychic trauma (p. 213). Breuer also observed: "Marriage brings fresh sexual traumas. It is surprising that the wedding night does not have pathogenic effects more frequently, since unfortunately what it involves is so often not an erotic seduction but a violation" (1893–1895, p. 246). Up until this time the "sexual factor" in Freud's theorizing had not necessarily meant specifically sexual violence.

Despite Breuer's recognition of sexual factors, what went on between Freud and Breuer behind the scenes bespoke theoretical tensions. In Freud's letter to Fliess on November 8, 1895 (Masson, 1985), he wrote: "Recently at the College of Physicians Breuer gave a big speech in my honor and introduced himself as a *converted* adherent to the sexual etiology. When I thanked him for this in private, he spoiled my pleasure by saying, 'But all the same, I don't believe it.' Do you understand this? I don't." (p. 151). Breuer's ambivalent comments in this speech were reported in several publications (cited in Masson, 1985):

> Breuer declares right at the outset of his presentation . . . that one is mistaken if one expected that he is speaking here as a coauthor, because the entire theory of repression is essentially Freud's property. . . . [H]e has witnessed the birth of the theory at first hand, though not without some opposition, but he now stands, as a result of Freud's illuminating explanations, as a convert before the assembly. . . . One point on which the speaker does not agree with Freud is the overvaluation of sexuality; Freud probably did not want to say that every hysterical symptom has a sexual background, but rather that the original root of hysteria is sexual. We do not yet see clearly; it remains only for the future, the masses of observations, to bring full clarification to this question; in any event, one must be grateful to Freud for the theoretical hints he has given us [p. 151, n. 1].

In his paper, "The Aetiology of Hysteria" (1896c), Freud voiced his debt to Breuer: "[W]e must take our start from Josef Breuer's momentous discovery: *the symptoms of hysteria . . . are determined by certain experiences of the patient's which have operated in a traumatic fashion and which are being reproduced in his psychical life in the form of mnemic symbols*" (1896c, pp. 192–193). But Freud set himself apart from Breuer (and Charcot) when he added:

> Breuer assumed—following Charcot—that even an innocuous experience can be heightened into a trauma and can develop determining force if it happens to the subject when he is in a special psychical condition—in what is described as a hypnoid state. I find, however, that there are often no grounds whatever for presupposing the presence of such hypnoid states. What remains decisive is that the theory of hypnoid states contributes nothing to the solution of the other difficulties, namely that *the traumatic scenes so often lack suitability as determinants* [1896c, pp. 194–195; emphasis added].

Freud then introduced the idea that "chains of memory," derived from earlier experiences awakened in association to the more recent experience, play a part in causing symptoms, and that, in the end, these are necessarily early and premature sexual experiences. Although Breuer's cathartic approach and Janet's chains of unconscious fixed ideas greatly influenced this conceptualization, the associationistic psychology of Johann Friedrich Herbart (1776–1841), who investigated the notion of quantitative relationships among ideas, may have played an even earlier role. Herbart's main concept was that mental processes can be explained by scientific laws, and he sought a "mathematical psychology" (Jones, 1953, p. 373). Regarding Herbart, in Gymnasium Freud had used Gustav Adolph Lindner's (1828–1887) 1872 textbook of empirical psychology (*Lehrbuch der empirisches Psychologie als inductiver Wissenschaft*), which examined how chains of associations diverged and converged in nodal points (Jones, 1953, p. 374; cf. Ramzy, 1956; Ellenberger, 1970, p. 489, 536; Sulloway, 1979, p. 67; Wozniak, 1992; Sand, 2002). Even if Freud did not extract much on Herbart from Lindner's book at that stage (when he was disinclined to read books on psychology), Freud had another likely influence regarding ideas about memory: In 1879 he was asked to translate some essays of John Stuart Mill (1806–1873), one of which dealt with Plato's theory of reminiscence, the revival of long-standing memories that had been forgotten (Ramzy, 1956). Freud remarked in 1933 that he had been greatly impressed by Plato's theory of reminiscence (Jones, 1953, p. 56).

In order to correlate his observations and to attempt to explain the physiological and psychical mechanism of hysteria, Freud had "come to regard the participation of sexual motive forces as an indispensable premiss" (1896c, p. 200). The sexual foundation provided both a biological and a psychological explanation for this theory of neurosis and thus could better meet objections that purely psychological constructs could not really explain psychopathology. He did not want to "overstretch psychogenicity" (1912, p. 248), and consideration of biological factors pleased his "medical conscience" (1925, p. 25; Sulloway, 1979).

In contrast, although Janet included the possible role of sexual traumas in his conceptualizations, he did not believe that all traumas causing fixed ideas were necessarily sexual (1914–1915). Janet and Freud later contested not only the matter of the specificity and uniformity of sexual factors but also the matter of priority in treating patients by having them recall their traumatic experiences. Freud claimed that his views derived from Breuer's use of the cathartic method, even before Freud went to Paris in 1885, and even though Janet's work on this topic was published in 1889, four years before Breuer and Freud's "Preliminary Communication" (Strachey, 1966, pp. 39–40; Freud, 1925, pp. 19–20; Breuer and Freud, 1893–1895, pp. xii–xiii, n. 2). In any event, already in his encyclopedia article on hysteria (1888a), Freud specified "conscious or unconscious ideas" associated with "a surplus of stimuli in the organ of the mind" for which "anything that alters the distribution of the excitations in the nervous system may cure hysterical disorders . . ." (p. 57).

THE SEXUAL MISE EN SCÈNE

During Freud's time there was a period of unique cultural fascination with both mental illness and sexual problems (Bettelheim, 1990). A manifest "cult of eroticism" arose with the decline of the ostensible

Victorianism that had prevailed until at least the middle of the century. This new spirit of the fin de siècle was especially evident in Paris and Vienna, which were centers for literature and the arts. In literature, Arthur Schnitzler (1862–1931), a Viennese physician-poet and contemporary of Freud's, independently wrote fiction on such subjects as infantile trauma and the sexual etiology of hysteria (Beharriell, 1962; Ellenberger, 1970, pp. 471–474). Eroticism dominated publications at all levels of literary quality and spanned fiction, medical writing, and pseudomedical articles (Ellenberger, 1970, p. 282; cf. Levin, 1978, p. 53). A burgeoning "scientia sexualis" paralleled the "ars erotica" as medicine assumed more of the role held by religious institutions in the regulation and control of sexuality (Wilson, 1982). According to Foucault (1978), particularly among the Victorian bourgeoisie, "Toward the beginning of the eighteenth century, there emerged a political, economic, and technical incitement to talk about sex . . . to pronounce a discourse on sex that would not derive from morality alone but from rationality as well . . ." (pp. 23–24). The discursive ferment gathered momentum from then onward into the late nineteenth century (p. 18). With the development of sexology, science sought to classify and reveal the secrets behind such entities as hysteria, childhood masturbation, prostitution, perversion, homosexuality, and nymphomania.

In 1886, Richard von Krafft-Ebing (1840–1902), professor of psychiatry and nervous diseases in Vienna and a world expert on sexual perversion, first published his widely read *Psychopathia Sexualis*, a landmark in the early sexology movement. Freud knew Krafft-Ebing personally and regularly received autographed copies of Krafft-Ebing's major works, including the fifth (1890) and later editions of *Psychopathia Sexualis*. In the ninth (1894) edition, Freud heavily marked details of cases histories with marginal emphases (Sulloway, 1979). It is noteworthy that Krafft-Ebing's schema of sexual aberrations included description of premature sexual excitement in childhood ("paradoxia"), such as masturbation, seduction of other children, and "other revolting vices" (Krafft-Ebing, 1886, pp. 36–37; Drinka, 1984, p. 174). As it happened, Charcot too had written directly about sexuality, collaborating with the eminent French psychiatrist Valentin Magnan (1835–1916) on an article published in 1882 entitled "Inversion du sens génital et autres perversions sexuelles" that included mention of sexual assaults (cited in Ellenberger, 1970, p. 300; Masson, 1984, pp. 28, 200).

Furthermore, as Masson (1984) elaborated, while studying at the Salpêtrière, Freud also visited the Paris morgue and likely witnessed cases involving both physical and sexual abuse in early childhood. At Charcot's home, Freud met Paul Camille Hippolyte Brouardel (1837–1906), the chair of legal medicine in Paris, and subsequently commented that "[Brouardel] used to show us from post-mortem material at the morgue how much there was which deserved to be known by doctors but of which science preferred to take no notice" (1913, p. 335).[3] Brouardel wrote a book on the rape of children and apparently collaborated with Charcot in investigating this subject, although the exact nature of their collaboration is unclear (Masson, 1984, p. 33). In his library Freud also possessed three major French works dealing with sexual violence, though he did not cite the authors in his publications of 1896 (Masson, 1984, p. 38). His exposure to sexual trauma of children was not restricted to Paris, for the topic was one highly publicized in the Viennese press, although apparently not very much until 1899 (Wolff, 1988). Even so, as Gay (1988) noted, sexual assaults on young girls, in particular by their fathers, had been discussed in public since the beginning of the nineteenth century. As early as 1821, the French psychiatrist Jean Étienne Esquirol (1772–1840) reported the case of a father's attempt at molestation of his 16-year-old daughter, leading to her breakdown and repeated attempts at suicide (p. 85n).

Freud worked for three years in a children's outpatient clinic. Eissler (2001, p. 53) suggested that it might have been there that Freud uncovered the building blocks of his formulations, particularly involving masturbation and neurasthenia (see also Bonomi's [1994] intriguing essay on the relevance of Freud's pediatric training for the origins of psychoanalysis). While in Berlin in 1886 Freud daily attended the polyclinic where Baginsky, a proponent of the idea that onanism was an important cause of childhood hysteria, taught (Bonomi, 1994). This

---

[3] Freud recalled one occasion in which Brouardel, who was discussing the indications by which one could judge the social rank, character, and origin of an unidentified body, said with apparent irony, "Les genous sales sont le signe d'une fille honnête" ["Dirty knees are the sign of a respectable girl."] (1913, p. 335; 1886, p. 8n). Freud also recalled how, at one of Charcot's evening receptions, Charcot and Brouardel were discussing a recent case involving a young married couple, when Charcot exclaimed, "Mais, dans des cas pareils c'est toujours la chose génitale, toujours . . . toujours . . . toujours" ("But in this sort of case it's always a question of the genitals—always, always, always."] (1914a, p. 14). Charcot apparently did believe that some unclear core of sexuality underlay hysteria, and this dim perception appears to have left a deep impression on Freud (Masson, 1985, p. 25, n. 1).

idea had a parallel with the seduction hypothesis, for, although mastur-bation had been considered to be one of the causes of neurasthenia according to George Miller Beard (1839–1883, 1869), Freud posited it to be the exclusive cause (Eissler, 2001, p. 53). Freud was intent on identifying exclusive etiologies for the neuroses, analogous to Koch's postulates in the pathogenesis of infectious disease (Freud, 1895a, p. 137; 1896c, p. 209; see also Eissler, 2001, chapter 2; Carter, 1980; Macmillan, 1992; Makari, this volume). In a letter to Fliess dated February 8, 1893, he wrote:

> It may be taken as a recognized fact that neurasthenia is a frequent consequence of an abnormal sexual life. The assertion, however, which I wish to make and to test by observation is that neurasthenia actually can *only* be a sexual neurosis. I (along with Breuer) have advocated a similar view in regard to hysteria. Traumatic hysteria was known; we then said every case of hysteria that is not hereditary is traumatic. The same holds for neurasthenia: every neurasthenia is sexual [Masson, 1985, pp. 39–40].

Freud was moving inexorably toward an exclusive cause for hysteria. Once he was able to move away from the hereditarian point of view, he could address himself to traumatic, sexual, and psychological pieces of the puzzle. Seduction occurring in early childhood and having de-layed effects became an exclusive cause incorporating all three of these elements.

"SEXUAL SCENES" FROM CHILDHOOD

Childhood sexual behavior had been identified by priests and educators for generations, even though physicians generally considered it un-common. Father Debreyne, a physician and moral theologian, pub-lished in the 1840s on the considerable frequency of infantile masturbation, sexual play between children, and the seduction of young children by wet nurses and servants. And Bishop Dupanloup of Orleans published a three-volume dissertation on education in 1866 in which he repeated how frequently sex play occurred among children (Ellenberger, 1970, pp. 295–296; Carter, 1983).

Eventually, the idea became prevalent that sexual disturbances could result from unconscious psychological causes whose origins stemmed from childhood (Ellenberger, 1970, p. 300). Benedikt emphasized the frequency of early sexual trauma in hysteria and the importance of fantasy life in normal and neurotic individuals. Even perversions, which had been considered due to constitutional factors (''degeneration theory''), were beginning to be attributed to specific experiences in childhood (1970, p. 299). In 1894, J. Dallemagne contended that many sexual deviations in adolescence resulted from childhood sexual experiences that were revived in puberty.

Also in 1894, Charles Samson Féré (1852–1907) gave examples of two women who in early childhood had been subject to sexual caresses by domestics without immediate effect. However, they reportedly had delayed sexual effects due to stresses later in life. Féré believed that similar effects could occur in cases of sexual seduction in infancy (cited in Ellenberger [1970, p. 299]; see also Masson [1984, p. 199]). As early as 1888, Freud was aware of Féré's investigations on hypnotism and hysteria (Freud, 1888b, p. 78) and subsequently cited Féré's published work on dreams and hysterical paralysis (Féré, 1886, 1887; Freud, 1900, p. 88, n. 1 [added 1914], p. 89) but did not mention the 1894 article on delayed sexual effects linked to seduction.

The next year, Wilhelm Stekel (1868–1940) published a paper, ''Coitus in Childhood'' (1895), which Freud noted having come across, adding that he ''had not had time to collect other published evidence; but even if it were only scanty, it is to be expected that increased attention to the subject will very soon confirm the great frequency of sexual experiences and sexual activity in childhood'' (1896c, p. 207).

It is unclear precisely when Freud postulated that *exclusively* sexual factors were the regular and specific cause of hysteria (Blass and Simon, 1994; Eissler, 2001). Nevertheless, *with the recognition of sexual factors and traumatic precipitants in neuroses, the stage was implicitly set for the role of childhood seduction.* Freud started to allude to seduction as early as 1893—coincidentally also the year in which Charcot died. Between 1895 and 1897 he attributed a major etiological role to it, situating the traumatic scenes of seduction chronologically further and further back in childhood (Laplanche and Pontalis, 1973, p. 404). Why did Freud conclude that the seductions necessarily occurred in childhood? For one thing, going back in time made logical sense, since, as noted above, Freud had already observed that "traumatic scenes so often lack suitability as determinants" (1896c, p. 195). Freud had a firm conviction about psychic determinism, namely, that all vital phenomena, including mental ones, are lawfully determined by principles of cause and effect (Sulloway, 1979, p. 94). Like Herbart, he dreamed of establishing mathematical relationships for mental processes. He sought a "formula" or "equation" in order to respond to critics of his ideas on sexual etiology.

Thus, he expanded the nature–nurture dichotomy into a four-factor "etiological equation."[4] The factors in this equation were "precondition" (innate or acquired disposition to subsequent illness), "specific cause" (one which is never missing in any case in which the effect takes place, e.g., childhood sexual assault), "concurrent cause" (e.g., factors such as exhaustion, fright, or anxiety that are not causative on their own), and "precipitating or releasing cause" (the most recent factor preceding the effect) (1895a, pp. 135–136; Garcia, 1987). If relatively recent traumatic memories were absent, exceedingly trivial, or indeterminate in a significant number of cases of hysteria, and if sexual factors were considered essential in the etiological equation, then it became a *logical necessity* to seek earlier sexual events that were not traumatic at that early time and for which the memory of the event was no longer in awareness. In addition to using theoretical arguments and clinical observations, he now had what amounted to a logical basis to prove his idea to any doubter (Blass and Simon, 1994).[5,6,7] The etiological equation was extremely important in Freud's

---

[4] In his letter to Breuer as part of the "Sketches for the 'Preliminary Communication' of 1893" (1892), Freud referred to the "pathological formula of hysteria . . . the series proposed by me" (p. 148). Elaborated into the "etiological equation" or "etiological series," this formula was his first explicit reference to what he later called a "complemental series."

[5] At the University of Vienna, Freud had studied philosophy with the psychologist–philosopher Franz Brentano (1838–1917), a specialist on Aristotle. Brentano contributed to Freud's development of psychoanalysis in several ways, including the former's belief that philosophy and the emerging scientific psychology could reach greater certainty regarding the truth or falsity of an idea through the use of both external perception and a kind of introspection that he called "inner perception" (*innere Wahrnehmung*) (Cohen, 2002). Furthermore, of Freud's five courses with Brentano, one was devoted to Aristotle and another to logic (Sulloway, 1979, p. 92, n. 27; Frampton, 1991). Aristotle's influence was great in many fields, but it was most extensive in logic. As noted by Ramzy (1956), if any of Freud's theories were unacceptable, this is not due to his argumentation but to his premises. This observation certainly applies to the seduction theory.

[6] The logical necessity of the argument follows only if no distinction is made between actuality and fantasy, a differentiation that significantly complicates the equation, as Freud came to realize. Furthermore, regarding the deferred effects of seduction, the theory developmentally assumed childhood asexuality.

[7] Regarding the influence of Charles Darwin (1809–1882) on Freud (Ritvo, 1990), Kris (1950a) observed that Freud's phylogenetic speculations followed the pattern of contemporary

thinking. He called it "the key that unlocks everything" (Draft C, probably written in April or May, 1894; Masson, 1985, pp. 45–46; May, 1999, p. 776).

Freud further argued that it is only ideas with a sexual content that can be repressed and that the traumas of childhood then operate in a deferred fashion, as though they were fresh experiences (1895b, pp. 166–167, n. 2). If it logically followed that earlier, repressed sexual scenes must be the specific cause (as well as an acquired preconditon) for hysteria, we still might ask why this earlier time must be in child-hood and not, say, in adolescence or even adulthood? Freud explained that "if the sexual experience occurs during the period of sexual imma-turity and the memory of it is aroused during or after maturity, then the memory will have a far stronger excitatory effect than the experi-ence did at the time it happened; and this is because in the meantime puberty has immensely increased the capacity of the sexual apparatus for reaction" (1895b, p. 167, n. 2).

However, there were clinical problems in the etiological equation for hysteria. These had to do with the recognition that childhood sexual innocence might not be strictly assumable and the possibility that not only hysteria but also perversion might be caused by seduction (Sullo-way, 1979, pp. 112, 303–315; Makari, 1997). The former problem Freud dealt with by "chronological requirements for their sexual scenes" (May 30, 1896, and December 6, 1896; Masson, 1985, pp. 187–190, 207–214) and by acknowledging nongenital, polymorphous perverse sexuality (December 6, 1896; Masson, 1985, pp. 207–214; Geyskens, 2001). The latter problem he addressed by positing an "in-verse equation" (Makari, 1997, p. 481) between neurosis and per-version.

"PROTON PSEUDOS," THE RECOGNITION OF FALSE PREMISES, AND TRANSFERENCE

Based on the etiological equation, seduction as the specific cause of hysteria was not only a clinical hypothesis but also a logical tour de

---

evolutionism and Darwinian tradition, but that the idea of studying the individual's past as a source of etiology grew entirely out of clinical data, initially focused on the repression of sexual traumas. Freud, however, may have been influenced as well by Darwin's contributions to child psychology (Sulloway, 1979, pp. 242–251). Moreover, Freud's logically synthetic reasoning itself suggests that the seduction theory was not derived from observational data alone.

force. Arguably, for all his empirical aspirations, at this stage Freud was primarily a builder of logical systems (Ramzy, 1956). Even before the seduction hypothesis could be empirically validated, Freud was "in a sphere of convictions that is relatively immune to factual observation" (May, 1999, p. 776). As Freud wrote to Fliess, "We cannot do without people who have the courage to think something new before they can demonstrate it" (December 8, 1895; Masson, 1985, p. 155). Theory building involves the use of fantasy, and Freud drew greatly on internal, affectively charged sources (May, 1999, p. 777), in addition to his intellectual prowess.[8]

By September 21, 1897, however, Freud had gone from zealous belief to grave doubt about the seduction theory (Masson, 1985, pp. 264–266). This change in his belief and various reasons for it have been widely recounted in psychoanalytic history (e.g., Sulloway, 1979, pp. 206–207; Masson, 1984; Simon, 1992; Good, 1995; Eissler, 2001; see, especially, Sulloway [1979, pp. 513–518] on Felix Gattel's [1870–1904] 1898 study (*Über die sexuelle Ursachen der Neurasthenie und Angstneurose*) testing Freud's theories and on the dating of Freud's reading of Albert Moll's [1862–1939] *Untersuchungen über die Libido Sexualis*, published in 1899, that may have influenced Freud's decision that the seduction theory was not correct.) In addition, there is a reason based on Freud's own likely logical reconsideration, which historically has received scant attention. It appears that Freud already knew, if only preconsciously, that he had made false premises in his logical reasoning about the requirement that there had been a presexual sexual shock. Evidence for preexisting recognition of an error appears in his "Project for a Scientific Psychology" (1895b), where he referred to the "Hysterical Proton Pseudos," written both in Latin script (p. 352) and in Greek (p. 356). Here, again, Freud

---

[8] In this respect, it is again noteworthy that the seduction theory arose more as a proposition than a clinical generalization. Contemporaneous sources regarding its origin are at variance with accounts claiming that Freud postulated the theory because most of his early female patients reported sexual abuse in early childhood (Freud, 1925, pp. 33–34; 1933, pp. 120; Esterson, 2002). Asking why Freud initially attached so much importance to his etiological formula, Stewart (1967, p. 36) pointed to the impetus it gave for further study but did not address the logical reasons and subjective factors that lay behind it. Macmillan (1992), on the other hand, noted how Freud spoke of the "logical and associative structure" of the neurosis. He did not define these terms but suggested their reference to the association between symptoms and causal memories (p. 130). While the coherence of the associative connections of the neurosis makes narrative sense, it is less clear how this coherence itself takes "logical" form, apart from the logical necessity of invoking childhood scenes in the first place.

used logical terminology, since the term *proton pseudos* appears in Aristotle's *Prior Analyticus* (later known as the *Organon*), which deals with the theory of syllogisms (1895b, p. 352, n. 1). What is striking in the present context is that Aristotle's "chapter deals with false premises and false conclusions, and the particular sentence asserts that a false statement is the result of a preceding falsity (*'proton pseudos'*)" (1895c, p. 352, n. 1; Barnes, 1984).[9]

Freud apparently intended to use this Greek term in the sense of a "false connection" between an affect and its symbol when a sexual idea has been repressed (see also Andersson, 1962, p. 196, who refers to "proton pseudos" as a "first lie"). "Proton pseudos" was not a passing issue for Freud, who mentioned "false connections" numerous times in various papers (see also Breuer and Freud, 1893–1895, pp. 67–70, n.1, 294, 302–303; 1894, pp. 52–53; 1896c, p. 218). He also identified a "false connection" as a *mésalliance* or *transference,* his first use of the latter term in a psychoanalytic sense (1893–1895, pp. 302–303).

Thus, if *proton pseudos* implied (albeit unwittingly) his own "false premise" and subsequent "false conclusion" in formulating the seduction theory, it suggests that transference played a role in arriving at this error. A recognition of transference then could be a factor in his reconsideration of the theory, which he did not abruptly abandon, nor did he forego a struggle with the issue of actual seduction (Blass and Simon, 1994; Good, 1995). Although clinical and epidemiological considerations also played a role in rejecting the seduction theory, Freud's wish for a logically necessary equation or syllogism, whose truth must depend on the truth of its premises, was a strong force behind his belief that he had found the key to the etiological equation, the *caput Nili,* the source of hysteria in seduction.

Regarding the subjective factors that shaped Freud's creation of the seduction theory, Eissler (2001) noted covert rivalry with Fliess and the approach of Freud's fortieth birthday in 1896. Forty at that time was no longer considered young. Freud likely anticipated that the end of his life was approaching and that he needed to justify it with a bold discovery. It was only weeks before this birthday that he boastfully announced the discovery of the origin of the Nile (pp. 144–145).

---

[9] In logic, if a premise is false, it can imply any conclusion whatever (Copi, 1961, p. 269).

His subsequent disbelief in the seduction theory had a subjective link to beginning in earnest his self-analysis in about July 1897 (Jones, 1953, p. 306; Sulloway, 1979, pp. 207–210).[10]

PRIMAL SEDUCTION

From a contemporary perspective, it is a curiosity that Freud used the word *seduction* (*Verführung*) to refer to a traumatic experience, even if it was traumatic by deferred effect. In contrast, as Masson (1984, p. 3) pointed out, Freud also employed various other terms to describe "infantile sexual scenes." These words include *Vergewaltigung* (rape), *Missbrauch* (abuse), *Angriff* (attack), *Attentat* (the French term, meaning an assault), *Aggression* (aggression), and *Traumen* (traumas). Masson noted that all of these terms indicate violence except for the word *seduction,* which he considered an unfortunate choice because it implies some form of participation by the child. However, by the term *seduction* what Freud meant (and what Masson in spite of himself subsequently cited [p. 52]) was a "passive sexual experience in the first years of childhood." In Freud's words: "Influenced by Charcot's view of the traumatic origin of hysteria, one was readily inclined to accept as true and aetiologically significant the statements made by patients in which they ascribed their symptoms to passive sexual experiences in the first years of childhood—to put it bluntly, to seduction" (1914a, p. 17).

In current usage, the term *seduction* can be regarded as an umbrella concept that includes seductive behavior, sexual harassment, coercive molestation, sexual abuse, and child rape (Blum, 1996). Although the term carries some benign or understated connotations that Freud, for one, had not intended, and although in recent years it has been caught up in some of the controversies and misconceptions about Freud's ideas on trauma, fantasy, and reality, the term also has the

---

[10] Commenting on Freud's identification with Moses, who received and then smashed the Tablets, Gay (1988, p. 316) called attention to Freud's life-long struggle for control over his speculative and destructive impulses. Such a struggle appears to apply in the example of the seduction theory, where Freud went from utter belief to disbelief and then to a reconstituted version. Just as Moses obtained a new copy of the Tablets, so Freud evolved a new theory of how the mind works.

advantage of a range and depth of meaning that speaks to the need for, and usefulness of, individual analytic exploration.

In an innovative extension of the original seduction theory, Jean Laplanche (1989, 1997) has set forth a theory of generalized seduction that encompasses the development of the child in relation to the mothering figure, who unconsciously communicates enigmatic messages to the child that are real (in the way that language, meaning, and the unconscious are real, even though they are not events) and can be seductive and traumatizing. The unconscious aspects of this relatedness Laplanche considers to be the hidden meaning of the theory of seduction, based upon enigmatic and asymmetric sexuality. In "primal seduction," the infant is unable to metabolize or assimilate the adult's seductively enigmatic communications. Primal seduction, as defined by Laplanche, is to be contrasted with two other types of seduction included in the general theory. The first is infantile, or pedophilic, seduction, designated as the "special theory of seduction." The other is precocious seduction, which occurs with the mother through her activities in the child's bodily hygiene (Freud, 1933, p. 120).

With the idea of primal seduction we have come full circle back to Genesis, where the naive Adam and Eve experienced a seductive enigma surrounding the Tree of Knowledge. In his quest for knowledge about the enigmatic cause of hysteria, Freud himself was seduced and experienced neurotic suffering. The seduction hypothesis was, in effect, an attempt at a scientific rendering of the Biblical story of Eden, a search for the *caput Bibliae* from which the origins of neurosis are traceable in mythic form. From this mythic point of view, the seduction theory was a veritable "scientific fairy tale." As with fairy tales, it contained hidden truth. Indirectly, the theory pursued a meaning contained in myth and thereby led to the development of psychoanalysis. To the extent that psychoanalysis is an exploration involving current expressions of early developmental experiences with others, it is a process seeking the individual mythic meaning of seduction.

REFERENCES

Abraham, K. (1909), Dreams and myths: A study in folk-psychology. In: *Clinical Papers and Essays on Psycho-Analysis.* New York: Basic Books, 1955, pp. 151–209.

Andersson, O. (1962), *Studies in the Prehistory of Psychoanalysis: The Etiology of Psychoneuroses and Some Related Themes in Sigmund Freud's Scientific Writings and Letters 1886–1896.* Stockholm: Svenska Bokförlaget.

Armstrong, K. (1996), *In the Beginning.* New York: Ballantine Books.

Barnes, J., Ed. (1984), *The Complete Works of Aristotle: The Revised Oxford Translation,* Vol. 1. Princeton, NJ: Princeton University Press.

Barron, J. W., Beaumont, R., Goldsmith, G. N., Good, M. I., Pyles, R. L., Rizzuto, A.-M., & Smith, H. F. (1991), Sigmund Freud: The secrets of nature and the nature of secrets. *Internat. Rev. Psycho-Anal.,* 18:143–163.

Beard, G. M. (1869), Neurasthenia, or nervous exhaustion. *Boston Med. & Surg. J.,* 80:217–221.

Beharriell, F. J. (1962), Freud's "double": Arthur Schnitzler. *J. Amer. Psychoanal. Assn.,* 10:722–730.

Benedikt, M. (1894), *Hypnotismus und Suggestion.* Leipzig: Breitstein.

Bettelheim, B. (1990), *Freud's Vienna and Other Essays.* New York: Alfred A. Knopf.

Blass, R. B., & Simon, B. (1994), The value of the historical perspective to contemporary psychoanlaysis: Freud's "seduction hypothesis." *Internat. J. Psycho-Anal.,* 75:677–693.

Blum, H. (1991), Freud and the figure of Moses: The Moses of Freud. *J. Amer. Psychoanal. Assn.,* 39:513–535.

———— (1996), Seduction trauma: Representation, deferred action, and pathogenic development. *J. Amer. Psychoanal. Assn.,* 44:1147–1164.

Bonomi, C. (1994), Why have we ignored Freud the "paediatrician"? The relevance of Freud's paediatric training for the origins of psychoanalysis. In: *100 Years of Psychoanalysis: Contributions to the History of Psychoanalysis,* ed. A. Haynal & E. Falzeder. Geneva, Switzerland: Cahiers Psychiatriques Genevois et Institutions Universitaires de Psychiatrie de Genéve, pp. 55–99.

Breuer, J., & Freud, S. (1893–1895), Studies on Hysteria. *Standard Edition,* 2. London: Hogarth Press, 1955.

Briquet, P. (1859), *Traité Clinique et Therapeutique de l'Hysterie.* Paris: J.-B. Baillere.

Carter, K. C. (1980), Germ theory, hysteria, and Freud's early work in psychopathology. *Med. Hist.,* 24:259–274.

———— (1983), Infantile hysteria and infantile sexuality in late nineteenth-century German-language medical literature. *Med. Hist.,* 27:186–196.

Charcot, J.-M., & Magnan, V. (1882), Inversion du sens génital et autres perversions sexuelles. *Archive de Neurologie,* 3:53–60, 4:296–322.

Chertok, L. (1970), Freud in Paris: A crucial stage. *Internat. J. Psycho-Anal.,* 51:511–520.

Cohen, A. (2002), Brentano, Franz (1838–1917). In: *The Freud Encyclopedia: Theory, Therapy, and Culture,* ed. E. Erwin. New York: Routledge, pp. 59–61.

Copi, I. M. (1961), *Introduction to Logic.* New York: Macmillan.

Crabtree, A. (1988), *Animal Magnetism, Early Hypnotism, and Psychical Research, 1766–1925.* White Plains, NY: Kraus International.

——— (1993), *From Mesmer to Freud: Magnetic Sleep and the Roots of Psychological Healing.* New Haven, CT: Yale University Press.

Crocq, L., & DeVerbizier, J. (1989), Le traumatisme psychologique dans l'oeuvre de Pierre Janet. *Annales Médico-Psychologiques,* 147:983–987.

Darnton, R. (1968), *Mesmerism and the End of the Enlightenment in France.* Cambridge, MA: Harvard University Press.

Descartes, R. (1649), *Les Passions de L'Âme,* tr. & ann. S. Voss. Indianapolis: Hackett, 1989.

Drinka, G. F. (1984), *The Birth of Neurosis: Myth, Malady, and the Victorians.* New York: Simon & Schuster.

Eissler, K. R. (1966), Review of *Die Wiener Medizinische Schule Im 19 Jahrhundert. Psychoanal. Quart.,* 35:127–130.

——— (2001), *Freud and the Seduction Theory: A Brief Love Affair.* Madison, CT: International Universities Press.

Ellenberger, H. F. (1965), Charcot and the Salpêtrière School. In: *Beyond the Unconscious: Essays of Henri F. Ellenberger in the History of Psychiatry,* ed. M. S. Micale. Princeton, NJ: Princeton University Press, 1993, pp. 139–154.

——— (1966), The pathogenic secret and its therapeutics. In: *Beyond the Unconscious: Essays of Henri F. Ellenberger in the History of Psychiatry,* ed. M. S. Micale. Princeton, NJ: Princeton University Press, 1993, pp. 341–359.

——— (1970), *The Discovery of the Unconscious: The History and Evolution of Dynamic Psychiatry.* New York: Basic Books.

——— (1973), Moritz Benedikt (1835–1920): An insufficiently appreciated pioneer of psychoanalysis. In: *Beyond the Unconscious: Essays of Henri F. Ellenberger in the History of Psychiatry,* ed. M. S. Micale. Princeton, NJ: Princeton University Press, 1993, pp. 104–118.

Esterson, A. (2002), Seduction theory. In: *The Freud Encyclopedia: Theory, Therapy, and Culture,* ed. E. Erwin. New York: Routledge, pp. 515–520.

Féré, C. (1886), Note sur un cas de paralysie hystérique consécutive à un rêve. *Soc. Biolog.,* 41: (Nov. 20).

—— (1887), A contribution to the pathology of dreams and of hysterical paralysis. *Brain,* 9:488.

—— (1894), Contributions à l'histoire du choc moral chez les enfants. *Bull. de la Soc. de Méd. mentale de Belgique,* 74:333–340.

Fine, R. (1979), *A History of Psychoanalysis.* New York: Columbia University Press.

Foucault, M. (1978), *A History of Sexuality, Volume 1: An Introduction,* tr. R. Hurley. New York: Vintage Books, 1990.

Frampton, M. F. (1991), Considerations on the role of Brentano's concept of intentionality in Freud's repudiation of the seduction theory. *Internat. Rev. Psycho-Anal.,* 18:27–36.

Freud, S. (1883a), July 12 letter to Martha Bernays. In: *Sigmund Freud: His Life in Pictures and Words,* ed. E. L. Freud, L. Freud, & I. Grubrich-Simitis. New York: Harcourt, Brace Jovanovich, 1978, p. 96.

—— (1883b), *Letters of Sigmund Freud,* ed. E. L. Freud. New York: Basic Books, 1969.

—— (1886), Report on my studies in Paris and Berlin. *Standard Edition,* 1:1–15. London: Hogarth Press, 1966.

—— (1888a), Hysteria. *Standard Edition,* 1:37–57. London: Hogarth Press, 1966.

—— (1888b), Preface to the translation of Bernheim's *Suggestion. Standard Edition,* 1:71–85. London: Hogarth Press, 1966.

—— (1892), Sketches for the "Preliminary Communication" of 1893. *Standard Edition,* 1:147–158. London: Hogarth Press, 1966.

—— (1892–1896), Preface and footnotes to the translation of Charcot's *Tuesday lectures. Standard Edition,* 1:129–143. London: Hogarth Press, 1966.

—— (1893a), Charcot. *Standard Edition,* 3:7–23. London: Hogarth Press, 1962.

—— (1893b), On the psychical mechanism of hysterical phenomena: A lecture. *Standard Edition,* 3:25–39. London: Hogarth Press, 1962.

—— (1894), The neuro-psychoses of defence. *Standard Edition,* 3:41–61. London: Hogarth Press, 1962.

—— (1895a), A reply to criticisms of my paper on anxiety neurosis. *Standard Edition,* 3:119–139. London: Hogarth Press, 1962.

—— (1895b), Project for a scientific psychology. *Standard Edition,* 1:281–391. London: Hogarth Press, 1966.

—— (1896a), Heredity and the aetiology of the neuroses. *Standard Edition,* 3:141–156. London: Hogarth Press, 1962.

—— (1896b), Further remarks on the neuro-psychoses of defence. *Standard Edition,* 3:157–185. London: Hogarth Press, 1962.

—— (1896c), The aetiology of hysteria. *Standard Edition,* 3:187–221. London: Hogarth Press, 1962.

—— (1899), Screen memories. *Standard Edition,* 3:299–322. London: Hogarth Press, 1962.

—— (1900), The Interpretation of Dreams. *Standard Edition,* 4. London: Hogarth Press, 1953.

—— (1907), Contribution to a questionnaire on reading. *Standard Edition,* 9:245–247. London: Hogarth Press, 1958.

—— (1908), Creative writers and day-dreaming. *Standard Edition,* 9:141–153. London: Hogarth Press, 1958.

—— (1912), Contributions to a discussion on masturbation. *Standard Edition,* 12:239–254. London: Hogarth Press, 1958.

—— (1913), Preface to Bourke's *Scatologic Rites of All Nations. Standard Edition,* 12:335–337. London: Hogarth Press, 1958.

—— (1914a), On the history of the psycho-analytic movement. *Standard Edition,* 14:1–66. London: Hogarth Press, 1957.

—— (1914b), The Moses of Michelangelo. *Standard Edition,* 13:209–236. London: Hogarth Press, 1955.

—— (1925), An autobiographical study. *Standard Edition,* 20:1–70. London: Hogarth Press, 1959.

—— (1933), New Introductory Lectures on Psycho-Analysis. *Standard Edition,* 22:1–182. London: Hogarth Press, 1964.

—— (1939), Moses and Monotheism: Three Essays. *Standard Edition,* 23:1–137. London: Hogarth Press, 1964.

—— (1954), *The Origins of Psycho-Analysis. Letters to Wilhelm Fliess, Drafts and Notes: 1887–1902,* ed. M. Bonaparte, A. Freud, & E. Kris. New York: Basic Books.

Garcia, E. E. (1987), Freud's seduction theory. *The Psychoanalytic Study of the Child,* 42:443–468. New Haven, CT: Yale University Press.

Gattel, F. (1898), *Über die sexuellen Ursachen der Neurasthenie und Angstneurose.* Berlin: August Hirschwald.

Gauld, A. (1992), *A History of Hypnotism.* New York: Cambridge University Press.

Gay, P. (1988), *Freud: A Life for Our Time.* New York: W. W. Norton.

Gelfand, T., & Kerr, J. (1992), *Freud and the History of Psychoanalysis.* Hillsdale, NJ: Analytic Press.

Geyskens, T. (2001), Freud's letters to Fliess: From seduction to sexual biology, from psychopathology to a clinical anthropology. *Internat. J. Psycho-Anal.,* 82:861–876.

Gilman, S. L. (1993), *The Case of Sigmund Freud: Medicine and Identity at the Fin de Siècle.* Baltimore: Johns Hopkins University Press.

Ginsburg, L. M., & Ginsburg, S. A. (1992), Paradise in the life of Sigmund Freud: An understanding of its imagery and paradoxes. *Internat. Rev. Psycho-Anal.,* 19:285–308.

Good, M. I. (1995), Karl Abraham, Sigmund Freud, and the fate of the seduction theory. *J. Amer. Psychoanal. Assn.,* 43:1137–1167.

—— (1996), Suggestion and veridicality in the reconstruction of sexual trauma, or can a bait of suggestion catch a carp of falsehood? *J. Amer. Psychoanal. Assn.,* 44:1189–1224.

Hacker, F. J. (1964), The reality of myth. *Internat. J. Psycho-Anal.,* 45:438–443.

Havens, L. L. (1973), *Approaches to the Mind: Movement of the Psychiatric Schools from Sects Towards Science.* Boston: Little, Brown.

Holy Bible: The Authorized or King James Version. Washington, DC: American Bible Society.

Janet, P. (1889), *L'Automatisme Psychologique.* Paris: Alcan.

—— (1914–1915), Psychoanalysis: III. Traumatic memories relative to sexuality. *J. Abnorm. Psychol.,* 9:153–187.

Jones, E. (1953), *The Life and Work of Sigmund Freud,* Vol. 1. New York: Basic Books.

King, H. (1993), Once upon a text: Hysteria from Hippocrates. In: *Hysteria Beyond Freud,* ed. S. L. Gilman, H. King, R. Porter, G. S. Rousseau, & E. Showalter. Berkeley: University of California Press, pp. 3–90.

Krafft-Ebing, R. von (1886), *Psychopathia Sexualis: With Especial Reference to the Antipathic Sexual Instinct,* 12th ed., tr. F. S. Klaf. New York: Stein and Day, 1965.

Kris, E. (1950a), The significance of Freud's earliest discoveries. In: *The Selected Papers of Ernst Kris.* New Haven, CT: Yale University Press, pp. 357–374.

—— (1950b), Notes on the development and on some current problems of psychoanalytic child psychology. In: *The Selected Papers of Ernst Kris.* New Haven, CT: Yale University Press, pp. 54–79.

—— (1954), New contributions to the study of Freud's *The Interpretation of Dreams:* A critical essay. In: *The Selected Papers of Ernst Kris.* New Haven, CT: Yale University Press, pp. 390–405.

Laplanche, J. (1989), *New Foundations for Psychoanalysis.* Oxford, U.K.: Basil Blackwell.

—— (1997), The theory of seduction and the problem of the other. *Internat. J. Psycho-Anal.,* 78:653–666.

——— Pontalis, J.-B. (1968), Fantasy and the origins of sexuality. *Internat. J. Psycho-Anal.,* 49:1–18.

——— ——— (1973), *The Language of Psycho-Analysis,* tr. D. Nicholson-Smith. New York: W. W. Norton.

Leach, E. (1970), The structure of myth. In: *Claude Lévi-Strauss.* New York: Viking Press, pp. 57–91.

Lehmann, H. (1966), Two dreams and a childhood memory of Freud. *J. Amer. Psychoanal. Assn.,* 14:388–405.

Lesky, E. (1965), *Die Wiener Medizinische Schule Im 19 Jahrhundert.* Cologne: Hermann Böhlaus Nachfolger.

Levin, K. (1978), *Freud's Early Psychology of the Neuroses: A Historical Perspective.* Pittsburgh: University of Pittsburgh Press.

López Piñero, J. M. (1963), *Historical Origins of the Concept of Neurosis,* tr. D. Berrios. Cambridge, U.K.: Cambridge University Press, 1983.

Macmillan, M. (1992), The sources of Freud's methods for gathering and evaluating clinical data. In: *Freud and the History of Psychoanalysis,* ed T. Gelfand & J. Kerr. Hillsdale, NJ: Analytic Press.

Makari, G. J. (1997), Towards defining the Freudian unconscious: Seduction, sexology and the negative of perversion (1896–1905). *Hist. Psychiatry,* 8:459–486.

Mandl, E. (1893), Wiener medizinische Club. Sitzung vom 11. Jänner 1893 [and] Sitzung vom 24. Mai 1893. *Internationale Klinische Rundschau,* 7:108–110, 868–869.

Masson, J. M. (1984), *The Assault on Truth: Freud's Suppression of the Seduction Theory.* New York: Farrar, Straus and Giroux.

——— Ed. & Trans. (1985), *The Complete Letters of Sigmund Freud to Wilhelm Fliess, 1887–1904.* Cambridge, MA: Belknap Press/Harvard University Press.

May, U. (1999), Freud's early clinical theory (1894–1896): Outline and context. *Internat. J. Psycho-Anal.,* 80:769–781.

McGrath, W. J. (1986), The dream of Joseph. In: *Freud's Discovery of Psychoanalysis: The Politics of Hysteria.* Ithaca, NY: Cornell University Press, pp. 26–58.

McGuire, W., Ed. (1974), *The Freud/Jung Letters.* Princeton, NJ: Princeton University Press.

Micale, M. S. (1993), Henri F. Ellenberger and the origins of European psychiatric historiography. In: *Beyond the Unconscious: Essays of Henri F. Ellenberger in the History of Psychiatry,* ed. M. S. Micale. Princeton, NJ: Princeton University Press, pp. 3–86.

Miller, J. A., Sabshin, M., Gedo, J. E., Pollock, G. H., Sadow, L., & Schlessinger, N. (1969), Some aspects of Charcot's influence on Freud. *J. Amer. Psychoanal. Assn.,* 17:608–623.

Moll, A. (1899), *Untersuchungen über die Libido sexualis.* Berlin: Fischer's Medicinische Buchhandlung.

Perry, C., & Laurence, J. R. (1984), Mental processes outside awareness: The contributions of Freud and Janet. In: *The Unconscious Reconsidered,* ed. K. S. Bowers & D. Meichenbaum. New York: John Wiley, pp. 9–48.

Ramzy, I. (1956), From Aristotle to Freud: A few notes on the roots of psychoanalysis. *Bull. Menninger Clin.,* 20:112–123.

Ritvo, L. B. (1990), *Darwin's Influence on Freud: A Tale of Two Sciences.* New Haven, CT: Yale University Press.

Rosenbaum, M., & Muroff, M. (1984), *Anna O.: Fourteen Contemporary Reinterpretations.* New York: Free Press.

Sand, R. (2002), Herbart, Johann Friedrich (1776–1841). In: *The Freud Encyclopedia: Theory, Therapy, and Culture,* ed. E. Erwin. New York: Routledge, pp. 254–256.

Schlessinger, N., Gedo, J. E., Miller, J., Pollock, G. H., Sabshin, M., & Sadow, L. (1967), The scientific style of Breuer and Freud in the origin of psychoanalysis. *J. Amer. Psychoanal. Assn.,* 15:404–422.

Shengold, L. (1979), Freud and Joseph. In: *Freud and His Self-Analysis,* ed. M. Kanzer & J. Glenn. New York: Jason Aronson, pp. 67–86.

Simon, B. (1992), ''Incest—see under Oedipus complex'': The history of an error in psychoanalysis. *J. Amer. Psychoanal. Assn.,* 40:955–988.

Stekel, W. (1895), Koitus im Kindesalter. *Wien. Med. Bull.,* 18:247.

Stewart, W. A. (1967), *Psychoanalysis: The First Ten Years, 1888–1898.* London: George Allen & Unwin.

Strachey, J. (1966), Editor's Note. *Standard Edition,* 1:39–40. London: Hogarth Press, 1966.

Sulloway, F. J. (1979), *Freud, Biologist of the Mind: Beyond the Psychoanalytic Legend.* New York: Basic Books.

Tatar, M. M. (1978), From Mesmer to Freud: Animal magnetism, hypnosis, and suggestion. In: *Spellbound: Studies on Mesmerism and Literature.* Princeton, NJ: Princeton University Press, pp. 3–44.

van der Kolk, B. A., McFarlane, A. C., & Weisaeth, L., Eds. (1996), *Traumatic Stress: The Effects of Overwhelming Experience on Mind, Body, and Society.* New York: Guilford Press.

Veith, I. (1965), *Hysteria: The History of a Disease.* Chicago: University of Chicago Press.

Waelder, R. (1962), Review of *Psychoanalysis, Scientific Method, and Philosophy: A Symposium,* edited by Sidney Hook. *J. Amer. Psychoanal. Assn.,* 10:617–637.

Wilson, E. (1982), Review of *The History of Sexuality, Vol. 1: An Introduction,* by Michel Foucault. *J. Amer. Psychoanal. Assn.,* 30:797–799.

Wolff, L. (1988), *Child Abuse in Freud's Vienna: Postcards from the End of the World.* New York: New York University Press.

Wozniak, R. H. (1992), *Mind and Body: René Descartes to William James.* Bethesda, MD: National Library of Medicine/American Psychological Association.

Part I

What Is the Seduction Hypothesis? Why Are We Talking About It Today?

Introduction

Chair: Owen Renik
Panelists: George Makari, Jay Greenberg
Discussants: Helen Meyers, Henry Smith

Owen Renik: Because seductiveness may be inherent in the psychoanalytic treatment situation itself, this alone establishes unquestionably the relevance of the topic for all of us. Analysis is often criticized as a field that is disposed to ancestor worship. Some members of the intellectual community consider us a little like the Collyer brothers,[1] who never throw anything away. But, at the same time, there is a benefit to historical review. The philosopher Santayana admonished us in the famous caution that ''Those who don't study the lessons of history are doomed to repeat them.'' This means not necessarily that history is studied so that it can be discarded as obsolete but that it is reviewed so that we can very carefully and selectively decide what is worth preserving.

---

[1] Ed.'s note: Homer and Langley Collyer were eccentric brothers who lived during the first half of the twentieth century in a New York City Fifth Avenue brownstone that was literally packed from floor to ceiling with a bizarre collection of every kind of object and junk they had accumulated through which ran a network of tunnels.

43

The notion, even the possibility, that Freud would consider fantasy as something generated by undischarged impulses links the concepts of fantasy to the biological theories of Freud's time. It therefore has to do with the dichotomy between fantasy and internal reality, which is closely related to the division between endogenous processes versus external reality associated with stimuli originating outside the self. Now, that is a dichotomy which is very relevant to our current topic. The alternative would be to consider the generation of constructs of reality as a holistic activity of the mind. Furthermore, Freud's confusion about actual adverse reality and psychic reality has something to do with his struggles personally to come to terms with the sexual aspect of the analytic relationship. This, too, is why today we should be talking about the seduction hypothesis.

1

The Seductions of History: Sexual Trauma in Freud's Theory and Historiography

George J. Makari, M.D.

A century ago Sigmund Freud wrote a letter to Wilhelm Fliess which has been seen as a critical turning point. Dated September 21, 1897, the letter details Freud's reasons for losing faith in his seduction theory for the creation of psychoneurosis. Guided by Freud's autobiographical accounts (e.g., Freud, 1906a,b, 1914a,b, 1925a,b), as well as the scholarly and editorial work of James Strachey (1953), Ernest Jones (1953), and Ernst Kris (1954), generations of psychoanalysts have seen this moment as a seminal one in which error was discarded, and Freud began to comprehend the central role of psychic fantasy rather than external reality in the origin of neurosis.

This paper was previously published in *The International Journal of Psycho-Analysis* (1998; 79:857–869). An earlier version was presented at the symposium.

Since 1984, this historiography has come under question. The tale of darkness yielding to light has been flipped on its head by a revisionist history; Jeffrey Masson (1984) and others have argued that in repudiating the seduction theory, truth was suppressed in favor of a socially palatable lie. By Masson's estimation, from its inception, psychoanalysis was cruelly predicated on the denial of real trauma.

As the unceasing commentary that has since taken up this controversy loudly attests (over seventy articles by my count since 1984), these differing views of history are no small matter (e.g., Panel, 1988; Powell and Boer, 1994; Izenberg, 1991; Eissler, 1993; Isräels and Schatzman, 1993). For, traditionally, psychoanalysts have looked to their past to help define their identities, both individually and communally. A history of our field's origins has been employed to mark boundaries, and adjudicate what was within and outside of "the" psychoanalytic domain. Hence, it would be naïve to venture any one history of Freud's seduction hypothesis without in effect considering one's own identity, imagining potential allies and disputants, and considering the ways one's interpretations may ramify within the broader contexts of contemporary psychoanalysis.

In the 1890s, when Freud was attempting to solve the riddle of hysteria, he faced a very similar situation. He was writing about highly contested ground, and any hypothesis was freighted with implications for his own identity within his intellectual, professional, and social communities. I propose to examine the seduction hypothesis by briefly outlining the claims that Freud put forth, and exploring some of the communal implications these claims carried. Of the numerous social identities that can be attributed to Freud in the 1890s, I will pursue only one, but it is one I believe to be central; that is, the fin-de-siècle Sigmund Freud was deeply concerned with his relationship to his medical and scientific community, whose dominant ideology was, of course, nineteenth-century natural science.[1]

---

[1] I will not pursue the ramifications of the seduction theory as it might relate to Freud's other identities as (to name a few) a male, bourgeois, Jewish, heterosexual, politically liberal Viennese husband, father, or son. For that reason, I will not take up the interesting but problematic question of the relationship between Freud's self-analysis and the seduction theory.

SEXUAL TRAUMA AND SPECIFIC CAUSATION IN NINETEENTH-CENTURY MEDICINE

In the 1860s, psychological medicine began to take up the notion of trauma. Heretofore the province of surgeons, trauma was now also conceptualized as the physical result of an overstimulating "nervous shock," generally the result of a fall or blow (e.g., Trimble, 1981; Healy, 1993). By the last decades of the nineteenth century, trauma entailed mental consequences as well as physical ones, and was widely associated with the pressures of modernity, specifically the rapid growth of industrial technology, and the effects of these technologies on the battlefield, in the factory, on city streets, and on railways.

Trauma theory then emerged, in part, as an environmental explanation for the nervous ills of modernity, and this theory was soon employed as a counterargument to another medical theory that attempted to comprehend those same ills: degeneration theory. In France and Germany, most alienists assumed that degenerative heredity was the ultimate cause of nervous illness. Freud avidly opposed degeneration theory and later confessed that his seduction hypothesis had been in part constructed as a direct challenge to degenerative theories of psychoneurosis (Masson, 1985, p. 265). Gilman (1985, pp. 191–216) has persuasively argued that as a Jewish, political liberal, Freud's hostility to degeneration theory was in good part due to his concerns about the anti-Semitic and socially conservative applications of this theory.

In *Studies on Hysteria*, Breuer and Freud explicitly framed their own contributions within trauma theory, saying they were extending Charcot's (1889) notions of traumatic paralyses by postulating traumatic hysterias (Breuer and Freud, 1893–1895). In that work, Freud reported cases where sexual traumas were important, but he did not publicly generalize from those findings (Breuer and Freud, 1893–1895). However, in October of 1895, he wrote privately to Fliess, venturing that: "Hysteria is the consequence of a presexual *sexual shock*" (Masson, 1985, p. 144).

So, notions of trauma and nervous shock and an opposition to degeneration theory were critical to Freud's early theory building on neurosogenesis. But there was also another crucial medical context that Freud's seduction hypothesis was predicated on: germ theory.[2] Following Koch's famous three postulates for isolating a specific infectious agent, Freud by 1895 began to believe that neurosis, like infectious disease, must have a specific cause (Freud, 1896a; Carter, 1980; Makari, 1998). While Freud allowed for precipitating causes, concomitant causes, and preexisting dispositions, he insisted that one specific cause *alone* determined the actual form of neurosis that would develop (1896a, p. 209). In 1895, Freud hypothesized that the specific cause of neurasthenia was adult masturbation, and the specific cause of *Angstneurose* was unconsummated sexual excitement (Freud, 1895).

In 1896, in his letters to Fliess, Freud began to put forward the hypothesis that the specific cause of hysteria was childhood sexual seduction (Masson, 1985, pp. 162–169). That same year, Freud (1896a,b,c) published this theory in three separate papers, and presented it at the Vienna Society for Psychiatry and Neurology. According to Freud, the presentation was given an "icy" reception; for the foremost sexologist in the world, Krafft-Ebing (1840–1902), called Freud's theory a "scientific fairy tale" (Masson, 1985, p. 184). Krafft-Ebing—who had become famous exploring pedophilia, necrophilia, and other disturbing philias—would not have been reacting with Wilhelmine horror to the impossibility of childhood sexual seductions. Rather, I believe there are two grounds on which Krafft-Ebing would have adamantly rejected Freud's new hypothesis. First, Krafft-Ebing like many of his colleagues put great weight on degenerative heredity as the basis of nervous ills. So, Krafft-Ebing would probably have responded like the reviewer in *The Alienist and Neurologist*, who scoffed at Freud's rejection of a "bad neuropathic endowment" as the ultimate cause of hysteria and condemned Freud for "the absurdity of such wildly conjectural, unproved and unprovable conclusions" (Hughes, 1896).

Krafft-Ebing would also have been deeply skeptical of Freud's more radical claim, borrowed from germ theory, that of specific causation. For Freud asserted that a prior sexual seduction was absolutely necessary for the creation of hysteria. That is, *no* cases of hysteria

---

[2] In nineteenth-century psychological medicine, the dominant model of pathogenesis involved the interaction between numerous exciting causes and constitutional predispositions, all of which could lead to one or more diseases. The extraordinary success of germ theory in France and Germany encouraged the adoption of a disease-specific notion of causation in the last years of the nineteenth century (e.g., Bynum, 1994).

could exist without a prior sexual seduction (1896a, p. 209). It was this same kind of totalizing claim that led to a renowned Munich physician, Leopold Löwenfeld (1847–1923), to dismiss Freud's earlier 1895 paper on the specific causes of neurasthenia and *Angstneurose* (Löwenfeld, 1895). Löwenfeld didn't contest the notion that sexual acts might assist in causing these illnesses, but he rejected Freud's claim for one specific etiology. Rather, Löwenfeld, like many authors on hysteria at that time, catalogued a long list of over twenty preconditions and exciting causes that *might* lead to either neurasthenia or hysteria (1894).

What becomes apparent in this disagreement is that the two physicians were appealing to different ideals that polarized late nineteenth-century Germanic medicine (Bonner, 1995). Löwenfeld, like Krafft-Ebing, privileged broad-based empirical observation, and like a careful taxonomist was content with listing and categorizing. Freud's claims, on the other hand, appealed to ideals rooted in his experience as a laboratory researcher; he generated a bold, even unreasonable, but highly specific hypothesis, that if true would reduce the huge complexity of the field to something much more meaningful and potentially preventable.

But given that Freud adhered to trauma theory and specific causation, we still must ask why Freud fastened on a *sexual* trauma, much less sexual *seduction*, much less sexual seduction in *childhood*? We know that a large medical literature on infantile hysteria linked its occurrence to infantile sexuality, generally the trauma of masturbation (Carter, 1983). In his pediatric work, Freud had been exposed to one of the major proponents of such theories, Adolph Baginsky (see Bonomi, 1994). And by 1895, Freud too had become convinced of the "preconditions of *sexuality* and *infantilism*" for the psychoneuroses (Masson, 1985, p. 162). Then, in his 1896 paper "The Aetiology of Hysteria," Freud claimed that in all eighteen hysterics he had treated, he had discovered a history of seduction (Freud, 1896c, pp. 199–200). There are those—like Masson (1984)—who take at face value the claim that these patients told Freud of their sexual abuse. But, as numerous authors have pointed out, there is a great deal of room for skepticism here, since Freud characterized these memories of abuse as repressed and unconscious. More recently, it has been suggested that these histories of seduction were inferential reconstructions organized in good part by Freud's zealous pursuit for confirmation of his theory (e.g., Schimek, 1987).

Whatever the origin of this hypothesis, the moment Freud began to consider pedophilic seduction as an etiology of hysteria, he immediately became engaged in the controversies of a larger medical discourse, sexology.[3] For in the work of Krafft-Ebing, Schrenck-Notzing, Tarnowsky, Binet, and others, there was a great deal of debate and discussion as to the frequency, causes, and results of childhood sexual seduction (e.g., Binet, 1887; Krafft-Ebing, 1892; Schrenck-Notzing, 1892; Tarnowsky, 1898). Freud not only knew of these sexological theories, he also seems in part to have substantially relied on them. For example, Freud at first followed the sexological consensus, represented by Krafft-Ebing, as to the identities of sexual abusers, who were felt to be primarily nursemaids, older children, and strangers (Freud, 1896a, p. 208). So in 1896, Freud was quite pleased when a patient of his confirmed the predictions ''by Krafft'' by returning to his village and identifying his nursemaid as his sexual seducer (Masson, 1985, p. 219).

But, sexological theories of seduction also presented Freud with a serious theoretical problem. For many environmentally oriented sexologists, following Albert von Schrenck-Notzing (1892), postulated that such sexual seductions of children created *not* hysteria, but, in their term, *perversion,* most commonly homosexuality (Makari, 1997a). From his letters to Fliess, we know that Freud, too, assumed this environmental theory of perversion to be true, and so he found himself in a quandary (Masson, 1985, p. 163). For how could sexual seduction be *the* specific cause of hysteria, if it also created sexual perversion?

To resolve this impasse, Freud put forth a synthesis, hypothesizing that sexual seduction led to repression and hysteria in women, and not repression but perversion in men (Masson, 1985, p. 212). With the presumption of universal bisexuality, this synthesis led to Freud's famous adage that hysteria (and later neurosis) was the negative of

---

[3] Masson (1984) has suggested that Freud may have known of forensics experts such as Tardieu who recognized the existence of childhood physical and sexual abuse, but Freud himself never referred to these authors in this regard. I argue that it is much more likely that Freud was influenced by notions of pedophilia and sexual abuse in the work of sexologists, many of whom Freud had studied and cited (Makari, 1997a).

perversion (Masson, 1985, p. 227), an equation that he never abandoned (Makari, 1997a).

Throughout 1896, Freud gradually extended and consolidated his hypotheses into a seduction *theory* of the etiology of perversion and all psychoneurosis (in which the specificity of the trauma in one of three developmental periods led to hysteria, obsessional neurosis, and paranoia). Most notable in these alterations, however, was the crucial and unprecedented shift that occurred on December 6, 1896 (Masson, 1985, p. 212). Six weeks after his father's death, Freud privately put forward a new hypothesis that bluntly took issue with sexological opinion; he argued that the perpetrator of sexual abuse was no longer nursemaids, strangers, and children as Krafft-Ebbing had suggested, but rather, the father.

No doubt this extraordinary hypothesis had great personal meaning for Freud. This bold theoretical leap also had implications for Freud's relationship to his medical community. While a good deal has been written on the horror with which such a theory would have been received in patriarchal Austrian society, there were other implications this theory held for Freud's medical community. To sustain this theory, Freud would have had to refute the conclusions of men such as Krafft-Ebing, whose clinical experience far outweighed his own. However, Freud displayed no concern in this regard. For he immediately seized upon this theory's power to undermine degeneration theory completely. Freud excitedly recognized that if seduction were due to a perverse father, then the sexually abused progeny of this same family would *seem* to carry a degenerative taint. "Heredity," Freud wrote to Fliess, seems more and more in fact to be "seduction by the father" (Masson, 1985, p. 212).

Knowledge, Matthew Arnold has proposed, is the result of contests. The seduction theory was born in a historical crucible that included an intensely creative and ambitious former researcher, now a pediatrically trained neurologist, Sigmund Freud, working with a group of late nineteenth-century Viennese patients, and thinking about these clinical experiences within the contested grounds of late nineteenth-century trauma theory, germ theory, and sexology. As the theoretician of seduction, Freud was defining himself within a number of registers that organized one's identity within the medical community of late nineteenth-century Vienna, as research imperialist armed with

Koch's postulates, as a foe of degenerative heredity, as a sexologist. But soon some of these relationships were to shift.

AFTER THE SEDUCTION THEORY: FREUD'S MASTURBATION HYPOTHESES

Throughout 1897, Freud published nothing that hinted at the broad theory of psychoneurosis and perversion he had been privately constructing. The first hint of trouble came in May, with Freud reporting the premature termination of a patient and the likely loss of another (Masson, 1985, pp. 243–244). In that same May letter to Fliess, Freud reported the arrival of a student from Berlin, Felix Gattel (1870–1904). Gattel was sent to Krafft-Ebing's clinic, where he interviewed a hundred consecutive outpatient cases, to test Freud's hypotheses for the specific causes of *Angstneurose* and neurasthenia. Gattel's findings must have been quite cheering to Freud, for this research seemed to lend support to Freud's contentions regarding the specific causation of both neurasthenia and *Angstneurose* (Gattel, 1898).

But there was also some potentially disturbing news in regard to hysteria. Gattel had attempted to exclude hysterics from his sample but nonetheless ended up with 17 percent of his subjects who had a hysterical component. Sulloway (1979) has suggested that this large number may have given Freud pause, insofar as a high incidence of hysteria would require a very high incidence of paternal sexual abuse.

As Gattel's study was in full swing, Freud complained of intellectual paralysis (Freud, 1895, pp. 253–254) and occupied himself with a trip he planned to Italy with his brother and Gattel. Upon returning from the trip, Freud wrote the famed letter of September 21, 1897, in which he cited four reasons for his loss of faith in the seduction theory. First, Freud cited the failure of his treatments; second, the unlikelihood of paternal seduction given the "realisation of the unexpected frequency of hysteria"; third, the indistinguishability of truth and fiction in the unconscious; and fourth, the fact that even in psychosis, memories of seduction did not emerge. And with this unhappy retreat, Freud was left wondering if in fact hereditary disposition was back at the center of the etiology of neurosis (Masson, 1985, pp. 264–265).

September 21, 1897, has, for most traditional and revisionist historians alike, marked the beginning of a great shift from sexual trauma theory to—here I shall name but a few prominent theories—(1) Freud's discovery of libido, the Oedipus complex, and infantile sexuality (e.g., Gay, 1988); (2) Freud's appropriation of the Fliessian id (Sulloway, 1979); or (3) the denial of the frequency and consequences of sexual trauma, and the beginning of Freud's cowardly reconciliation with his medical community (Masson, 1984, p. 110). But in the hurry to reach for broader meaning, important details have been swept aside.

After his letter of September 21, 1897, despite one moment of doubt in December of that same year, Sigmund Freud did abandon the seduction *theory*. However, Freud did not totally reinvent himself, nor did he reinvent all of his concomitant theoretical positions within his discursive communities. Freud held the same positions on degeneration, the import of childhood, and still believed that external sexual trauma was etiological in the neuroses. But Freud abandoned one important assumption that had been foundational to his seduction theory, the notion of specific causes (on this point I am in agreement with Eissler [1993]).

This is made clear by a close examination of the first revision of the seduction theory, which Freud put forth in October 1897. There, Freud attempted to rebuild a theory for the creation of hysteria, and the crucial modification he made was that he now envisioned "large, general framing motives" with "fill-ins" that may "vary according to the individual's experiences" (Masson, 1985, p. 274; Masson and Schröter, 1986, p. 295).[4] That is to say, Freud shifted from a specific cause to a general category of causes. These causes were still sexual and traumatic, but now Freud referred generally to early infantile "sexual experiences" of various sorts. In this October 1897 theory, early sexual stimulation by whatever means led to "longing," fantasy, and later more traumatic sexual overstimulation through masturbation. Freud postulated that hysteria would only develop if such masturbation was repressed (Masson, 1985, p. 275; Masson and Schröter, 1986, p. 296).

---

[4] In German, Freud wrote: "In der Determinierung ahnen mir grosse allgemeine Rahmenmotive, möchte ich sie nennen, und andere, Füllmotive, die nach den Erlebnissen des Einzelnen wechseln" (Masson and Schröter, 1986, p. 295).

So, while, in his September 21, 1897, letter, Freud listed four grounds for the repudiation of the seduction theory, including pragmatic-clinical, epidemiological, and epistemological problems, the *one* aspect of that theory he almost immediately modified thereafter was the claim that paternal sexual seduction was the specific cause of hysteria.[5] That modification, of course, would contend with the problem of the "unexpected frequency of hysteria," which would, via Freud's notion of specific causation, require a high incidence of paternal sexual abuse.

Eight years later, in 1905, when first writing publicly of his repudiation of the seduction theory, Freud denied that he had exaggerated the "frequency or importance" of sexual seduction, only that he had not recognized that some who had been sexually abused remained normal (1905b, p. 190; 1905c, p. 91). In 1906, Freud noted that his caseload was skewed by a preponderance of patients where "sexual seduction . . . played the chief part in the history of the patient's childhood;" hence, he "over-estimated the frequency of such events" (1906a, p. 274; 1906b, p. 153).[6] Freud did add that at the time he was also unable to distinguish with certainty between "falsifications made by hysterics in their memories of childhood and traces of real events," but added that he learned to explain these phantasies as fending off real memories of masturbation (1906a, p. 274; 1906b, p. 153). In 1907, Freud wrote to Karl Abraham suggesting that the key factor for his loss of faith in the seduction theory was discovering that sexual traumas were quite common (Abraham and E. L. Freud, 1965, p. 2).

Despite the confusing lack of consistency in Freud's reasoning in these early accounts, a common strand remains. The central issue Freud wrestled with was epidemiological evidence regarding seduction and hysteria, probably coming at least in part from Gattel, that made paternal seduction implausible as a specific cause. The pressure raised

---

[5] I do not agree with Masson (1984), Blass (1992), and Rand and Torok (1997), who suggest that Freud maintained the seduction theory long after the autumn of 1897. For without the notion of a specific cause there was no Freudian seduction theory. To my mind, the confusion lies in the distinction between a narrow hypothesis that seduction in childhood was pathogenic (a notion which I believe Freud never relinquished), and the much more sweeping, as well as more specific theory by which seduction created certain neuroses or perversions when it was experienced actively or passively at certain points of development in boys or girls.

[6] Note here that Freud does not deny that the patients had been sexually abused, only that his small sample size had led to an erroneous generalization. But, as Blass and Simon (1992, p. 172) point out, Freud here directly contradicts his 1905 account by suggesting that he had mistaken the frequency of such attacks.

by this evidence, I would suggest, forced Freud *subsequently* to reconsider the truth value of his historical data.

Furthermore, rather than quickly fixing upon sexual fantasy and drive as causative in psychoneurosis, Freud over the next three years continued to think of the etiology of hysteria as traumatic. However, during this transitional period, he shifted his focus more and more from seduction to the overstimulating trauma of masturbation with its attendant fantasies (Makari, 1997b, 1998). Masturbation—an act poised between psyche and soma—and its later repression were increasingly the real, crucial traumatic element in the creation of hysteria, as is illustrated in Freud's interpretation of Ida Bauer's hysteria in the Dora case (1905a). Some time between 1901 and 1903, Freud reconceptualized masturbation as not traumatic, but rather indicative of nascent infantile sexuality, and with that reconceptualization Freud made the shift from a trauma theory to one based on sexual drives. This is not the place to examine fully my argument for the transitional role of masturbation in Freud's work (Makari, 1997b, 1998), but I raise this little-noted transitional phase to suggest that an immediate and easy linkage between the demise of the seduction theory and the creation of libido theory with its focus on wishful fantasies is not fully warranted.

THE SEDUCTIONS OF HISTORY

In our understanding of the rise and fall of Freud's seduction theory—degeneration, trauma theory, germ theory, sexological opinion, incidences, statistics, Gattel, masturbation—all of these historical details have more or less been eclipsed by another set of concerns. Debates about Freud's seduction theory have become debates, *not* about some of these somewhat strange-to-our-ears late nineteenth-century topics, but rather one very attuned to our postmodern times, the issue of historical truth and fantasy.

How did historical truth become the most prominent theoretical issue surrounding the fall of the seduction theory? Following Blass and Simon (1992), I would suggest that this shift can be traced in Freud's own historical accounts. In his earliest private account in September of 1897, Freud laid out pragmatic clinical, epidemiological, and epistemological problems with the seduction theory. However, in his earliest public accounts, as we have seen, Freud primarily attributed his renunciation of the seduction theory to epidemiological kinds of problems of a kind that I have argued were particularly important to the status of Freud's theory in the medical community.[7] In 1914, Freud's account shifted its emphasis. Problems related to specific causation, incidences, and skewed samples were dropped in toto. While Freud in 1914 did say that this etiology broke down "under the weight of its own improbability and contradiction in definitely ascertainable circumstances," he did not elaborate, instead highlighting how his adherence to trauma theory led him naïvely to accept the "statements made by patients" in which they ascribed their symptoms to seduction. Hence, "analysis had led back to these infantile sexual traumas, and yet they were not true. The firm ground of reality was gone." Freud then described a radical conceptual shift, in which he recognized that "if hysterical subjects trace back their symptoms to traumas that are fictitious, then the new fact which emerges is precisely that they create such scenes in *phantasy*," and from there Freud tells us, childhood sexuality came to light (1914a, pp. 17–18; 1914b, pp. 55–56).

It is an elegant and exciting history of discovery, based on an attempt to grasp an elusive reality from illusion. It is also an account that Ernest Jones has rightly called a "dramatic" one that does not quite tally with the historical record that exists in the Freud–Fliess correspondence (Jones, 1953, p. 267). What accounts for the change in emphasis from Freud's earlier historical accounts? This is an important question given that Freud's 1914 account can be seen as a historiographic turning point that in good part organized subsequent accounts (e.g., 1896b, n. 1; 1896d, n. 1; 1925a,b; 1933a,b).[8] For in these post-1914 texts, Freud minimized or dropped epidemiological reasons for

---

[7] A closer examination of the confusing and contradictory claims Freud put forth between 1905 and 1907, would be enriched by context; that is, Freud had different rhetorical and theoretical agendas when writing a private letter to Fliess, the *Three Essays on the Theory of Sexuality*, a private letter to Karl Abraham (who in 1907 was still employing the seduction theory), and a chapter in a book by Löwenfeld (1894).

[8] For instance, in a 1924 footnote, Freud wrote that "at that time I was not yet able to distinguish between my patients' phantasies about their childhood years and their real recollections. As a result, I attributed to the aetiological factor of seduction a significance and universality which it does not possess. When this error had been overcome, it became possible to obtain insight into the spontaneous manifestations of the sexuality of children . . ." (1896b, n. 1, p. 168; 1896d, n. 1, p. 385). How this error had been overcome, how Freud learned to distinguish fantasy from reality, none of this is mentioned. In his 1925 autobiographical sketch, Freud reported being "at last obliged to recognise

shifting from a theory based on first-hand accounts of sexual trauma to fantasies derived from libido. Instead, Freud's post-1914 accounts give the impression that his rejection of false claims of seduction, after a period of confusion, led directly to his recognition of the truth of sexual libido, despite the years of struggle and complicated theorizing that separated these two events. Though Freud does make reference to a transitional period of feeling "helpless bewilderment" (1914a, p. 17; 1914b, p. 55) and "at a loss" (1925a, p. 34; 1925b, p. 60), he rhetorically suggests that the recognition of the falseness of a hysteric's claims of seduction via a simple and brilliant reconceptualization resulted in the emergence of the truth of Freud's libido theory.

So how can we account for the shifts in historiography regarding the seduction theory? Blass and Simon argue that Freud, prior to 1914, was still waiting for his theory of fantasy to be on more secure phylogenetic and biological ground before placing it at the core of psychoanalysis. Only after 1914 did he dare put so much weight on the import of fantasy in the development of his theory, they argue (Blass and Simon, 1992, pp. 176–177). Perhaps. But I would suggest another interpretation. In his earliest published accounts, Freud was still writing to, for, and against members of his own medical community. His 1905 *Three Essays* account was in a book addressed to sexologists; his 1906 (1906a,b) account was published in a volume edited by none other than the enemy of specific causation, Leopold Löwenfeld. These accounts spoke to Freud's medical community in their language, highlighting their concerns, and touching on the issues that aligned, defined, included, and excluded members. But in 1914, looking back at the same events, and writing in a psychoanalytic journal, Freud wrote a quite different history for a different community. His struggles for recognition within the medical community of Vienna were over; he was famous. Freud's readers were no longer physicians interested in incidences, germ theory, and specific causes. Now, Freud was the leader of a movement. But it was a movement that Freud feared might fragment because of the challenges put forth by Alfred Adler and Carl Jung, both of whom continued to call their endeavors psychoanalysis

that these scenes of seduction had never taken place, and that they were only phantasies . . ." (1925a, p. 34; 1925b, p. 60). This realization left Freud "at a loss," but then resulted in his understanding of childhood sexuality (1925a, p. 34; 1925b, p. 60), but again no mention of how Freud was made to realize the untenability of these claims of seduction, nor what lay on the road between seduction and libido. In a 1933 lecture on femininity, Freud wrote of being "driven" to recognize that the tales of seduction were "untrue," that is, derived from fantasies and "not from real occurrences" (1933a, p. 120; 1933b, p. 128). But "driven by what?" the reader is left wondering.

after splitting with Freud (Stepansky, 1983; Kerr, 1993). It is in this context that Freud wrote his pivotal 1914 history of the seduction theory, for it appears, of course, in none other than Freud's written response to those splits, "On the History of the Psycho-Analytic Movement" (1914a,b). This essay has been aptly described by Phillip Rieff as "a masterpiece of polemic" meant to "exclude, on his [Freud's] own terms, those among his disciples who had already departed on terms he could no longer permit to be theirs" (1966, p. 79). It is an essay intended to forcefully segregate historical developments that were true to psychoanalysis from those that were false.

In that 1914 essay, Freud intended to define the essential postulates of psychoanalysis, and then demonstrate how neither Adler's nor Jung's theories could be considered psychoanalytic. His initial approach, however, was not via arguments over theory, but rather by recounting the history of the origins of psychoanalysis. In so doing, Freud took up the history of the "hypothesis of infantile sexuality" (1914a, p. 17; 1914b, p. 55). After recounting his history, including the discovery of sexual libido, from the ruins of the seduction theory, Freud wrote: "I think that by thus unrolling the story of the development of psycho-analysis, I have shown what it is, better than by a systematic description of it" (1914a, pp. 20–21; 1914b, p. 59).

It is therefore hardly surprising that the history Freud unrolled in this polemic differed markedly from his account to Fliess in 1897, or the accounts he addressed to a medical audience in the first years of the twentieth century. For Freud, the purpose of this 1914 history was to make his sexual libido theory absolutely central to the origins and development of psychoanalysis. Dissenters to sexual libido theory such as Adler and Jung might have argued that many major tenets of psychoanalysis had been known before Freud set out his libido theory in 1905, and hence one could claim to be a psychoanalyst and not subscribe to libido theory. Freud and his followers felt differently. For them, September 21, 1897, became a "historical beginning" that left the followers of Jung and Adler for dead.

But in writing this polemical and streamlined history, Freud left a somewhat distorted impression for future generations of readers who looked to his 1914 document for an account of the development of psychoanalytic theory. The elegance of this simple formulation—accusations of past seductions are really sexual fantasies—resulted in subsequent accounts downplaying or ignoring any post-1897 transitional period in Freud's etiological thinking. Jones described Freud's discovering the truth of infantile sexuality when he repudiated the seduction theory in September of 1897 (1953, p. 322).[9] Strachey agreed that Freud discovered infantile sexuality in the fall of 1897, but added the complicated thesis that it "took some years, however, for him to be entirely reconciled to his own discovery" (1953, p. 128). Even more misleading was the fact that some readers took Freud's 1914 account to mean that for Freud claims of seduction were always false, and that in his model external trauma was pathogenically irrelevant, despite his numerous statements to the contrary (i.e., Freud, 1896, n. 1, p. 168).

But his 1914 history notwithstanding, Freud did not hold such a simplistic view. In 1916 and 1917, before an audience made up of the general faculty of the Vienna Medical School, Freud put forth, not a history, but a statement of theory in which he refused either–or dichotomies. While putting forth his belief that little girls' phantasies of seduction by their father are "no doubt" imaginary, he simultaneously suggested that phantasies of being seduced are of "particular interest because so often they are not phantasies but real memories," and "you must not suppose, however, that sexual abuse of a child by its nearest male relatives belongs entirely to the realm of phantasy" (1916–1917a, p. 370; 1916–1917b, p. 385).[10] Before this medical audience, Freud extended the notion of pathological trauma to include fantasy, and hence presented a more nuanced account of his theory that did not fit the polemical needs of his historical account in 1914.

And so Freud's seduction theory is inextricably bound up with the problems of history. Should we believe our patients' histories, should we believe Freud's, Jones's, Masson's, should you believe mine? The history of Freud's seduction theory forces us to consider

---

[9] Jones's claim has been repeated in numerous histories. To my mind, it is based on a fundamental confusion between Freud's still unintegrated thinking on dreams and normal psychology as opposed to his thinking on pathogenesis. The seduction theory was a theory of pathogenesis, and while Freud began to understand aspects of the oedipal situation and incestuous desires in dreams in late 1897, at this point he did not consider these to be pathogenic. Freud made this clear in the Dora case, where he commented on the commonality of oedipal feelings, suggesting that there must be either a constitutional aberrance, seduction, or masturbation to make such oedipal feelings pathological (1905a; Makari, 1997b).

[10] I would like to acknowledge Henry Smith for pointing me to this passage. Interestingly, Freud also argued in these lectures that the pathogenic effect of seduction and fantasy were the same (1916–1917a, p. 370; 1916–1917b, p. 385), a notion that has been dropped in most accounts but is to be found in Fritz Wittels's history (1931, p. 84). In my view, there is no justification for the reading of this position back into Freud's thinking during the 1890s.

such questions, foregrounding our postmodern suspicion regarding the
way truth claims may be organized by our personal and communal
desires and identities, while at the same time by the very gravity of
its matter—childhood sexual trauma—refusing us this easy out, forcing
us to reconsider the responsibility we have to continue our always
flawed efforts to recapture both the disquieting and reassuring, the
strange and familiar from our past.

REFERENCES

Abraham, H. C., & Freud, E. L., Eds. (1965), *A Psychoanalytic Dialogue:
The Letters of Sigmund Freud and Karl Abraham.* New York: Basic
Books, 1965.

Binet, A. (1887), Le fétichisme dans l'amour. *Rev. Philosophique,*
24:143–167, 252–274.

Blass, R. (1992), Did Dora have an Oedipus complex? *The Psychoanalytic
Study of the Child,* 47:159–187. New Haven, CT: Yale University
Press.

——— (1994), The value of the historical perspective to contemporary psychoanalysis: Freud's seduction hypothesis. *Internat. J. Psycho-
Anal.,* 75:677–694.

——— Simon, B. (1992), Freud on his own mistake(s): The role of seduction
in the etiology of neurosis. *Psychiatry & the Humanities,*
12:160–183.

Bonner, T. N. (1995), *Becoming a Physician: Medical Education in Great
Britain, France, Germany and the United States, 1750–1945.* New
York: Oxford University Press.

Bonomi, C. (1994), Why have we ignored Freud the "paediatrician"? In:
*100 Years of Psychoanalysis: Contributions to the History of Psycho-
analysis,* ed. A. Haynal & E. Falzeder. Geneva: Cahiers Psychiatriques Genevois.

Breuer, J., & Freud, S. (1893–1895), Studies on Hysteria. *Standard Edition,*
1. London: Hogarth Press, 1955.

Bynum, W. F. (1994), *Science and the Practice of Medicine in the Nineteenth
Century.* Cambridge, U.K.: Cambridge University Press.

Carter, K. C. (1980), Germ theory, hysteria and Freud's early work in psychopathology. *Med. History,* 24:259–274.

——— (1983), Infantile hysteria and infantile sexuality in late nineteenth
century German-language medical literature. *Med. History,*
27:186–196.

Charcot, J. M. (1889), *Lecture on the Diseases of the Nervous System,* Vol. 3, tr. T. Savill. London: New Sydenham Society.

Eissler, K. (1993), Comments on erroneous interpretations of Freud's seduction theory. *J. Amer. Psychoanal. Assn.,* 41:571–584.

Freud, S. (1895), On the grounds for detaching a particular syndrome from neurasthenia under the description 'anxiety neurosis.' *Standard Edition,* 3:85–115. London: Hogarth Press, 1962.

—— (1896a), Heredity and the aetiology of the neuroses. *Standard Edition,* 3:141–156. London: Hogarth Press, 1962.

—— (1896b), Further remarks on the neuropsychoses of defense. *Standard Edition,* 3:157–185. London: Hogarth Press, 1962.

—— (1896c), The aetiology of hysteria. *Standard Edition,* 3:187–221. London: Hogarth Press, 1962.

—— (1896d), Weitere Bemerkungen über die Abwehr-Neuropsychosen. *Gesammelte Werke,* 1:377–403. London: Imago, 1952.

—— (1898), Sexuality in the aetiology of the neuroses. *Standard Edition,* 3:259–285. London: Hogarth Press, 1962.

—— (1905a), Fragment of an analysis of a case of hysteria. *Standard Edition,* 7:1–122. London: Hogarth Press, 1953.

—— (1905b), Three Essays on the Theory of Sexuality. *Standard Edition,* 7:123–243. London: Hogarth Press, 1953.

—— (1905c), Drei Abhandlungen zur Sexualtheorie. *Gesammelte Werke,* 5:27–145. London: Imago, 1942.

—— (1906a), My views on the part played by sexuality in the aetiology of the neuroses. *Standard Edition,* 7:269–279. London: Hogarth Press, 1953.

—— (1906b), Meine Ansichten über die Rolle der Sexualität in der Ätiologie der Neurosen. *Gesammelte Werke,* 5:147–159. London: Imago, 1942.

—— (1914a), On the history of the psycho-analytic movement. *Standard Edition,* 14:1–66. London: Hogarth Press, 1957.

—— (1914b), Zur Geschichte der psychoanalytischen Bewegung. *Gesammelte Werke* 10:43–113. London: Imago, 1946.

—— (1916–1917a), Introductory Lectures on Psycho-Analysis. *Standard Edition,* 16. London: Hogarth Press, 1961.

—— (1916–1917b), Vorlesungen zur Einführung in die Psychoanalyse. *Gesammelte Werke,* 11. London: Imago, 1946.

—— (1925a), An autobiographical study. *Standard Edition,* 20:1–70. London: Hogarth Press, 1959.

—— (1925b), Selbstdarstellung. *Gesammelte Werke,* 13:31–96. London: Imago, 1948.

———— (1933a), New Introductory Lectures on Psycho-Analysis. *Standard Edition,* 22:1–182. London: Hogarth Press, 1964.

———— (1933b), Die Weiblichkeit. In: *Neue Folge der Vorlesungen zur Einführung in die Psychoanalyse. Gesammelte Werke,* 15:119–145. London: Imago, 1946.

Gattel, F. (1898), *Über die sexuellen Ursachen der Neurasthenie und Angst-neurose.* Berlin: August Hirschwald.

Gay, P. (1988), *Freud: A Life for Our Time.* New York: W. W. Norton.

Gilman, S. (1985), *Difference and Pathology: Stereotypes of Sexuality, Race and Madness.* Ithaca, NY: Cornell University Press.

Healy, D. (1993), *Images of Trauma: From Hysteria to Post-Traumatic Stress Disorder.* London: Faber & Faber.

Hughes, C. H. (1896), Review of "The aetiology of hysteria." *The Alienist & Neurologist,* 17:519–520.

Isräels, H., & Schatzman, M. (1993), The seduction theory. *Hist. Psychiat.,* 4:23–59.

Izenberg, G. N. (1991), Seduced and abandoned: The rise and fall of Freud's seduction theory. In: *The Cambridge Companion to Freud,* ed. J. Neu. Cambridge, U.K.: Cambridge University Press, pp. 25–43.

Jones, E. (1953), *Sigmund Freud, Life and Work,* Vol. 1. New York: Basic Books.

Kerr, J. (1993), *A Most Dangerous Method: The Story of Freud, Jung and Sabina Spielrein.* New York: Knopf.

Krafft-Ebing, R. (1892), *Psychopathia Sexualis, with Especial Reference to the Antipathic Sex Instinct,* 7th ed., tr. C. G. Chaddock. Philadelphia: F. A. Davis, 1893.

Kris, E. (1954), Introduction. In: *The Origins of Psychoanalysis: Letters to Wilhelm Fliess, Drafts and Notes: 1887–1902.* New York: Basic Books, pp. 33–34.

Löwenfeld, L. (1894), *Pathologie und Therapie der Neurasthenie und Hyst-erie.* Wiesbaden: J. F. Bergmann.

———— (1895), Über die Verknüpfung neurasthenischer und hysterischer Symptome in Anfallsform nebst Bemerkungen über die Freudsche Angstneurose. *Münchener Med. Wschr.,* 42:282–285.

Makari, G. J. (1997a), Towards defining the Freudian unconscious: Seduction, sexology and the "negative of perversion" (1896–1905). *Hist. Psychiat.,* 8:459–485.

———— (1997b), Dora's hysteria and the maturation of Sigmund Freud's the-ory of transference: A new historical interpretation. *J. Amer. Psy-choanal. Assn.,* 45:1061–1096.

———— (1998), Between seduction and libido: Sigmund Freud's masturbation hypotheses and the realignment of his etiologic thinking (1897–1905). *Bull. Hist. Med.,* 72:638–662.

Masson, J. M. (1984), *The Assault on Truth: Freud's Suppression of the Seduction Theory.* New York: Farrar, Straus & Giroux.

———— Ed. (1985), *The Complete Letters of Sigmund Freud to Wilhelm Fliess, 1887–1904,* tr. J. M. Masson. Cambridge, MA: Harvard University Press.

———— Schröter, M., Eds. (1986), *Sigmund Freud Briefe an Wilhelm Fliess, 1887–1904.* Frankfurt: S. Fischer.

Panel (1988), The seduction hypothesis. Reported by A. Marans. *J. Amer. Psychoanal. Assn.,* 36:759–772.

Powell, R., & Boer, D. (1994), Did Freud mislead patients to confabulate memories of abuse? *Psychological Rep.,* 74:1283–1298.

Rand, N., & Torok, M. (1997), *Questions for Freud: The Secret History of Psychoanalysis.* Cambridge, MA: Harvard University Press.

Rieff, P. (1966), *The Triumph of the Therapeutic: Uses of Faith After Freud.* Chicago: University of Chicago Press, 1987.

Schimek, J. G. (1987), Fact and fantasy in the seduction theory. A historical review. *J. Amer. Psychoanal. Assn.,* 35:937–966.

Schrenck-Notzing, A. von (1892), *Therapeutic Suggestion in Psychopathia Sexualis,* tr. C. G. Chaddock. Philadelphia: F. A. Davis, 1895.

Stepansky, P. (1983), *In Freud's Shadow: Adler in Context.* Hillsdale, NJ: Analytic Press.

Strachey, J. (1953), Editor's note. *Standard Edition,* 7. London: Hogarth Press, 1953.

Sulloway, F. (1979), *Freud, Biologist of the Mind.* New York: Basic Books.

Tarnowsky, B. (1898), *The Sexual Instinct and Its Morbid Manifestations from the Double Standpoint of Jurisprudence and Psychiatry,* tr. W. C. Costello & A. Allinson. Paris: Charles Carrington.

Trimble, M. (1981), *Post-Traumatic Neurosis: From Railway Spine to Whiplash.* New York: Wiley.

Wittels, F. (1931), *Freud and His Time,* tr. L. Brink. New York: Liveright.

invoked neurology far too soon in the explanatory chain, foreclosing the possibility of further psychological exploration. The theory that Freud, even at an early stage in his career, hoped to create required some way to anchor the entire history of hysterical illnesses in psychic experience. He needed to construct a chain of events that led from the symptom back to its cause. Breuer's findings did this so far as individual symptoms were concerned. Freud needed to construct a similar chain that would lead beyond the symptom, that could explain the predisposition to be so deeply affected, even traumatized, by events that could be quite ordinary.

Freud's theoretical need converged with a clinical finding: As he did more and more analyses the chain of remembered events stretched farther back into the earliest days of childhood. Ultimately, it led to an original scene of sexual arousal at the hands of another person, and Freud could write that "at the bottom of every case of hysteria there are *one or more occurrences of premature sexual experience*, occurrences which belong to the earliest years of childhood" (1896b, p. 203).

Seduction, the most general term that Freud used to describe these premature sexual experiences, was the sine qua non of the psychoneuroses. By occupying this etiological role, it became one of a handful of organizing concepts that Freud developed over the course of his career to anchor his theorizing and to direct further psychoanalytic exploration. These concepts are among the most fertile and generative in the history of ideas. Freud had an ability to think in a way that engaged the interest of psychoanalysts and others interested in psychoanalysis over the course of many decades, and that continues to do so today. That today we continue to debate an idea that Freud abandoned after only a few years, stands as proof of the power of these central organizing concepts.

Consider some of the other concepts, drawn from various periods in Freud's career: trauma, the Oedipus complex, primal scene, castration, libido, psychic structure. Each of these served as a core from which Freud spun out an intricate web of ideas about psychodynamics, internal and external experience, and pathogenesis. But despite their centrality, and despite how foundational they are for a massive body of data and theorizing, there is something marvelously elusive about all of them. Freud's thinking was always delicately poised between the literal and the metaphoric, a quality that goes a long way toward explaining its enduring power. Consider the exquisite ambiguity of some critical ideas. Libido is a chemical substance in the *Three Essays on the Theory of Sexuality* (1905), but it is also an aspect of the drive theory that Freud called ''our mythology, magnificent in its indefiniteness'' (p. 95). Psychic structure is, concretely, a part of cerebral anatomy that he assumed would eventually become visible through dissection (1923), but it is also something that we learn about only when we invoke ''the witch metapsychology.'' The threat of castration can be something that adults use to control their children's masturbation or other distressing behavior; viewed in that light it refers to words that are literally and frequently uttered. But it can also point to a common, even ubiquitous experience of the child's, not merely a fantasy in the usual sense of the term but a way of organizing and contextualizing a range of feelings about growing, or wanting, or hating.

With any of these central concepts, attempting to take them either as simply literal or as simply metaphor eviscerates them. Consider castration: Taken as an actually uttered threat, it seems an archaic and even foolish idea in our contemporary Western culture. But thinking of it merely as a concoction of the child's, collapsing it into mere fantasy, enfeebles it as well. When we do that, we lose the sense of the origin of the experience in relationship to the other, in the child's fear of adult retaliation for becoming competent or sexual. Whatever richness the concept has depends upon our ability to maintain it simultaneously in various universes of discourse. Freud's ability to do this consistently was an important aspect of his unique genius.

That is why conferences can (and in most cases have) been held on the topics ''What is trauma?'' or ''What is the primal scene?'' or ''What is psychic structure?'' And it is fascinating that it is impossible for an analyst to come up with an answer to any of these questions without touching upon a great deal (possibly everything) about the way he or she thinks about all of the most important issues in psychoanalysis. Think seriously about how we conceptualize libido or castration (even if the concepts play little or no role in our own psychoanalytic vision) and we will have discovered a great deal about where we stand as analysts.

The generative ambiguity of so many Freudian concepts reflects Freud's own intellectual playfulness, a capacity he applied to his struggles with some of the gravest concerns about human experience. Despite the recent, justified criticism of him for embracing an always suspect and now largely discarded positivistic philosophy of science, Freud was never one to insist on operationalizing his terms. Looking at the first appearance of any of his major organizing concepts reveals him at play, considering various meanings, exploring connotations, valuing a term's potential over its precision. It can be maddening at times, because Freud refuses to guide the reader carefully through his various usages. His need to engage his ideas at their fullest—including an intense commitment to whichever connotation he is working with at any given moment—always takes precedence over the reader's need to understand them.

This characterization of Freud, however, requires a kind of warning label. In speaking of him as playful, I am referring to the way he thought, not necessarily to the way he wrote. As we will see when we look at his writing about seduction, his words can be misleadingly vehement, even dogmatic; they convey a sense of certainty that belies an underlying openness to the many implications of the ideas he is developing. Freud did not necessarily articulate all of these implications; it is our guess whether or not he was actually aware of them. Perhaps he was especially wary about acknowledging the various possibilities inherent in his ideas (and the consequent uncertainty of any one of them) to a public audience that he always considered hostile and suspicious. But the many implications are there, and they keep his ideas as alive today as they were a century ago.

Before I address the seduction hypothesis specifically, I want to spend a moment on Freud's concept of trauma—closely related to seduction, of course, and central to the view of neurosis spelled out in *Studies on Hysteria* (Breuer and Freud, 1893–1895). In passages that appear close to each other, Freud seems to be thinking about trauma in two related but quite different ways. On the one hand, the term could refer to the overwhelming impact of external events—deaths, life-threatening illnesses, accidents, and so on. But the term can also refer to something else—to the moment at which some mental event (an idea, a feeling, a wish, a memory, a fear) is experienced as incompatible with what Freud called the "dominant mass of ideas,'' the sum total of everything that can be known consciously. Viewed thus, trauma refers to the experienced incompatibility itself; Freud makes no judgment about how weighty or innocuous the idea or the event that gave rise to it might be in any objective sense.

Thus, at the very outset, the concept of trauma in and of itself raises a range of questions about the etiology of neurosis. It points simultaneously to an external event and an internal conflict, and arouses our curiosity about the relationship between the two. Within the realm of external events, it points simultaneously to the extraordinary and the ordinary, again raising questions about how various events affect mental life. (Contemporary emphases on the role of dissociation in both normal development and pathogenesis reflect our continuing interest in the traumatic potential not only of extraordinary but also of ordinary events.) But typically for him, Freud made no effort to distinguish between these various uses of the term (or even to note that he had different things in mind). He was quite comfortable just to move back and forth between the various resonances that the concept of trauma evoked in his own thinking, to move between outside and inside, between the commonplace and the awe inspiring, between the literal and the metaphor.

So what of the seduction hypothesis? Like trauma and Freud's other organizing concepts, it is richly and confusingly ambiguous at its core. I will try to show this, although in his writings Freud typically used the term and the theory to refer, quite concretely, to specific events. But despite this, I find that any attempt to take what Freud had in mind too literally ends with the hypothesis crumbling in our hands.

Despite its importance in the history of psychoanalysis, seduction appears centrally in only three papers, all published in 1896. In ''Further Remarks on the Neuro-Psychoses of Defence,'' Freud tells us that the pathogenic events covered by his theory must have occurred before the age of 8 or 10, and that *"their content must consist of an actual irritation of the genitals (of processes resembling copulation)"* (1896a, p. 163). In ''The Aetiology of Hysteria,'' he reiterates the idea that the seductions consist of ''stimulation of the genitals, coitus-like acts, and so on . . .'' (1896b, p. 206). He specifies three situations in which such acts may take place: They may be perpetrated by adults who are strangers, by someone the child knows such as a governess, tutor, or relative; or by one child upon another (p. 208). In his descriptions of these events Freud typically characterizes them as attacks, or assaults, or abuse.

These words fit the phenomena, but when he spoke generally of the pathogenic sexual experiences of childhood, the word he used was *seduction,* which is a translation of the German *Verführung,*[1] which is comparable to our English word, and refers to something that we typically think of as happening between consenting adults. The difference in connotation between the word and the event as Freud described it is striking; the contrast highlights the ambiguities in Freud's thinking about his clinical findings and about how he was using them theoretically. Why, for instance, did Freud not speak of an "abuse theory of hysteria," or a "molestation theory"? What does it mean to seduce a child anyway?

The various possibilities become even more intriguing in light of the subsequent history of the seduction theory. Within a year and a half of publishing "The Aetiology of Hysteria," he announced in a letter to Fliess that, "I no longer believe in my *neurotica*" (Masson, 1985, p. 264). He gave several reasons for abandoning the theory, including two that are particularly interesting. "Surely," he writes, "such widespread perversions against children are not very probable" (p. 264). This is striking in light of his published assertion eighteen months before that "it seems to me certain that our children are far more often exposed to sexual assaults than the few precautions taken by parents . . . would lead us to expect. . . . It is to be expected that increased attention to the subject will very soon confirm the great frequency of sexual experiences and sexual activity in childhood" (1896b, p. 207).

Equally interesting, in light of his categorization of the various relationships between the attacker and the child is a second reason for giving up the theory. Freud was unable to accept what he called "the surprise that in all cases, the *father* . . . had to be accused of being perverse" (Masson, 1985, p. 264). This assertion is difficult to understand, because there is nothing in the published material that implicates the father "in all cases." Even Freud's 1925 footnote in *Studies on Hysteria,* in which he admits that when the book first appeared he had

---

[1] I am grateful to Drs. Mark Blechner and Joerg Bose for chasing down and translating the references to seduction in Freud's German text.

withheld information about the fathers' involvement in two cases, does not address all the various kinds of molestation that he had described in other reports (Breuer and Freud, 1893–1895, p. 134n, p. 170n).

What could have led Freud, in such a short period of time, to change his opinion about the frequency of child sexual abuse? He cites neither clinical nor epidemiological evidence for the shift. Perhaps even more startling—what evidence led him to conclude that in all cases the child's father was the perpetrator? On this point, he never even acknowledged that he had rethought his earlier formulations.

But the mystery goes even deeper. Questions arise not only about *why* Freud changed his mind, but also about *how completely* he actually changed. In a letter to Fliess written on December 12, 1897 (two and a half months after the ''I no longer believe in my *neurotica*'' letter) Freud says, ''My confidence in paternal etiology has risen greatly.'' He then cites an analysis in which the analyst treated the patient ''in such a manner as not to give her the slightest hint of what would emerge from the unconscious and in the process obtained from her, among other things, the identical scenes with the father'' (Masson, 1985, p. 286). This seems to imply that despite what appears to be a total renunciation of his former views, Freud continued to believe that seductions of some sort were central in creating the disposition to hysteria. Could we say that Freud never gave up his belief in the idea of seduction itself, but that instead he pursued subtleties and ambiguities of a concept that he had once taken too literally?

I believe this possibility is supported both by Freud's odd use of the term *seduction* and by the perplexing history of the concept. Each of these suggests that Freud spent a lifetime groping for and playing with the implications of an idea that he could not fully grasp in 1896, when he was only just beginning to create psychoanalysis. Early on Freud saw that sexual abuse was both common and devastating; this he never forgot or ignored. But perhaps, when he hit upon the idea of seduction, he had opened an even wider door.

In saying this, I certainly do not mean to deny the reality of what occurred between parent and child. Quite the contrary, doing so would collapse the memory of seduction into a fantasy or into a defensive attempt to avoid memories of masturbation. This would eviscerate the concept, just as denying the reality of castration threats would eviscerate that central Freudian hypothesis. Freud verged on doing this when he turned his attention almost exclusively to fantasized seductions. But opening the wide door does raise the possibility that not all seductions need refer to the same kinds of events. Some of the events implicated are aggressive, violent, and abusive; Freud described these vividly and called them assaults or attacks. But not all are.

What might it mean to think of a nonabusive, but still potentially traumatic, seduction? Recall that one of Freud's definitions of seduction is "an actual irritation of the genitals." It is obvious, of course (and was recognized by Freud in his 1931 paper on "Female Sexuality") that genital irritation is ubiquitous, that it is a facet of the care given to every child. In this paper, Freud refers to the mother as a "seductress," using a version of the same word that 35 years earlier he had used in framing the original hypothesis. This implies that loving parental care may be one piece of the puzzle that Freud was trying to put together in the 1890s. The thought seems unlikely on its face, but perhaps there is more to be said.

Recently, the French analyst Jean Laplanche, addressing the sorts of ambiguities that I have been describing, has proposed what he calls the "general theory of seduction." Laplanche puts it this way: "What is important in the scenes of seduction is that the adult transmits a message in it, that he 'makes a sign' from his own unconscious. . . . What I describe as the driving force of all the scenes of seduction is a universal fact: the intervention of the adult other, with his sexual unconscious" (1997, p. 660).

For Laplanche, the essence of seduction is the confrontation of the child with the otherness of his or her objects. I believe we can take this even further. Recall Freud's vision of the child's earliest experience of the external world. It is a vision that runs through all his writings, and that is epitomized in this formulation from his paper on "Negation": "What is bad, what is alien to the ego and what is external are, to begin with, identical" (1925, p. 237). This grim, brooding perspective decisively colored Freud's ideas about the nature of object relations. Something would have to draw the child's interest away from an "all-good" inner world and toward an originally hated world of other people. And Freud is quite clear about what this is: The child is drawn out by what people have to offer, especially by their ability to gratify drive-derived needs. It is in this spirit that Freud, reviewing the analysis of Little Hans in *Inhibitions, Symptoms and*

Anxiety (1926), could write that "Repeated situations of satisfaction have created an object out of the mother" (p. 170).

It does not require too great a leap of imagination to think that creating oneself as an object by providing satisfaction is a kind of seduction. Putting this another way, every child is seduced into human relatedness itself—including, importantly, the sexual relatedness that Laplanche emphasizes. Everyday care, with its bodily and emotional stimulation, arouses powerful feelings. The pleasures involved in ordinary genital stimulation play a special role in seducing the child into an affectionate and even passionate relationship with his or her caretakers.

Perhaps Freud's strongest formulation of this sort of seduction emerges in his discussion of the Oedipus complex in the biography of Leonardo da Vinci (1910a). There he writes that the child's incestuous object choice "usually follows some clear indication from its parents, whose affection bears the clearest characteristics of a sexual activity. . . . As a result a father prefers his daughter and a mother her son; the child reacts to this by wishing, if he is a son, to take his father's place, and, if she is a daughter, her mother's" (1910b, p. 47). Here, unlike in more formal conceptualizations of the Oedipus complex, Freud makes it clear that the parent leads the child. There would be no sexual engagement with the parent, he argues, no Oedipus complex at all, if there were no libidinally tinged parental affection in the first place. "Sexual activity" in this formulation originates with the adult, and the child reacts to it. It is a seduction, and in such seductions lie both the greatest potential for living a fully realized sexual—and relational—life, and also the greatest danger of falling ill.

So we have arrived at the proposition that seduction as a concept and a hypothesis is so intriguing because it resonates with our experience in so many different ways. There are many seductions. Some are necessary, some are tragic. Some are brutal, some are kind. Some are physically violent, others may be hard even to notice as they are happening, but (by dint of the psychopathology of the participating adult) are psychologically devastating. Some invite the child into full (if delayed) libidinal and relational participation in the adult world, others foreclose the possibilities forever. I believe that Freud hinted at each of these seductions, and ruled out none of them. We are talking about the seduction hypothesis today, one hundred years later, because it evokes the awesome forces that bring about the creation and the destruction of human desire and human relatedness.

REFERENCES

Breuer, J., & Freud S. (1893–1895), Studies on Hysteria. *Standard Edition,* 2. London: Hogarth Press, 1955.

Freud, S. (1896a), Further remarks on the neuro-psychoses of defence. *Standard Edition,* 3:157–185. London: Hogarth Press, 1962.

———— (1896b), The aetiology of hysteria. *Standard Edition,* 3:187–221. London: Hogarth Press, 1962.

———— (1899), Screen memories. *Standard Edition,* 3:299–322. London: Hogarth Press, 1962.

———— (1901), The Psychopathology of Everyday Life. *Standard Edition,* 6. London: Hogarth Press, 1960.

———— (1905), Three Essays on the Theory of Sexuality. *Standard Edition,* 7:123–243. London: Hogarth Press, 1953.

———— (1910a), Leonardo da Vinci and a memory of his childhood. *Standard Edition,* 11:58–137. London: Hogarth Press, 1957.

———— (1910b), Five lectures on psycho-analysis. *Standard Edition,* 11:1–55. London: Hogarth Press, 1957.

———— (1923), The Ego and the Id. *Standard Edition,* 19:1–66. London: Hogarth Press, 1961.

———— (1925), Negation. *Standard Edition,* 19:233–239. London: Hogarth Press, 1961.

———— (1926), Inhibitions, Symptoms, and Anxiety. *Standard Edition,* 20:73–172. London: Hogarth Press, 1959.

———— (1931) Female sexuality. *Standard Edition,* 21:221–243. London: Hogarth Press, 1961.

Laplanche, J. (1997), The theory of seduction and the problem of the other. *Internat. J. Psycho-Anal.,* 78:653–666.

Masson, J., Ed. (1985), *The Complete Letters of Sigmund Freud to Wilhelm Fliess: 1887–1903.* Cambridge, MA: Belknap/Harvard University Press.

Discussion of "What Is the Seduction Hypothesis? Why Are We Talking About It Today?"

Helen C. Meyers, M.D.

Seduction is defined as the act of enticing or tempting or leading astray into a wrong, though I do not think it needs always to involve wrong. The very concept of seduction is seductive: History and its retelling are seductive. And Freud's writings are seductive—but this is for developing a bright new science, not for evil. I suspect Greenberg is more intrigued, or seduced, by the concept; Makari, more by the study of the history of the hypothesis.

Why are we talking about the seduction hypothesis, a hypothesis about the etiology of hysteria, which had a rather short heyday in the 1890s? What is to be learned from a study of history and its retelling?

One reason for our interest is the present upsurge of reports of sexual abuse of children by caretakers and parents—some reported spontaneously and early; some supposed "memories" recovered in support groups or during treatment (which may be genuine memories or may be transference phenomena); and some gathered by implication. The old discarded theory has been resurrected and the old questions have resurfaced. How frequent is actual paternal seduction, how much is it the child's fantasy or "wish" or false reconstructed memory, how traumatic is it? What was Freud's thinking on this? Was the old seduction hypothesis correct after all—not, perhaps, for the specific etiology of hysteria but in terms of a more sophisticated understanding of the traumatic impact of parental seduction in the development of neurotic or borderline pathology? Some people have suggested that current "revelations" and insistence on the high frequency of parental child seduction is related to Masson's "exposé," his questioning of Freud's abandoning of the seduction hypothesis for political reasons. Be that as it may, it seems we have come about almost full circle.

The other reasons for our revisiting the seduction hypothesis relate to the past: (1) As analysts we are intensely interested in the past and how and where things come from; what seems to have happened and how and why the stories change over time in the retelling. (2) Studying Freud's old theories in detail, their development and their origins, their evidence, their rejection, gives us a chance to study the workings of a great, creative mind. (3) Hearing what kind of data and evidence were used then to create or discard a hypothesis can help guide us in principle as to how to evaluate our current hypotheses, and helps us to know what to expect from that kind of data. (4) Studying the specific issues and materials involved in this specific theory, then, may help in our reevaluating these same issues currently, avoiding repetition, and encourage viewing the issues from a current perspective; in particular addressing issues of external trauma versus internal instinctual trauma, external event versus inner fantasy, objective reality versus psychic reality, and finally, the question of historical truth.

Both Makari and Greenberg elucidate some of these issues, although the two papers are very different. I suspect that the two authors may not differ all that much substantively, but their approach to the topic is from very different perspectives—each worthwhile, each revising history, reflecting their own "beliefs and wishes," as Greenberg puts it, quoting Freud. In accord with his contemporary views,

Greenberg approaches this with broad strokes, seeing more of an implied balance and interpenetration of external traumatic events and inner fantasy throughout Freud's work from the very beginning, including viewing the seduction hypothesis, in these balanced terms. For evidence he uses Freud's deliberately ambiguous and often contradictory use of words and concepts. He also proposes the interesting idea that, if we enlarge the concept of seduction to include all manner of relational and sexual enticements by the adult, thus treating the seduction hypothesis more as a metaphor than literally, this theory can be seen as the first of a series of broad organizing concepts used by Freud in developing psychoanalysis.

Makari, on the other hand, presents us with a careful, detailed historical tour through the seduction hypothesis to its final revision, documenting each step with Freud's writings and letters and guiding us step by step, with amazing scholarship, through Freud's discoveries, evidences, and data used, the criticism and opposition he met with from his peers in medicine and sexology—peers whose acceptance he so badly needed to start with—his deliberations and struggles, his doubts, contradictions, confusions, and changes of mind, and his eventual rewriting of history. I meant to engage Makari in a high-level academic historical debate, but there really is nothing I would add to or would question in this intriguing and serious academic piece of research, from which I have learned a lot. To Makari the historical facts are, as he sees them, interesting and essential. However, we must be acutely aware that each story told is only *one* story.

Implied in all of this, as well as in many other articles on the subject since Masson, is a refutation of Masson's accusation, in his book *The Assault on Truth*, that Freud abandoned a well-documented hypothesis and suppressed facts for political reasons, though this is not the only point. The hypothesis, actually, was never well documented; these were not facts and stories told by the patients spontaneously, but stories constructed or reconstructed by Freud to which the patients more or less reluctantly agreed—though often without conviction. As Freud put it to Fliess, they often did not really feel it even after their acceptance. Because of this, Freud himself had many doubts about his hypothesis throughout its short life and began to no longer believe in his *neurotica*—his specific sexual, traumatic etiologic theory

for hysteria and other neuroses—as explained in his famous letter to
Fliess on September 21, 1897. He felt that something had to be wrong
with his theory, because, using it, he had not been able to cure a single
case of hysteria; nor could he believe there were that many fathers
perverse enough to seduce their children. Indeed the seduction hypothesis itself was a bit muddy from the very beginning, taking several
forms during the time of its ascendancy. First, Freud postulated some
repressed traumatic sexual experience in early childhood as the specific
etiology. Then he stipulated that this experience took the form of a
seduction by an adult in the household, such as a governess, a stranger,
or another child. The seduction later in childhood called forth the
repressed memory of an earlier sexual experience, originally not traumatic, but now making the new experience traumatic by the weight
of association (*après coup*). Finally, the villain, the seducer, became
the father in "all cases" according to Freud—to his own dismay—although this was never really documented in detailed case histories.
When Freud did drop this hypothesis as the specific etiology for hysteria, he did not drop the idea of the traumatic impact of such early
sexual experiences, but kept them as contributing or conditioning factors. Indeed, this was not an abrupt shift but a slow, vacillating process,
as Freud turned from external causative events to the importance of
internal fantasy and libido theory. Furthermore, as Makari points out,
in the transition phase there appeared to be another in-between step
where Freud considered masturbation and masturbation fantasy (i.e.,
traumatic event *and* fantasy) as the main trauma leading to neurotic
illness—before finally stressing that fantasy was predominant. This is
an important intermediate step, showing Freud's transitional thinking
as he struggled with the issues, a step much neglected in the historical
analytic literature. We have to thank Makari for bringing it to our
attention and teasing out the evidence for it. Of course, some authors
claim that Freud never fully dropped the seduction theory, but Makari
points out that in 1914, writing his historical sketch for an analytic
audience, Freud not only repudiated this theory fully, but rewrote the
history of how and why and when this came about.

Makari attributes this change in attitude and rewriting of history
by Freud to the fact that Freud was now writing for an analytic audience and no longer needed to court the medical community. While
this may have played a part, I am not so sure of its centrality in Freud's

motivation. I believe there was a genuine intellectual shift in Freud's understanding, which he wished to stress and admit to and which he *wished* he had thought of earlier, enough so to convince himself that he had done so.

Now to some of the important larger issues that were generated by the seduction hypothesis and that are still speculative and controversial today, which are what this symposium is about: trauma, reality, fantasy, memory, and historical truth.

I am in agreement, theoretically and clinically, with what I think is Greenberg's suggestion that there is always an intertwining of external traumatic event and internal traumatic fantasy, although I do not think that Freud would have agreed with this from the beginning in his seduction hypothesis. And even though later Freud was willing to accept causes combined from internal fantasy and eternal events, he would continue to fluctuate between the inner and outer as the predominant causative trauma. It seems to me, however, that while there can be rape and force and violence without mutual consent, there cannot be *seduction* or *enticement* or *Verführung* without something in the seducee responding to the seduction in the first place—a wish, a need, a fantasy. Looking at it the other way around, it seems to me also, that while there can be projection or externalization of an inner fantasy, of an unacceptable part of oneself onto an outer object (projective identification), there would have to be something coming from that object to lend itself to being a good object to be projected onto. Indeed, Laplanche, as quoted by Greenberg, proposes a general theory of seduction with the adult always first transmitting a signal, a seductive message from his or her sexual unconscious. I am also intrigued with Greenberg's enlarged, almost all-inclusive concept of seduction; a child will be attracted to what people have to offer, will be drawn to the one who is able to gratify its needs and desires; and thus the gratifying mother, in a way, creates herself as a desirable object, as a kind of seducer or *seductress,* the term used by Freud later on in 1931. An interesting idea—think of myself as a seductress! Nevertheless, however interesting this may be, it is not quite the same as the concrete seduction Freud had in mind in his seduction theory of 1896.

Greenberg is, I think, also correct about Freud's ambiguity of terms, his lack of clarification about contradictory ideas. This is, I believe, at times purposeful on the part of Freud, to avoid reification or rigidity, or the narrowing of concepts, as demonstrated in Greenberg's examples or in Freud's term *ich,* which he uses interchangeably for *I,* the person, the self, and the ego without further explanation. It is, I think, sometimes inadvertent but at other times necessary as Freud develops new ideas, a sign of his flexibility. At other times, I believe it is, as Makari suggests, due to Freud writing for a different audience with different purposes in mind.

Now, none of this really answers for us the question of the relative impact, quantity, or quality, of "real" external trauma versus that of internal fantasy—a question still controversial and hotly debated today. Nor will we, I am afraid, reach an answer here. Many analysts, particularly child analysts, will tell us that it is important to search out the real mother–child interaction, the real external traumatic events—that indeed the impact of a real trauma on the child is very different from the traumatic impact of inner fantasy, due to instinctual needs and conflicts. An actual sexual abuse by a parent, they argue, accordingly, is very different from such a fantasy in its traumatic impact and must be brought out and validated in treatment or support groups. Now I agree that a real trauma is different from a fantasy, but the traumatic *impact* of the same event will differ in different children in terms of their inner life, their state of development, their unconscious fantasy. An external real event may influence the inner fantasy, a seduction or a deprivation may intensify an instinctual wish or impulse, a deprivation may even erotize an earlier nonerotic need; but, in the long run, objective reality has meaning to the child only in the way it is processed to become psychic reality, and what counts is psychic reality. What is reconstructed is psychic reality.

To complicate matters further, there is not only the question of reality: What is reality, objective, subjective, or psychic reality? But also, whose reality are we talking about: the child's, the parent's, the patient's, the analyst's? These are questions that have plagued philosophers for centuries and analysts only more recently (having let go of Freud's view of "objective reality" in the psychoanalytic situation and the analyst as the "objective" observer, and instead playing with such controversial concepts as intersubjectivity). There is also the related question of truth. Makari speaks of the historian's search for historical truth, as well as the falsification of history, of stories told and retold differently for conscious purposes and unconscious reasons. Some theorists even claim there is no historical truth, only narrative truth, only stories told. When we think how hard it is to get at the truth in the here and now, in the newspapers or on the couch, how difficult it is to get to the truth of the past. Can we believe the stories told by patients, stories told by the analyst? Freud claimed in 1914 that he, at first, "naively" believed his patients' tales of paternal seduction, yet he forgets that earlier he actually created some of these stories by re-interpreting what patients told him. Sometimes they were not the patients' own stories but sometimes they were, but even when they were, memory is not reliable; it plays tricks on us. Memories often are screens, defensive telescoping of events and false condensations of events and places and affects, or projections of one's wishes and desires. "I remember the place well" says memory—"You couldn't, it never existed" says reality. And yet, of course, we must and do believe our patients' stories—this is not "naivete," as Freud put it, but an essential analytic stance, because we are not there to search out historic truth in our patients' accounts. A "truth," if it exists, would have no relevance, since we are interested in the only meaningful reality, the inner meaning, the psychic reality of the patient—his or her subjective experience and inner truth, which needs exploration, recognition, and validation.

So, while the seduction hypothesis as such has been discarded, the questions that gave rise to it and the questions that were generated by it, have continued to be of importance. And seduction itself in whatever form—traumatic or generative, violent or gentle—continues to be with us.

On Literal Misreadings and Reconstructed Truths

Henry F. Smith, M.D.

Late in the fourth act of *King Lear*, the old man Gloucester, his eyes gouged out, is alone with his son Edgar, whom he does not recognize. He knows the king, whom he loves, is mad, and from what he calls his "huge sorrows," he cries out:

> Better I were distract.[1]
> So should my thoughts be sever'd from my griefs,
> And woes by wrong imaginations lose
> The knowledge of themselves [IV, vi, 288–291].

In this terrifying image of trauma, notice how precise Shakespeare is about the defense against unbearable affect. He speaks of severing thought from feeling. Nearly 300 years later in one of his first published papers, Freud (1894) would write about separating what he

---

[1] mad.

called an incompatible idea from the intolerable affect it has aroused, a defensive process that would lead in turn to hysteria, phobia, obsessional neurosis, and finally, when all else failed, psychosis. Maybe the critic Harold Bloom (1994, 1998) is right. Maybe Shakespeare was Freud's model.

We have two very different papers to discuss. Makari, who has thus far contributed more than anyone else I know to illuminating the ten-year period in Freud's thinking that is the starting point for this symposium, with his unusual capacity to think his way into the historical context of the decade, tells us yet again that what we thought was simple is not so, that more was going on to shape Freud's ideas than we realized, and that Freud's thinking took more detours than we—and perhaps even Freud in retrospect—knew. As with an interpretation that reminds us of the nature of reality, something we knew but had, in our fantasy, set aside, our primary response can only be "of course" and gratitude for being given a piece of the truth.

If it is true that every writer inevitably misreads his predecessors (Bloom, 1994; Smith, 1997, 2001), how are we to understand Makari's presentation? For the quality of misreading, or, as Greenberg puts it, the influence of one's own "beliefs and wishes," is difficult to impute to Makari. It would seem that what he has given us is simply a meticulous historical reading. But here we must make room for the concept of selectivity. Makari's interpretation is a misreading only in the sense that it leaves out, as he himself tells us, other aspects of the multiply determined events on which he focuses. Such are the limitations of any focus of attention, a limitation built into the nature of discourse itself.

But that selectivity, and the particular scrutiny that informs it, has some hazards. Might the very literalness of a reading that emphasizes only certain of the details, in some sense misrepresent the events themselves, their passions and confusions? I will return to this general issue in a moment.

For now, I want to raise a related and more specific concern about Makari's reading. He comments on the profound theoretical shift when Freud "argued that the perpetrator of sexual abuse was no longer nursemaids, strangers and children as Krafft-Ebing had suggested, but rather, *in all cases,* the father."[2] Makari dates this change to the

---

[2] Ed. note: In the published version (Makari, 1998), the phrase *in all cases* was deleted (p. 860; see p. 51 of this volume).

December 6, 1896, letter to Fliess. But in that letter Freud wrote only that "it seems to me . . . *more and more* that heredity is seduction by the father". The phrase *in all cases* does not appear until the famous September 21 letter, ten months later, in which he renounces the seduction theory: "Then the surprise that in all cases, the *father,* not excluding my own, had to be accused of being perverse" (Masson, 1985, p. 264). I say this not to quibble but because it is critical to Makari's thesis that Freud had latched onto paternal sexual seduction as the specific cause *in all* cases of hysteria, and because by September 21, 1897, the meaning of this most important sentence is highly ambiguous.

In the letter of September 21, the sentence I have quoted is the *second* reason Freud offers for giving up his theory of specific seduction—the first being his therapeutic failures—and it is a point that puzzles Greenberg as well, because, as he says, "Nothing in the published material implicates the father 'in all cases.' " In reviewing the German, it appears that Masson's translation, contrary to the earlier Mosbacher and Strachey translation (Bonaparte, Freud, and Kris, 1954), is a literal one.[3] But its meaning, even in English, is ambiguous. Does Freud mean that from his own perspective, based on his observations of patients and his theory of the specific cause of hysteria, the father had to be accused in all cases? This is the literal reading that supports Makari's thesis. Or does Freud mean that everyone, including himself, accuses the father of being perverse, in other words, that it is a universal fantasy? In this light, listen to the earlier translation: "Then there was the astonishing thing that in every case . . . blame was laid on perverse acts by the father" (Bonaparte et al., 1954, p. 215). A third interpretation, which I believe is in keeping with the events surrounding the September letter, is that Freud suspected from his own self-analysis, as well as from his patients, that it was a universal fantasy that children accuse their fathers, which, if taken as veridical, would mean that all fathers would have to be so accused. Consider the literal translation again with this in mind: "Then the surprise that in all cases, the *father*, not excluding my own, had to be accused of being perverse." This latter view would weight more heavily the evidence of

---

[3] I am grateful to Axel Hoffer and Peter T. Hoffer for their help with the German text.

Freud's self-analysis and his own recently discovered aggressive fantasies toward his father and would give more textual support for Freud's
emphasis on the significance of fantasy at this time.

It would not then be surprising that in a rapid sequence of letters,
Freud would announce three weeks later his discovery of an Oedipus
complex lurking in his own fantasies, which he judged to be a universal
phenomenon of childhood, and, four weeks after that, he would elaborate, again from his self-analysis, the universal nature of infantile sexuality. Something was changing rapidly in Freud's thinking at the time,
something to do with the nature of fantasy.

It seems to me we arrive here at one of the difficulties of retrospective research, one with which Freudian scholarship has been particularly fraught, namely that in trying to build a particular historical
argument, we may read too literally a text that is not meant to bear
such acuity and hence not allow it to have its usual compliment of
ambiguity, an ambiguity which in its natural setting borrows on the
good will of the epistolary relationship. Ambiguities and contradictions are ordinarily allowed to coexist in the text of a letter as they do
in the life of the mind; the letter writer relies on the personal relationship with his or her reader to clarify them, not always successfully to
be sure.

Greenberg tells us from the start that his reading will be consistent
with his own "beliefs and wishes" and his own particular niche in
contemporary psychoanalysis. He points out that this is in keeping
with Freud's thinking about childhood memory and with historical
writing in general. I would suggest that the sort of secondary revision
to which Greenberg refers is a fundamental property of mind, and I
am sure he would agree. But it is usually a property that is thought to
occur *unconsciously,* whereas Greenberg seems content that it be not
only inevitable but also a conscious and deliberate process: "The history and interpretation of the seduction theory that I intend to develop
reflects my own 'beliefs and wishes.' " This is what he sets out to do,
and it is what he achieves, as he selects aspects of Freud's thinking
that show us the roots of Freud's interest in object relations and that
seem to lead inevitably to a relational point of view, a relational point
of view based on Freud.

Greenberg also tells us that "Freud's thinking was always delicately poised between the literal and the metaphoric." Although there

is an elusive, ambiguous, and at times frankly confused quality to Freud's thinking, Greenberg's view of it as metaphorical is easier to justify when he telescopes Freud's work from beginning to end, taking, for example, Freud's uses of the word *seduction* over a thirty-five-year period to infer that Freud had in mind such a range of possibilities all along. If Makari immerses himself in the historical details of a single decade, Greenberg takes bits from different parts of the Freudian edifice. Although I agree with Greenberg that there are distinct themes in Freud's thinking that we can trace from beginning to end, I do not think one can piece together earlier moments and later ones, as if they all belonged in the quilt, without losing the sense of Freud's theoretical development and his not-so-delicate struggles with his own critical thinking. As Makari has documented, Freud's search for specific cause was *not* a struggle over metaphor.

Greenberg, moreover, tells us that he has in mind Freud's thinking, not his writing. It is a little difficult to know what data he uses for Freud's thinking, since all we have is Freud's writing. Even the letters, valuable as they are, are examples of his writing in a particular context to a particular person. If Greenberg means that in some of Freud's papers, including his letters, we feel that he reveals his thinking more than he does in others, I agree.

But as I read these early papers I would say that Freud's thinking at this point is anything but poised, or if poised it is the poise of an elephant sitting on a fence, not so comfortable a place to rest, and always threatening to collapse beneath him. At times confused, at times tortured, it is characteristic of Freud's style throughout his work that he repeatedly seems to be thinking out loud, trying to make his way between what appear at first to be two diametrically opposed positions before sometimes reaching a synthesis. Often he leaves us dangling between the two, as in his later debate over whether transference love is real or not real (Freud, 1915). We hear it now in his struggle over whether the stories he is being told by patients are real or not real, whether events are internal or external, whether the lesion is environmental, something done *to* the patient, or constitutional, something *in* the patient. I suggest that these struggles on Freud's part grip us because they are familiar to us as struggles that every clinician inevitably retraces with every patient, given the invariant challenges of the clinical situation and the nature of human experience.

Metaphor it seems to me is also a property of mind, an inescapable part of our thinking. It is, as Arlow (1979) has pointed out, at the heart of the concept of transference and embedded in the very derivation of the word. One can make a case, I believe, that it was only through the crucible of these years, as Freud was exploring the ubiquity of fantasy, that he came to appreciate more fully the nature of metaphor itself and its elaboration in the phenomenon of transference.

If both Makari and Greenberg, then, raise questions about what we can ever know about ''the 'events' of the afternoon on the staircase,'' in Ernst Kris's evocative words (1956, p. 73), I would like to highlight some aspects of this topic that are increasingly being buried in the avalanche of reinterpretation to which Makari has alluded. For, brilliant as Makari's teasing out the historical context is, and however much I agree in principle with Greenberg's view of the ambiguity in Freud's writing, the critical dilemmas that altered Freud's theories and the clinical implications of those theoretical shifts are not always clear to me from their accounts.

To locate Freud's initial inclinations we cannot do better than to return to the unfinished Project of 1895.[4] Here we find the roots of Freud's interest in object relations, which Greenberg has been seeking. Here in this neurophysiological fantasy, Freud suggests that it is in relation to the child's first satisfying object, which is simultaneously his first hostile object, that a human being learns to think (Freud, 1895, p. 331). Here too we find the roots of the concept of infantile sexuality, of the importance of wishes—he was analyzing his own dreams at the time—and of his explorations of fantasy. But predominantly in this piece we hear Freud trying to explain the relationship between external and internal excitation, and the problem of how to defend against internal stimulus overload; that is, unpleasure. Freud reasoned that one can avoid the input from external reality simply by closing one's eyes, but one cannot shut down the internal pathways so easily. Internal stimuli were relentless and might overwhelm individuals unless they could defend against the discomforts of such stimuli in some other way. One defense might be to imagine some satisfaction in fantasy, hallucinatory wish fulfillment, if you like, another to feel that what

---

[4] I am grateful to my colleague Bonnie Smolen, Ed.D., for suggesting the significance of the Project in this regard.

was coming from inside was really originating outside. I suggest that from the beginning Freud was struggling with the natural human inclination to externalize, to look for external causes and external solutions, a problem that every school of psychoanalytic technique has addressed in its own unique way ever since—the Kleinians built their metapsychology around it. Freud's own wish for external solutions was lived out in his struggle with the seduction theory.

Next we shift to the late spring of 1897, when Freud began a more systematic self-analysis. He was in the midst of an intense relationship with Fliess, and his father had died the previous fall, at which time he had written, "the old man's death affected me deeply. . . . I feel now as if I had been torn up by the roots" (Bonaparte et al., 1954, p. 170). In short order he discovered his own aggressive fantasies toward his father. And now his theory of neurosogenesis was breaking down in part because, as Makari points out, the numbers did not add up. But there was another factor that troubled him. His patients were not getting better. In fact they were quitting analysis. He was worried not only about his dashed hopes for fame but also how to pay his bills. Throughout his life Freud's clinical failures were always an impetus to rethink his theories. As the attempt to uncover the hidden memory of the event, along with its affect, was not giving him therapeutic leverage, Freud was increasingly looking to internal causes.

As I read the material of this period, this is a man in the midst of a personal and intellectual crisis, not unlike those periods of creative ferment when a person's internal world and ideas are all in a jumble; such states are familiar to us from our own psychoanalytic experience both as patients and as analysts.

So Freud renounces his *neurotica,* his theory of the specific cause of hysteria, and he continues his search both inside and outside, along a not so steady path, as Makari has detailed. Makari ends his paper (as presented at the symposium) with Freud's position in his 1914 history, repeated with some changes in 1925, in which Freud seems to deliver a revised version of the events of 1897 and the years that followed in accordance with his own "beliefs and wishes," as Greenberg puts it, to emphasize his discovery of the importance of fantasy. What are we to make of this? Makari cites the changed historical, political, and personal context.

But remember, Freud's version of the events was always changing, even as they were happening. Now he was looking to an external
cause, now to an internal one; first the father was *not* the perpetrator,
then he *was,* then he *wasn't,* then he *was* again, and then again maybe
it was masturbation after all. I would suggest that Makari's view that
Freud eliminated points of view that had fallen out of contextual favor
is accurate but does not consider the possibility that Freud's reconstructive lens may yield not only distortion but also a kind of insight.
Like reconstructions in analysis, which do not give us historical truths,
retrospection may lead us to truths not contained in the literal details
of the time. When we say, "So *that's* what was going on," it may not
always bespeak self-deception. When Freud looked back after twenty
years might he not be giving us a more cohesive, selective account of
what was confusing to him at the time?

If we note the roots of Freud's interest in fantasy before and
after this ten-year period, rather than explaining the 1914 account as
a contextual *revision,* we might view both his masturbation theory and
the literalness of his seduction theory as a contextual *detour* from his
ongoing personal preoccupation with internal events, a detour encouraged by the social and scientific climate, not to mention Freud's idealization of Fliess, who was, it turns out, thoroughly preoccupied with
masturbation.

Mindful as we are of conscious politically motivated revisions
and the unconscious tricks that time plays on memory, we must leave
room, I believe, for what we might call *reconstructed truths,* when the
patterns in one's own life sometimes appear more clearly in retrospect
than they did at the time of the event. I suggest that these truths,
like the truths we discover in psychoanalysis, are different both from
historical and from what has been called narrative truth. They are the
history of a reconstructed life, with an affective immediacy that is
shaped by the exigencies of both the past and the present.

To judge how far Freud traveled in his clinical approach, bear in
mind that if his seduction theory once told him to try to uncover
memories of forgotten traumas, his masturbation theory told him to
encourage prophylaxis. Thus Freud wrote in 1898, "To break the patient of the habit of masturbating is . . . one of the new therapeutic tasks
which are imposed on the physician who takes the sexual aetiology of
the neurosis into account" (p. 275). Not exactly a subtle and textured

approach. Do we really expect him in writing the history of psycho-analysis to say, "For a time I thought the solution was to get people to stop masturbating"? Some truths are better left for dead.

While Makari's account (as presented at the symposium) of Freud's revisions stops with 1914, only two years later in his introductory lectures at the University of Vienna, yet another context to be sure, Freud (1916) elaborates on the confusion he once felt, which is still alive in him, not at all cleaned up. Listen to his dilemma, which is, I submit, every clinician's dilemma:

> If the infantile experiences brought to light by analysis were invariably real, we should feel that we were standing on firm ground; if they were regularly falsified and revealed as inventions, as phantasies of the patient, we should be obliged to abandon this shaky ground and look for salvation elsewhere. But neither of these things is the case: the position can be shown to be that the childhood experiences constructed or remembered in analysis are sometimes indisputably false and sometimes equally certainly correct, and in most cases compounded of truth and falsehood [p. 367].

And then he adds the most telling comment of all: "It is difficult to find one's way about in this."

This is what Freud discovered, this sense of being lost between and within the mix of reality and fantasy. It is still alive for him twenty years later because it is alive in every psychoanalytic situation. We all retrace Freud's steps every day, regardless of our own preferred theoretical allegiance, as we try to sort out the mix of what is "real," what is "fantasy," and how they are compounded together. What Freud did was to shift the analyst's focus of attention, not to fantasy *instead* of reality but to that mix of the two we call psychic reality. As he put it in this same 1916 lecture, "In the world of the neuroses it is psychical reality which is the decisive kind" (p. 368).

Until the end of his life Freud (1939) maintained that trauma might in theory result either from terrible external events or from a highly fragile temperament, but that in real life what we invariably see are combinations of the two factors, forming what he called a "complemental series." In every patient less of one factor would be balanced by more of the other.

If Freud was from the beginning seeking syntheses of external and internal, some of our difficulty with all of this has been our own tendency to dichotomize fantasy and reality. The complemental series was a synthesis Freud postulated by stepping back from the clinical situation. Up close it is not so easy. In this light, over thirty years ago Jacob Arlow (1969a,b) captured a metaphor which has been useful to several generations of clinicians. I am thinking of the two movie projectors. You remember Arlow was walking outside his house on Thanksgiving Day. Inside, the family was entertaining the children with cartoons. Outside, Arlow could see the images projected onto a white translucent window shade, and, always the psychoanalyst, he wondered what might be the effect if another projector were simultaneously projecting images from the outside, the two synchronized in such a way as to create clear but blended images, mixtures of fantasy and reality, or psychic reality, if you like. I would like to suggest that this *is* what the clinician sees, and it is what Freud saw, something compounded of truth and falsehood, as he put it, that made it so difficult for him to find his way.

But, before I close, there is another more synthetic view of fantasy, which, even in his letters to Fliess, Freud was beginning to consider. I am thinking of fantasy as a compromise combining all the components of conflict: wish, defense, fear of punishment, and the external reality that is always being processed and registered. In this view fantasy is the very life of the mind itself, the activity of the mind processing reality, with fantasy and reality forming a seamless unit. In this sense fantasy is the lens through which we view the world. It is, in the end, all we know. Thus, Arlow tells us that every act of perception is an act of creation, a view increasingly corroborated in the neurosciences.

So when Greenberg says he is trying not to collapse the memory of seduction into "mere fantasy," at that moment he and I have a different view of fantasy. Rather than being dichotomized with reality, I would regard fantasy as a complex, ubiquitous phenomenon, which organizes and integrates, binds conflict, and constructs a view of the world.

Just before he died Merton Gill (1994) wrote, "It remains true that the great discovery peculiar to psychoanalysis, the internal factor in the sense of unconscious fantasy, is the one psychoanalysis must zealously protect" (p. 28). Even if we concede that Shakespeare got there first, as we search for new ways to understand our patients, let us not forget the unique window Freud gave us into the nature of internal fantasy and its interplay with external reality. It is *not* that seductions do not occur but the way we study them that was revolutionary. Freud shifted our focus of attention. Something was added in 1897, not taken away. Something new.

REFERENCES

Arlow, J. A. (1969a), Fantasy, memory, and reality testing. *Psychoanal. Quart.,* 38:28–51.

——— (1969b), Unconscious fantasy and disturbances of conscious experience. *Psychoanal. Quart.,* 38:1–27.

——— (1979), Metaphor and the psychoanalytic situation. *Psychoanal. Quart.,* 48:363–385.

Bloom, H. (1994), *The Western Canon: The Books and Schools of the Ages.* New York: Harcourt Brace.

——— (1998), *Shakespeare: The Invention of the Human.* New York: Riverhead Books.

Bonaparte, M., Freud, A., & Kris, E., Eds. (1954), *The Origins of Psychoanalysis: Letters to Wilhelm Fliess, Drafts and Notes: 1887–1902,* tr. E. Mosbacher & J. Strachey. New York: Basic Books.

Freud, S. (1894), The neuropsychoses of defence. *Standard Edition,* 3:41–61. London: Hogarth Press, 1962.

——— (1895), Project for a scientific psychology. *Standard Edition,* 1:281–397. London: Hogarth Press, 1966.

——— (1898), Sexuality in the aetiology of the neuroses. *Standard Edition,* 3:263–285. London: Hogarth Press, 1962.

——— (1914), On the history of the psycho-analytic movement. *Standard Edition,* 14:1–66. London: Hogarth Press, 1957.

——— (1915), Observations on transference-love. *Standard Edition,* 12:157–171. London: Hogarth Press, 1958.

——— (1916), Introductory lectures on psycho-analysis. *Standard Edition,* 16. London: Hogarth Press, 1961.

——— (1925), An Autobiographical Study. *Standard Edition,* 20:1–70. London: Hogarth Press, 1959.

——— (1939), Moses and Monotheism: Three Essays. *Standard Edition,* 23:1–137. London: Hogarth Press, 1964.

Gill, M. M. (1994), *Psychoanalysis in Transition: A Personal View.* Hillsdale, NJ: Analytic Press.

Kris, E. (1956), The recovery of childhood memories in psychoanalysis. *The Psychoanalytic Study of the Child,* 11:54–88. New York: International Universities Press.

Makari, G. J. (1998), The seductions of history: Sexual trauma in Freud's theory and historiography. *Internat. J. Psycho-Anal.,* 79:857–869.

Masson, J. M., Ed. & Tr. (1985), *The Complete Letters of Sigmund Freud to Wilhelm Fliess, 1887–1904.* Cambridge, MA: Belknap/Harvard University Press.

Shakespeare, W. (1606), King Lear. In: *Arden Shakespeare.* London: Routledge, 1989.

Smith, H. F. (1997), Creative misreading: Why we talk past each other. *J. Amer. Psychoanal. Assn.,* 45:335–357.

——— (2001), Obstacles to integration: Another look at why we talk past each other. *Psychoanal. Psychol.,* 18:485–514.

General Discussion and Audience Questions

Owen Renik: George Makari has given a thoughtful, comprehensive, and cogent account of the origins of Freud's theories of pathogenesis and their relationship to the science of his day. If we approach Makari's presentation with what I consider to be an analytic attitude—namely, not to engage in a historical exercise for its own sake but to learn from this review of history what we can that helps us evaluate current psychoanalytic ideas—then I think that his presentation generates a couple of questions. Of the science of Freud's day, what still remains valid for us, and what has become obsolete? What kind of innovations do his theories indicate for us? In terms of the psychology of Freud's relationship to his community, does any of that remain relevant for us still, and should it be considered in thinking about our cultural and intellectual surround?

Jay Greenberg has provided a playful and creative discussion of Freud's playful creativity. He set the stage beautifully for us to consider the seductiveness which may be inherent in the psychoanalytic treatment situation itself, which alone establishes unquestionably the relevance of the topic for all of us still. Harry Smith has stated in the best sense a strong and provocative position that, in certain respects,

directly challenges Greenberg's and Makari's presentaions and gives
a tremendous amount to respond to, which we will hear about shortly.

Helen Meyers's take on the two presentations is considerably
different from Harry Smith's and generates, at least in my mind, a
very constructive tension. I am glad that she explicitly named the
implicit dialogue with Jeffrey Masson and his critique and also questioned to what degree Freud's revision of his thinking was an attempt
to find alliance with the medical community of his time, which remains
a very important consideration about which anyone who tries to pursue
analysis has to be mindful. It underlies the ''how I learned to drive''
aspect of our subject.

GEORGE MAKARI AND JAY GREENBERG
RESPOND TO THE DISCUSSIONS

George Makari: In fact, I find myself agreeing with a good deal of
Harry Smith's discussion, but I feel that the issue of selectivity and
readers' misreading is a serpent that is often in danger of biting its
own tail. As psychoanalysts we are extremely good at making things
much more complicated and at times much more confusing than need
be. It is not always a helpful strategy for doing history. What I would
suggest is that a number of Harry Smith's statements are inferences,
and I would love to see the references that he could marshal in support
of them. They are interesting inferences, and, as I said, I was going
to cover one specific issue: Freud's relationship to his medical community and the way I thought those matters might be interesting in helping
us understand shifting theory. Smith went to many other aspects of
Freud—his relationship to his father, his own self-analysis—all interesting and important topics but nothing I was going to be discussing.
More importantly, on the very specific issue of paternal seduction,
which is a very minor aspect of my paper, I still disagree with Smith.
I do believe that Freud considered the shift from nursemaids and older
children to the father to be a rather complete one. Nonetheless, that
is a matter for reference and data from whatever texts are available
to us, some of which are available to us as notes in Freud's own hand
in the Library of Congress. But that aside, the most important point I

would make is that I agree: Things are extraordinarily complicated. As analysts with persons on the couch, we think about how we can understand the multiple determinants of motivation. As a historian, though, I think it is extremely risky to have that strategy. One of the things I was hoping to bring out in my paper was precisely the way in which we have to struggle not with either fantasy and reality or with historical truth and subjective idealism, but with a combination of the two. I think the only guard that we have is to try to say something true about history—and I think it is crucial to try, knowing that you are going to fail. It reminds me of the old line of Malcolm Forbes: "The guy with the most toys wins." Well, in historical scholarship, "The guy with the most footnotes wins." It is an extreme position and a caricature, but going to the data, including the contextual data, is absolutely crucial.

I thank Helen Meyers for her kind words. One of the things I was trying to do was to make more problematic and not so easily dichotomize the notion of intellectual versus political motivation. My strategy was to think about intellectuals in a community. There are litmus tests called *controversies* that one could track throughout the history of many disciplines, including psychoanalysis. Thus, the idea that Freud might have been doing something only for political reasons is not one that I would subscribe to. I think it is much more complicated. The concern I have is that we might try to ratify a different Freud, one that accommodates our assumptions about what we want Freud to be because it is what we think psychoanalysis today should be. Historical work constantly reveals to you how strange history is as well as how familiar it is—how disturbing it is and how sometimes it doesn't add up to the things we would like it to add up to. So in that sense I disagree with some of my copanelists about the intent of this panel.

Jay Greenberg: In my paper I was picking up less on the historiography, of course, and more on the second question that the panel was asked to address: Why are we talking about the seduction hypothesis today? Why, in effect, are we talking about a hypothesis that Freud held and evidently abandoned within a very short period of time—and trying to make the concept of seduction lively in terms of the way that we currently think about our patients? I think that Harry Smith is doing the same thing. The one objection that I would have is that, in talking about his version of seduction, he used some of Freud's organizing concepts like psychical reality and fantasy as if they had a unitary meaning and as if they could resolve the debate. If we were to discuss the meaning that seduction has for each of us, we would have to do a similar analysis of terms like *psychical reality* and *fantasy*.

Everyone except me talked about the seduction hypothesis, as Freud framed it, in terms of its relationship to the medical community. I was quite explicit in talking about Freud attempting to develop a psychological theory of hysteria that freed it in many ways from a kind of neurological bias, something that George Makari also referred to in terms of the degenerative hypothesis. But Freud's goal was to create a story of hysteria as a sequence of experiences that were psychologically lived through. It struck me as less than surprising that I was talking about Freud as a psychologist and everyone else on the panel was talking about Freud as a physician. From our starting point, it shows how much our current beliefs and wishes and desires to claim Freud and to establish particular relationships to him influence the way that we look at the history.

Owen Renik: A question from the audience: Do you agree with Helen Meyers's implication that Freud's *Sehnsucht* (longing), undischarged by masturbation, is already a form of fantasy?

George Makari: Well, it's an interesting question what *Sehnsucht* refers to. To me it remains ambiguous in that particular formulation in October, but over the next eighteen months or so it became clear that Freud believed that sexual fantasy and masturbation are absolutely crucial. Without taking up too much time, this refers to the debate in sexology. The basic debate was this: If you claim masturbation as such a pathogenic act, how is it any different from coitus? Big problem, right? The claim made by people who wanted to protect masturbation as a pathogenic agent said that is so because of sexual fantasy. The fantasy that one has to create with masturbation to overthrow reality is actually the single most important pathogenic part of it. So it is in that context that I argue elsewhere, within the broad framework of what happens in masturbation, that fantasy increasingly is put front and center as the pathogenic agent more so than the actual physical stimulation.

Helen Meyers: I was really referring more to it being a transitional notion where he holds onto a concrete event as well as blaming the fantasy content for its pathogenic aspects. That issue deals with the notion of how masturbation also can be healthy and not traumatic. It depends on the fantasy that goes with it, as George Makari has noted.

Owen Renik: The notion that Freud would consider fantasy as being generated by an undischarged impulse links the whole idea of fantasy to Freud's biological theories of the time. In my mind, it therefore refers to the dichotomy between fantasy and internal reality, which is closely related to endogenous processes versus external reality related to stimuli originating outside the self. Now, that's an important dichotomy and one that was referred to a number of times in the discussion. In Smith's discussion it was assumed that the dichotomy has value, as, for example, in Arlow's metaphor of the two projectors, one being external, the other being internal. The alternative is to consider the generation of constructs of reality as a holistic activity of the mind. So, I would like to know the panelists' sense of the value of that dichotomy and its relation to the subject of the day.

Henry Smith: My point about the two projectors was in response to the way in which Jay Greenberg mentioned ''mere fantasy'' throughout his paper. We talk about these matters in different ways all the time. As analysts, we construct them in different ways in order to achieve different kinds of therapeutic leverage. There are moments in my own experience when I'm with a patient and I think, ''Oh, there's a fantasy that is very persistent, and, if I can point it out to the patient, she'll get a slightly different sense of it, so she can hold onto it and it won't be quite so interwoven with whatever the external reality is.'' One doesn't even have to know what the external reality is. It is not that the analyst has to be the judge of what's out there, but if there's something that one hears repeatedly, thematically, it is often useful to clarify. The reason I said that there's another, even more synthetic way of thinking about it, is precisely the point you are making, I think, Owen. But at other moments in the analysis and at other moments in the way the analyst is thinking, perhaps pervasively throughout every moment, the analyst's own fantasies are inevitably wedded with how he or she perceives the world. It's true for all of us. And that becomes something that is also true for the patient. We try in various ways to help the patient understand this more holistic view of the world and as many of the ingredients that go into it as we can. It's a complicated process, but I think one is often shifting epistemological perspectives, if you like. It may be dirty pool, but I think that's what you do in life.

Helen Meyers: It is not only a dichotomy; it is much more complicated than two. As is well known, I am very hepped up on the concept of psychic reality. Freud's use of the term *psychic reality* referred to the internal, instinctual unconscious. It wasn't the way we or I use the term, referring to the end result of input from everywhere. But even external reality is filtered and processed by the particular frame of reference, the particular glasses you wear, by psychic reality. Even unconscious fantasy is filtered by another process, so that screen in the middle isn't just external projection and an internal projection, but each step is already doubly filtered through a particular window and a particular view, so that the end result is such an amalgam and so complicated. It isn't just inner and outer that are acted upon.

Jay Greenberg: I don't believe in "mere fantasy" anymore than I believe in "mere reality." Some of these epistemological distinctions, which are endlessly arguable, are probably best addressed by asking about the way things get talked about in analysis: the way that a particular analyst hears a particular analysand's associations and the way that analyst responds to the associations. We could avoid the attempt to solve insoluble epistemological questions by paying more attention to the qualities of interaction that develop around different people's way of approaching those questions.

Owen Renik: Could Freud's *confusion*—your word, Jay Greenberg—about seduction be due to his denial of his countertransferential responses to female patients, in which he was the ubiquitous parental seducer? Would that be an explanation for his "confusion"?

Jay Greenberg: It would be an explanation. I certainly wouldn't privilege it over any number of other explanations. But I would say that it would make an important point about Freud's attitudes toward what is inherently seductive about the psychoanalytic situation. This is something, by the way, that he acknowledged in *Studies on Hysteria* (Breuer and Freud, 1893–1895). At the end of the section of studies on technique in *Studies on Hysteria,* he made it quite clear that the psychoanalytic situation was a seductive one and that some of the transferential and other experiences that emerged were a result of the nature of the situation itself. By the time of the *Introductory Lectures on Psycho-Analysis* (1916–1917) he was quite at pains to deny this issue; there he talked about transference developing where there was nothing to entice. That is a backtracking from his early sense of what was going on in the psychoanalytic situation. So I think it is clear that Freud was troubled by the intimacy and the seductive element of two people closeting themselves together, closed off from public scrutiny.

Owen Renik: Freud seemed to have seduced and traumatized his patients. In the 1895 "On Hysteria," patients are seen in a sanitarium. He bathes and massages them himself and then does a therapy session. It seems to me that if a contemporary therapist massaged his patient at a resort hotel and then had a session with her, in her hotel room, the session material could be filled with stories of seductive trauma, and so on.

To summarize, the questions relate to whether Freud's confusion about actual versus psychic reality had something to do with his struggles personally to come to terms with the sexual aspect of the analytic relationship. At that juncture Freud was really engaging in a hypnotic relationship with his patients. His hypnotizing patients was informed by a different theory and clinical approach proceeding from it.

Also, when Freud realized that actual traumatic sexual seduction was not universally true, he had two choices: (1) to build a theory based on an infantile fantasy, in terms based on built-in drives; or (2) that actual trauma of a psychic nature, not necessarily sexual, did frequently occur and was experienced in erotized terms—not a surprising synthesis of loving feelings with painful psychic interactions. Why did Freud disregard this second possibility?

George Makari: Well, it's an intriguing second possibility, but I think that we can generate a great number of hypotheses in our position right now in the late twentieth century, much of it piggybacked on the history of psychoanalysis and Freud's positions. When we ask a question like that, we have to wonder: Is this a theory that was in any way available to people at that time? Is Freud responsible for every theory we can think of now? And why shouldn't he have thought of it then? There is a danger of putting our present concerns, assumptions, and knowledge back into the late eighteen nineties, which was a very different time, a very different place.

Owen Renik: There seems to be a certain consensus around Makari's response.

All right, another question: Would the panelists agree that Harry Smith's utilization of the term *fantasy*, as articulated by Arlow, is an example of the kind of identity that Makari noted in Freud's original formulation of the causally specific seduction hypothesis?

George Makari: I think I understand this question. The questioner is asking if Harry Smith's reference to Arlow's very famous metaphor was, in fact, not only just a reference but also a symbolic alliance with an important set of thoughts, ideas, and people in contemporary psychoanalysis?

Owen Renik: I presume it is not just a psychobiographical suggestion about Smith; I presume it is an effort to ask whether there is an implicit acceptance of a certain set of attitudes and assumptions about the world that is exemplified in accepting and using the term *fantasy*. I think Greenberg touched on it, and it was part of my question really about the fantasy/reality dichotomy.

Henry Smith: Of course, I think that it's many things. There is the debt I feel to Arlow for having articulated something that has been useful to me. It is very much along the lines that Makari is talking about in terms of one's own identifications and idealizations in the context in which one is writing. It is also something that I use methodologically, both based on identification and based on what appears to me to be useful. I added a further piece, however, because I actually think that Arlow stays a little too focused on the two projectors rather than the four or five or fifty that Helen Meyers began to talk about, and rather than what I think of as the more seamless and synthetic view of fantasy and perception that is contained in the notion of compromise. I suspect that Arlow would agree.

Helen Meyers: What is so intriguing about what we are addressing is the notion that all our interpretations, presentation, fantasies, and intellectual convictions are predicated partially on our own desires and wishes, internal drives, and identifications. We cannot necessarily get to any kind of an objective evaluation of anything because we are all subjectively impulsed. That Smith reacts to what Arlow taught him thus would be a given. That he has tried to go beyond it is a given too, but how much one goes beyond these things is always a question. He was referring to Makari seeing his view of Freud from his interpretation and Greenberg seeing his view of Freud from his interpretation—and the interesting thing is that we actually talk to each other.

Owen Renik: Yes, and that Socrates was a convicted seducer of youth doesn't prevent his ideas from being of enduring value. Of course, for that reason it raises interesting questions about whether it makes sense for us to try to avoid being seductive as analysts or whether that also is something that has to be taken into account as inevitable.

Next question: In psychoanalysis, when we talk about seduction we seem to focus on how children experience or fantasize about it. We speak of its developmental significance. Are we less willing to focus on why adults seduce and what are their sexual fantasies about children? And if we are, why? In other words, are we avoiding thinking about the reverse of the Oedipus complex?

Helen Meyers: No, because we were all talking about the very fact that all parents seduce their children, in their own way. Greenberg was talking about it, Laplanche was talking about it, I was talking about it, Makari was talking about it, Smith was talking about it. And we are all very much aware of the seduction of the analyst and the seduction of the parent and the sexual fantasies that they have, both unconscious and conscious. And I don't think there is anything wrong with that.

Jay Greenberg: I agree with a good deal of what Meyers is saying but would add that in our way of looking at things there is probably a bit of a retreat from some of our own countertransferences in the analytic situation. In each instance, there is a history. There is still a contemporary tendency to feel that the analyst's unconscious motivations can either be factored out or be resolved by careful self-scrutiny. So I think that there is a tendency to look away from the adult–analyst role in some of these seductions.

Owen Renik: Makari's application of techniques and perspectives derived from intellectual history provides an intriguing addition to the reading of Freud's early works. Given that the study of Freud's work is usually an important aspect of psychoanalytic training, how might an intellectual history approach be integrated into psychoanalytic education? Also, how might integration of other intellectual disciplines, for example, philosophy of science, enrich psychoanalytic education?

George Makari: Well, I don't think that to be a psychoanalyst one has to be an intellectual historian. But what I would hope for is that we do the best that we can, knowing again that we will fail to understand Freud's process—the process by which he came to his theories and abandoned his theories, because I do think that is extremely important, as well as understanding the content of what we think Freud said and did. So in that sense, it is impossible to read Sigmund Freud by reading just the *Standard Edition*. If so, I believe it is really important to place Freud in context. As time passes that is an increasingly forgotten art. Especially before World War II and the huge exile, Freud's readers spoke the same language as Freud, they grew up in the same culture, and they knew many of these references without needing to be taught them. Especially here in the United States, for our generation of analysts, increasingly that's not something we can assume at all. A little bit of context goes a long way.

Owen Renik: With regard to a question of Freud's massage and hypnotic technique and the influence on a generation of sexual fantasies and ''memories,'' which came first: the change in technique, that is to say, the shift from hypnosis to free association, or the change in the theory, that is to say, the abandonment of the seduction theory?

George Makari: The shift in technique certainly came first, because it is already talked about in *Studies on Hysteria*, which is 1893 to

1895. The abandonment of the theory in the letters to Fliess doesn't come until 1897.

Owen Renik: How do you place in relation to the present discussion the work which led the American Psychiatric Association to recognize the role of real trauma in posttraumatic stress disorder and gross stress reaction?

George Makari: That's really a story in itself. The crucial event was World War II and combat trauma. But World War I and World War II were the defining events that brought trauma back into psychiatric thinking, and it also reached American psychoanalytic thinking.

Helen Meyers: I don't think that really changes a great deal, because what we were talking about still applies—that the emphasis on external trauma has a great deal to do with our wish to externalize causes and blame. But it makes it easier for us at least to have the various roles of it spelled out. It would be interesting if we could come to more of a consensus on some of these concepts.

Henry Smith: I agree completely with a comment Makari had made about postmodern suspicion, which was partly what I had in mind. I think that we are all wonderful second and third guessers, trying to find what might have been there. I have a hunch that if Freud were listening to us he would say, "What's this all about? Yeah, I did all that back then. I was very confused. Something came out of it. What came out of it was what I said came out of it. And now we are doing it very differently. What's the fuss all about?" That does not mean that we slight the question that came up about posttraumatic stress disorder (PTSD). As I understood it, the questioner was asking, "Have we bypassed something? Was Freud onto something way back when that we have disregarded, and that may be more relevant to how we think of that kind of massive trauma now?" I agree with what Meyers said, but I think the answers are not in on that yet—for example, whether different neurological pathways are involved, and how much dreams are different in PTSD than in other situations. I think Freud was onto certain things way back when. But what we do as psychoanalysts is primarily from the synthesis that he arrived at later on.

Owen Renik: The panel was posed two questions. They were: What is the seduction hypothesis and why are we still talking about it? And the answer is that we don't know, but we know that it is something important.

REFERENCES

Breuer, J., & Freud, S. (1893–1895), Studies on Hysteria. *Standard Edition,* 2. London: Hogarth Press, 1955.

Freud, S. (1916–1917), Introductory Lectures on Psycho-Analysis. *Standard Edition,* 16. London: Hogarth Press, 1961.

Part II

Analysts at Work with Patients Whose Lives Are Characterized by the Traumas of Everyday Life

Introduction

Chair: Arnold M. Cooper
Panelists: Jacob A. Arlow, Scott Dowling,
   Marylou Lionells, Anna Ornstein
Discussant: Robert Michels

Arnold M. Cooper: It is, of course, apparent by now that the actual topic of this conference is trauma—seduction being one version of it that Freud stumbled on early in his career. Many of you are aware that Arnold Rothstein, program chair for this symposium, has us all working on a topic which has long held special interest for him. He was the editor of a volume called *The Reconstruction of Trauma: Its Significance in Clinical Work,* issued in 1986 as part of a series of the American Psychoanalytic Association. I contributed a paper to that volume which, by fortunate coincidence for me, is germane to our topic, and I will draw upon some of my comments at that time in introducing this panel.

In my 1986 paper, I quoted two definitions on trauma. The *Oxford English Dictionary* defined trauma as "a wound of external bodily injury in general." Laplanche and Pontalis (1967) in their dictionary defined psychic trauma as "an event in the subject's life defined by its intensity, by the subject's incapacity to respond adequately to it, and by the upheaval and long lasting effects that it brings about in the psychical organization."

Freud later said, "We apply it [the term *trauma*] to an experience which within a short period of time presents the mind with an increase of stimulus too powerful to be dealt with or work off in the normal way, and this must result in permanent disturbances of the manner in which energy operates" (1916–1917, p. 275).

Following this and Kardiner's (1941) later definition of war neurosis, one could say that a psychic trauma, quoting myself, "is any psychological event that abruptly overwhelms the ego's capacity to provide a minimal sense of safety and integrative intactness, resulting in overwhelming anxiety or helplessness or the threat of it and producing an enduring change in the psychic organization" (p. 44). In recent years, trauma to the psyche has taken on new significance both in psychoanalysis and psychiatry. With no lack of psychological trauma in the last half of the twentieth century, there has been a flood of research on posttraumatic stress disorder since its inclusion in the *Diagnostic and Statistical Manual* (DSM) (American Psychiatric Association, 1994). This research has demonstrated rather conclusively the long-term consequences of psychic trauma occurring at any age, it has increased our knowledge of some of the factors that are protective as well as of those that increase vulnerabilities, and it has revealed an extraordinary frequency of early trauma. It almost seems now, if we believe some of the statistics being put forth, that childhood sexual abuse should be considered a commonplace trauma of everyday life, rather than a special event.

Trauma is clearly related to the later development of a range of personality disorders, with particular emphasis on borderline personality disorder and dissociative disorders. Interestingly, these researches also suggest that far more significant than sexual abuse—no one speaks any longer of sexual seduction—are neglect and physical abuse. In most studies, sexual abuse is seldom found alone. Households in which intrafamilial child sexual abuse or seduction occur are, quite obviously, those in which the child is either inadequately protected or not cherished.

There is, however, no one-to-one relationship of abuse or neglect to the later development of disorders. Here is where Freud's complemental series comes into play. In 1914, explaining his complemental series, Freud said that "*disposition* exaggerates impressions which would otherwise have been completely commonplace and have had no effect, so that they become traumas giving rise to stimulations and fixations; while *experiences* awaken factors in the disposition which, without them, might have long remained dormant and perhaps never have developed" (p. 18). In this view, trauma per se has no special significance and refers merely to what it was that touched off a neurotic process. Some children, constitutionally sturdy, develop adequate personality structure even under adversity, while others succumb to relatively mild assault. Of equal or greater importance than the proximate potentially traumatic event are the subsequent life course, and the preexisting or subsequent conflicts. A significant question arises: What are the events of later developmental life that provide opportunities for healing or exacerbation of early injury? The concept of *Nachträglichkeit* provides for the possibility of long quiescence after a traumatic event, before some new trauma, perhaps minor in itself, disturbs a fragile equilibrium and begins a pathological process.

This is where fantasy, conflicts, unconscious mental life generally, as well as the nature of the environment, fill in the gap. Everyday, possibly traumatic, events exert their effects through the way in which they are mentally processed. Severe trauma, however, because it overwhelms mental processes, and perhaps directly and permanently affects brain connections, may make ordinary mental processing and the creation of defense and coping mechanisms unavailable.

One could ask if any life, whether that of a patient or otherwise, is not characterized by what appear to be traumas of everyday life? Walking in the park this past weekend, I passed a couple walking with a probably 1½-year-old child in a stroller sobbing his head off, screaming at the top of his lungs with the parents saying, "We'll be home soon," as the mother is reaching to take the child into her arms with the child seeming inconsolable. A little further along another couple were jogging with a child in a jogging stroller who was screaming at the top of her lungs with the parents obviously trying to jog as fast as they could to get the kid home. Are these children being traumatized? They certainly looked as if they could not be more miserable or feel more injured. So one might say that all lives are characterized by the traumas of everyday life. What is it that makes our patients distinctive?

Analysts have long recognized that much of what they deal with does not fit a strict definition of trauma, and so we have tried to stretch the concept of trauma to include such things as strain trauma, stress trauma, cumulative trauma, and so on, in addition to shock trauma. Anna Freud in the 1967 volume on trauma edited by Sidney Furst said:

> Like everyone else, I have tended to use the term "trauma" rather loosely up until now, but I should find it easy to avoid this in the future. Whenever I am tempted to call an event in a child or adult's life "traumatic," I shall ask myself some further questions. Do I mean the event was upsetting; that it was significant for altering the course for further development; that it was pathogenic? Or do I really mean traumatic in the strict sense of the word, i.e., shattering, devastating, causing internal disruption by putting ego functioning and ego mediation out of action [p. 242]?

She also, however, went on to say that it is only in retrospect that we can know what events were shattering. I suggested in 1986 and will suggest again here that we do ourselves a disservice by confining our thinking to considering a single form of etiology (i.e., trauma), no matter how many modifiers we add to the term. Medicine, in addition to trauma, ascribes etiology to genetic deficiencies, nutritional failures of many kinds, invasions by other organisms, excessive stress, unpredicted damaging growths, inborn metabolic anomalies, perinatal injury, poorly formed organs, as well as traumatic injury. We might do better to follow such a model. We would do far better in clarifying our thinking and ordering our therapies if we consider that there are multiple etiologies of neurosis, not only trauma.

The term *trauma* tends to obscure our etiologic search. A child who has deviant needs in an ordinary environment will be improperly responded to and may be considered traumatized, but that label turns our attention away from pinpointing the origin of the difficulty. It makes a difference in understanding development whether an ordinary environment failed to respond to a deviant child or whether an ordinary child was inappropriately responded to by a deviant environment.

Kohut (1971), in effect, initiated a view of multiple origins for neurotic psychopathology with his concept of psychological deficit, implying that failure of adequate empathic nutrition stunted the growth of psychological organs. We also expect that there might be pathologic psychological consequences from such states as chronic overstimulation as well as understimulation, excessively aggressive environments, excessively unstructured environments, and so on. As Kohut's example indicates, viewing pathology as stemming from varieties of etiologies will likely lead us, as it already has, to explore varieties of technical procedures, perhaps more precisely tailored to diagnosis and etiology. Although this notion is anathema to some, I believe it is to be welcomed.

Our panel addresses the effects of these everyday painful events that no one escapes either in early childhood or later, and that are unpredictable in their effects, inflicting deep damage on some, leaving others unscathed, and spurring still others to extraordinary, sometimes almost superhuman, achievements. Psychoanalysts, of course, only have the opportunity to examine those who are damaged—we rarely see healthy persons. We do, however, see individuals whose degree of damage from trauma is incommensurate with the event as seen from the outsider's point of view. While most analysts today would say that it is the patient's experience of events that determines what the event was, I suggest that we retain our curiosity about *why* events were experienced as they were—even beyond what conflicts were touched—so that we may one day know more about psychic structure formation than we know now.

REFERENCES

American Psychiatric Association (1994), *Diagnostic and Statistical Manual of Mental Disorders,* 4th ed. (DSM-IV). Washington, DC: American Psychiatric Press.

Cooper, A. (1986), Toward a limited definition of psychic trauma. In: *The Reconstruction of Trauma: Its Significance in Clinical Work,* ed. A. Rothstein. Madison, CT: International Universities Press, pp. 41–56.

Freud, A. (1967), Comments on trauma. In: *Psychic Trauma,* ed. S. S. Furst. New York: Basic Books, pp. 235–245.

Freud, S. (1914), On the history of the psycho-analytic movement. *Standard Edition,* 14:1–66. London: Hogarth Press, 1957.

———— (1916–1917), Introductory Lectures on Psycho-Analysis. *Standard Edition,* 15 & 16. London: Hogarth Press, 1961.

Kardiner, A. (1941), *The Traumatic Neuroses of War.* New York: Hoeber.

Kohut, H. (1971), *The Analysis of the Self.* New York: International Universities Press.

Laplanche, J., & Pontalis, J.-B. (1967), *The Language of Psycho-Analysis.* New York: W. W. Norton, 1973.

Oxford English Dictionary, Compact Edition (1971), s.v. ''trauma.'' New York: Oxford University Press.

Rothstein, A., Ed. (1986), *The Reconstruction of Trauma: Its Significance in Clinical Work.* Madison, CT: International Universities Press.

3

Trauma and Pathogenesis

Jacob A. Arlow, M.D.

If the hysterical patients of psychoanalysts suffer mainly from reminiscences, then it may be said that analysts suffer even more so from their history. After the lapse of one hundred years, what need is there for us to reconsider the seduction hypothesis? It was a conjecture Freud made when he was first beginning to investigate the causes of hysteria. At that time he had no reliable method for studying psychopathology. Eventually he came to recognize that he had not distinguished sufficiently between fact and fantasy in his patients' material, nor had he appreciated fully how his method of treatment inevitably introduced the element of suggestion. But above all, he was still thinking in terms of the prevailing developmental concepts of the times, namely, that sexuality began with adolescence. Therefore, whatever his patients recalled from childhood concerning sexual interest or arousal had to be the consequence of stimulation by an older, more experienced person, a seducer. Ultimately Freud saw that this was not the case. This is not to say that seduction never took place: It did then as it does now, but it was not the inevitable and essential element in the etiology of hysteria.

Without actual experiences of sexual seduction, sexual wishes and sexual fantasies nevertheless had appeared in the childhood memories the patients presented to him. It was in this manner that Freud arrived at the threshold of the theory of childhood sexuality. Since that time, childhood sexuality has, in fact, become a commonplace, even a popular concept. A consequence of this realization was that, so far as the etiology of hysteria was concerned, an actual experience of seduction is neither essential nor always present. It would seem that by now this concept should have been accepted as an incontrovertible principle, but in truth this is not the case, as witness the title of this symposium.

How then to account for the persistent influence of a hypothesis a full century old? There are, I believe, many reasons for this. In what follows I shall discuss a few of them.

To begin with, there is something appealing, something intriguing, about the seduction hypothesis. It begins with the assumption that a crime has been committed, though as yet unreported (i.e., it has not yet been discovered). It is a crime perpetrated against a defenseless child, usually a female. Under such circumstances, psychoanalytic treatment becomes like a detective story, a mystery to be solved. The victim is known, but the precise crime and the criminal remain to be unmasked. During the heyday of its popularity in the late 1940s and early 1950s, this is exactly how psychoanalysis was portrayed. The analyst was seen working very much in the spirit of a detective, perceiving in derivative "memories" a crime being recapitulated in the transference wishes and fantasies. Thus, for example, in the best manner of an investigating detective, Ingrid Bergman, in the movie *Spellbound,* using clues and even revisiting the scene of the "crime," cures her depressed, confused, and very handsome patient. True to the traditions of Hollywood, as well as to the popular appeal of misconceptions of transference, analyst and patient fall in love. Examples of this trend may be gleaned from all of the popular cultural media of that time.

Quite interestingly, and somewhat paradoxically, support for the seduction hypothesis was revived by Jeffrey Masson (1984) as part of an assault upon Freud's character and professional ethics. If Masson is to be believed, Freud abandoned the seduction hypothesis, not on the basis of clinical findings, but as part of an effort to exonerate the surgical bungling of his friend and confidant, Wilhelm Fliess. However one may choose to interpret the controversy over Fliess's professional competence and Freud's attitude toward it, one clear result of Masson's charges has been to focus interest on the seduction theory to a degree that rivals, or perhaps even exceeds, the attention given to that theory when it was first promulgated. At the same time, in many quarters, this controversy was seized upon as part of an attempt to discredit psychoanalysis in general.

Not surprisingly, there is also a political aspect to the controversy. The fact that the victim of seduction was usually a powerless, female child rendered the seduction hypothesis a convenient metaphor to dramatize the real and actual exploitation of women in society. Articulating the image of woman as victim, the seduction theory could be a useful weapon in the agenda of some political activists.

Even if the seduction theory was wrong, there was something about it that appealed to analysts. It served as a model for a clearly defined, specific etiology for psychological disturbances. To those analysts who entered the field from the medical profession (and at the beginning they constituted the overwhelming majority), the concept of a precise cause for the various forms of psychopathology was a welcome and familiar concept. In fact, the conceptual model which Breuer and Freud used in their *Studies on Hysteria* (1893–1895) was that of a foreign body embedded in the matrix of the tissues, a concept close to their interest and experience in histology and pathology. The memory of the seduction, now repressed, was like a foreign body in the psyche, growing by accretion and drawing into its structure thoughts and memories associated to it by similarity, contiguity, and contrast.

This understanding of the pathogenesis of neurotic symptoms had major implications for a theory of cure and, therefore, for a theory of technique. As Freud said repeatedly, even as late as his paper ''Constructions in Analysis'' (1937), the role of therapy is to recover the cause of the illness by having the patient recall the painful event or events, long forgotten, but persistently active. In other words, the technical goal of treatment was to recover the memory of certain events that were presumed to be the cause of the illness. The seduction hypothesis served as a model for later theories of discrete and specific pathogenesis. It centered on a concept of a specific trauma.

While an actual experience of seduction does not constitute the inexorable trauma of hysteria, there remain many other events that are considered inherently and powerfully pathogenic. For example, following Freud's (1918) elaborate reconstruction of the Wolf Man's experience at the age of 11 months, sustaining the shock of viewing parental intercourse, the primal scene has become the most frequently cited example of trauma, especially of shock trauma. In discussing Freud's reconstruction of the trauma in the case of the Wolf Man, Blum (1994) points out that many other experiences have to be taken into account: the Wolf Man's early pneumonia and malaria; a father who was manic-depressive; a mother who was hypochondriacal; a sister who had seduced him; in addition to his having viewed animals having intercourse and being castrated. Blum then notes,

> When one considers the wealth of material, the intricate and interlacing sets of experience, the single afternoon of exposure to the primal scene is clearly set within a background of stress and strain in a special developmental and cultural setting. The primal scene trauma can also be understood as both screen memory and an explanatory method for a far more complicated pathogenesis [p. 46].

In effect, these observations by Blum challenge the central significance of the primal scene as the traumatic factor in the case. Furthermore, the question remains: Why and how could an 11-month-old child have retained in memory the sensory impressions of viewing his parents' physical activities and integrated them later into a complex of fearful and vengeful fantasies? What is traumatic for an individual at one point in development may not be traumatic at another developmental phase.

Nevertheless, ever since Freud's observations of the traumatic effect of the primal scene on the Wolf Man, that kind of experience has been the most consistently adduced example of psychic trauma. By far the most comprehensive review and assessment of the issue has been made by Esman (1973). His conclusion was, while primal scene content, derived either from observation or fantasy, seems to be a universal element in the mental life of postoedipal humans, evidence that observation of parental intercourse is per se traumatic to the child is not convincing; certainly no specific pathological formation can be ascribed to it. The "sadistic conception" of the primal scene, supposed to be inevitable, appears to be largely, if not entirely, determined by other elements in the parents' behavior—in particular, by the amount of overt, violent aggression they exhibit. The child's response to such observations will be determined in large measure by the cultural setting and emotional set that surrounds him (p. 76).

Edelheit (1974) noted that the "primal scene schema" derives from fantasy as well as from actual observation and that psychic events external to it will determine its evolution in normal or pathological directions. He does not suggest that it is in itself traumatic or pathogenic. In this respect, Beres (1969) made the sobering observation that what to the analyst appears traumatic may not have been so to the patient. He also raised the issue "whether we do not, as a result of our cultural background, regard certain experiences as traumatic to the child, which in other cultures do not lead to symptom formation or other pathology" (p. 135). Do we not in similar vein in our own culture assume that experiences of a certain type are inevitably traumatic? To be sure, there are limits to what the average individual can be expected to sustain, but there are many and surprising exceptions to this rule. As Anna Ornstein (1985), and others too numerous to mention, have demonstrated from the Holocaust experience, just as we marvel at how some individuals may sustain and master seemingly overwhelming physical and psychological assault, so also are we struck by how fragile and vulnerable others may be in the face of the inevitable frustrations and untoward vicissitudes of experience that we as humans share in common. It was for this reason that I was confused and perplexed when the original invitation for me to participate in this symposium said the topic was to be "Analysts at Work with Patients Whose Lives Are Characterized by the Traumas of Everyday Life."

One person's mouse may be another person's dragon. In one case, the trauma may have been an actual event. In another case, it may have been a fantasy. In some instances, a certain type of painful event may be a spur to achievement, while for someone else the same event may result in inhibition or symptom formation, and in many instances, in an apparently contradictory but nonetheless common result; what finally develops may be a combination of stimulation and achievement, on one hand, and inhibition and symptom formation, on the other.

Aphoristically one may say trauma is as trauma does, or as Brenner (1986) pointed out, "One can define trauma only with reference to its effects on the psyche. Something which has a harmful, deleterious effect on psychic functioning, or psychic development, or on both,

is by definition, traumatic'' (p. 197). This becomes possible because
of the way an experience or a set of experiences (i.e., a relationship)
impinges on preexisting psychic conflicts (Fenichel, 1945). That is a
fundamental principle which is often overlooked. How valid, then, we
may ask, is the distinction we try to draw between the traumas of
everyday life and the dramatic or shocking traumas experienced by
other patients? This is the question I propose to address in the clinical
material that follows.

The patient was a 31-year-old housewife, married, with two children. She came into treatment because of feelings of depersonalization
and derealization. She had frequent attacks of overwhelming anxiety,
bordering on paralyzing panic states, in which her hands would feel
numb and paralyzed. She had a sensation of the lights dimming and
of the entire scene before her eyes receding. She was extremely irrita-
ble and was unable to discipline her children, so that she found herself
continually screaming at them. She was markedly depressed and given
to spells of uncontrollable but silent crying. During the course of the
treatment, numerous additional complaints and problems emerged, of
which the patient had either not been aware at the beginning of treatment or which were not sufficiently pressing at the time for her to
enumerate. Among these symptoms was a whole series of compulsions
about the use of the bathroom. She could only use the bathroom in
her own home with comfort. She had a form of agoraphobia and
claustrophobia, and felt uncomfortable in unfamiliar surroundings. The
patient was particularly sensitive about being overheard in private activities, especially those connected with going to the bathroom. Situations or scenes of violence and excitement, such as in the movies or
on radio programs, filled her with acute anxiety.

At first I hesitated to take her into treatment because of the possible diagnosis of schizophrenia but, after a number of introductory
interviews, I concluded that the appropriate diagnosis was masochistic
hysterical character with obsessive and compulsive features. To play
safe, I had a Rorschach test done on the patient and felt relieved when
the test results corresponded with the diagnosis I had made.

The patient had an older sister and a younger brother. Her father,
a man of humble beginnings, was immensely successful in business.
He was kind and affectionate and particularly attached to the patient.

On the other hand, the mother was a peculiar person, whose life revolved around her own and her children's bowel habits. She foisted many of her own bathroom rituals upon the children, examining their stools and establishing regimens of mineral water and enemas. She insisted upon cleanliness and control and would chastise and humiliate any child who made a mess with a bowel movement. Thus, it is clear that the patient's preoedipal history was characterized by repeated, small, but cumulative trauma of a type hardly rare in the training of young children. During her oedipal years, the patient had two experiences of witnessing the primal scene. Both of them took place while the family was on holiday, occupying more cramped quarters than they did at home. Although the patient's memory of these events was rather hazy and, in large measure, was reconstructed from details surrounding the experience, the effect upon the patient was profound. The patient was left with an impression of intercourse as an extremely wild, sadomasochistic assault. And, finally, there was the element of the patient's disappointing marriage to a cold, detached, indifferent, insensitive husband. The patient felt that her marriage had been a grievous mistake, but she could not get herself to do anything about it because she could not admit to her parents that she had "made a mess" of her life.

Thus, it may be said that the patient had three sets of traumatic experiences, one preoedipal, involving the vicissitudes of toilet training; the second oedipal, involving the terrors of the primal scene fantasies; and finally, the continuous deprivation and frustration resulting from a loveless marriage. How is one to classify these traumas on a comparative scale? Painful as such experiences are, they are far from rare, and the first two, at least, represent the kind of challenges that many, if not most, children growing up have to negotiate in the tender years of their lives. Yet, judging from the effects these experiences had upon the patient and her development, one would say that the traumas were severe indeed. There was nothing extraordinarily dramatic in the nature of the experiences which had such a deleterious effect upon this patient's development.

By way of comparison and contrast, I cite the case of a man, roughly the same age as this patient, who sought treatment for feelings of discomfort and discontent. He was mildly depressed and chronically unhappy. Outstandingly brilliant, with expertise in the fields of economics and politics, he nevertheless felt inferior and a chronic outsider because of his humble beginnings as "a little Jewish boy from the lower East Side." Employed in a prestigious Fortune 500 company, he did not report any experiences of discrimination but nevertheless felt like an outsider.

During the second preliminary interview, he said something, the full important of which I did not appreciate until sometime later in the treatment. Originally he had consulted with a senior analyst, one of the outstanding figures in the field, whose reputation as a leading therapist was universally recognized. The patient had been disappointed when this analyst could not take him into treatment because he had no time. The patient recognized, nevertheless, that, in any event, he would not have been able to pay that analyst's fee. Accordingly, the patient was referred to me. In the middle of the second interview, the patient suddenly interrupted the process of history taking and said he really would have preferred to be in treatment with the senior analyst, rather than with me, even though he knew that he could not afford to pay for it. I did not examine the issue with him at the time, largely because I felt it was a judgment with which I could hardly disagree.

It was not until several months into the analysis that I came to understand the full import of the patient's judgment, when he described what was the most significant and traumatic event in his life. This was the background. The patient's parents were immigrants from eastern Europe; the mother was a homemaker and the father worked in a store. There was a brother two years the patient's senior. According to the family story, the patient fell ill when he was a few months old, and the doctor prescribed some medication. The father went into the cold, wintry night to fill the prescription and contracted a respiratory illness, from which he died shortly thereafter. Unable to manage, the mother moved with her two children into the home of her sister. Her sister's family consisted of the husband and two young boys, each a few years older than the patient and his brother. The patient's mother went to work while the aunt stayed home and took care of the children.

A charming story, usually quoted by the family to indicate the patient's precocity and verbal facility, exemplifies the patient's concept of the family situation at the time. Someone came to the door one day and asked the patient if his mother was in. He answered,

"Which mother do you mean, the mother who stays at home or the mother who goes to work?" To him they were all one family. All the children called the uncle "papa," and the two women in the household were seen as mothers. This was the patient's illusion of the social structure in which he lived. One day the inevitable took place. The four boys were engaged in some childhood altercation, with our patient receiving the worst of it because he was the youngest and the weakest. Crying bitterly, he said to his two older cousins, "You just wait till papa comes home. I'll tell him what you did to me, and you'll get it." To this, his cousins replied, "He's not your papa. He's our papa. You don't belong to him." The patient was overwhelmed and confused and couldn't wait for his mother to come home. He told her about the mean things the cousins had said to him and, to his immense shock, she said it was true; it was not his papa, it was their papa. He became furious. "Where, then, is my papa?" he wanted to know. The mother tried to explain, but to no avail. Finally she took him to a photograph and said, "This is your papa." At this he flew into a rage. "This is not a papa, it's a picture. Where is my papa?" She tried the usual explanation, "He has gone away," but had to admit that he would never come back. "Then where is he?" the patient wanted to know. As she tried to explain death and burial, the patient could not be mollified. He wanted to be taken to the cemetery to see where his father was. Whether they actually went to the cemetery when he was a little boy or whether it was just a fantasy, the patient knew he wanted to get a shovel and dig his father out of the ground. The tragic shock that this little 3½-year-old sustained could be summed up in a single sentence: On one day he lost two fathers.

In much of his life thereafter he was on the trail of the true and false father: the true father, with whom he could have a loving, secure relationship which he had missed; the false, abandoning father, whom he would punish and kill. In his conscious fantasy life, in his relationship with authority figures, and in the transference, the patient lived out derivative representations of this fundamental conflict. Because I was a second analyst, not the real one whom he wanted, I was mostly the subject of his hostility, scorn, and vengefulness.

Compared with the unusually tragic misfortune that this patient experienced, what happened to my woman patient certainly seems like the effects of the trauma of everyday life. Nonetheless, the injurious effects of the woman patient's early experiences were far more deleterious and incapacitating than the dramatic, devastating nature of the trauma that the little 3½-year-old boy experienced. To me the conclusion seems clear. Trauma is not inherent in the nature of the experience alone. What is crucial is the impact that the event has on total psychic functioning, how it impinges on the previous, existing conflicts, which give rise to conflictual unconscious fantasy concepts and attempted solutions to the untoward events visited upon the child. It is in the nature of the unconscious conflicts so generated, and the effective or ineffective measures taken to subdue their consequences, that the significance of the trauma concept is to be found. It cannot be ascribed simply to the quality and nature of the actual happening or interpersonal relationships alone. We can appreciate this principle very clearly if we consider the different responses that people have to such everyday traumas as, let us say, divorce, or even to the seemingly more significant traumas like becoming aware of being an adopted child. One must also take into consideration the vicissitudes of fate. Childhood trauma is not always followed immediately by damaging psychological consequences. Very often the underlying conflicts may have minimally recognizable effects upon the character structure and personality of the individual until an event later in life supervenes, an event which by its nature resembles or confirms unconscious concepts and fantasies related to the original trauma. These secondary events in themselves constitute, as it were, a replication of the original trauma.

The search for a specific etiology for the uncovering of a traumatic event or relationship in childhood may dominate one's theory of cure and, therefore, the actual technical practice in analytic treatment. If the memory cannot be recalled and, as Freud stated, it has to be reconstructed, it would seem that the pursuit of a narrative reorganization of the patient's life story in the course of treatment represents an offshoot of the failed attempt to recall the pathogenic event of childhood (Schafer, 1983). Instead of pursuing a memory that cannot be recalled or reconstructed, an attempt is made to reorder the patient's vision of his history into a meaningful whole.

There are compelling, practical reasons to reconsider and to understand more clearly the concept of trauma. It is an important factor in any consideration of pathogenesis and, accordingly, inevitably defines the techniques we employ in clinical practice. In order to understand what to do to get our patients well, we have to have a better idea of what made them ill in the first place.

REFERENCES

Beres, D. (1969), Review of *Psychic Trauma,* ed. S. Furst. *Psychoanal. Quart.,* 38:132–135.

Blum, H. (1994), *Reconstruction in Psychoanalysis: Childhood Revisited and Recreated.* Madison, CT: International Universities Press.

Brenner, C. (1986), Discussion of the various contributions. In: *The Reconstruction of Trauma: Its Significance in Clinical Work,* ed. A. Rothstein. Madison, CT: International Universities Press, pp. 195–203.

Breuer, J., & Freud, S. (1893–1895), Studies on Hysteria. *Standard Edition,* 2. London: Hogarth Press, 1955.

Edelheit, H. (1974), Crucifixion fantasies and their relation to the primal scene. *Internat. J. Psycho-Anal.,* 55:193–199.

Esman, A. (1973), Primal scene: A review and reconsideration. *The Psychoanalytic Study of the Child,* 28:49–81. New Haven, CT: Yale University Press.

Fenichel, O. (1945), *Psychoanalytical Theory of Neurosis.* New York: W. W. Norton.

Freud, S. (1918), From the history of an infantile neurosis. *Standard Edition,* 17:7–71. London: Hogarth Press, 1961.

——— (1937), Constructions in analysis. *Standard Edition,* 23:255–269. London: Hogarth Press, 1964.

Masson, J. (1984), *The Assault on Truth: Freud's Suppression of the Seduction Theory.* New York: Farrar, Strauss, and Giroux.

Ornstein, A. (1985), Survival and recovery. *Psychoanal. Inq.,* 5:99–130.

Schafer, R. (1983), Construction of the psychoanalytic narrative: Introduction. *Psychoanal. & Contemp. Thought,* 6:403–404.

4

Psychological Trauma of Everyday Life

Scott Dowling, M.D.

Psychological trauma is best understood as a felt sense of abject help-lessness when confronted by an external event. To consider psycholog-ical trauma is to explore and discuss one important category of the relationship of the individual to the external world, of the connections and impact of the psychological world of "otherness" or "out-sideness" to the psychological world of "me-ness." Discussion of the human experience of me-ness and otherness involves us in the enig-matic issues of subject versus object, subjective versus objective, inner versus outer, relational versus empirical, and mind versus body. These have been recurrent concerns of psychoanalysis for the past hundred years and of Western philosophy since the time of Plato. As psychoan-alytic empricists we do not doubt a physical basis for all expressions of life. Psychoanalysis investigates and describes psychological functions and does not describe or attempt to speculate about the physiology that underlies these functions. We call these psychological functions

129

mind, their physical underpinnings *the body,* and the broader physical world *external events* or *external reality.* We utilize concepts and language consistent with our functional concerns rather than with physiological concerns. We are like the well-trained music or dance critic who describes the progression and characteristics of a musical or dance performance—but who does not delve into muscular and neurological descriptions of the performance.

Psychoanalytic discussion remains within its own language and concepts to avoid confounding physiological and functional concepts. We are in danger of violating this useful convention when we combine these two frames of reference, for example, when we define psychological trauma as "a state of helplessness that results when an external event overwhelms the mind (or ego)." The statement conflates the psychological mind with something outside the mind, an external event or reality, asking if the latter can overwhelm the former. When discussing psychological trauma, "overwhelming by an event" implies a force from a real, material, external event disrupting a vulnerable mind. Psychological consistency is achieved if we emphasize the psychological aspect of the event (its meaning) and the psychological result (a disorganization or disruption of psychological functioning)." Thus, for example, we can say that "psychological trauma is an experience whose meaning includes a sense of extreme helplessness."

Physical trauma is a disruption of physical structural boundaries. Decapitation by guillotine is a Cartesian means of execution, effecting a permanent separation of mind from body. A massive stroke, a gunshot to the brain, or a decapitation will interrupt functions of the brain, including the functions we call mind, by destroying the physical structure of the brain. These events are physical traumas and may occur without psychological trauma, which is not comparable to death by guillotine or oxygen starvation. If we look to the regulatory activities at the boundaries of physical biological entities, we find a more clinically useful analogy. A cell or other biological system responds to variations in the surround, from nutritive to poisonous, with homeostatic responses that allow for preservation and integrity. Psychological trauma is an extreme regulatory response of a functional biological system, the mind, to impingements upon its integrity. Less extreme responses provide for alertness and readiness for flight. It is a response which can be sufficiently disruptive to gain designation as *trauma* when anxiety or panic, hypervigilance, flashbacks, and dream repetition immobilize the individual and are no longer adaptive in usual life settings. This view of psychic trauma as an extreme regulatory measure, with both the advantages and disadvantages of such measures, is both strikingly different and more clinically useful than a viewpoint that emphasizes force and counterforce. A regulatory framework allows us to approach answers to such questions as, ''What is the psychological impingement and why is it viewed as an extreme danger? What is the contribution of past experience in defining this as a dangerous event? What functions are endangered or immobilized? How can I, as a therapist, change the endangering event or help this individual to establish a more effective regulatory response?''

This approach also helps us avoid the pitfalls of a repressed memories versus unconscious fantasy debate that asks, ''Are the memories of trauma an encoding of actual events or are they the product of fantasy?'' The functional approach spotlights a third alternative, that memories of trauma are like all other memories: They are a product of both external event and psychological processing of that event, including the ubiquitous influence of fantasy. Memories of trauma are constructions in which both an event and an active shaping and fantasizing mind have a place in forming the experience of that event. If we equate psychological trauma with unconscious fantasies, we sidestep the patient's experience of impingement; if we equate it with the external event, we sidestep the influence of meaning and unconscious fantasy.

Person and Klar (1994) have pointed out ''the different ways in which repressed and dissociated memories may be encoded and forgotten, remembered, reexperienced or reenacted'' (p. 1079). They remind us of the importance of dissociative vertical splitting in isolating traumatic experience from other psychological experience. Such vertical splitting is a wholly different regulatory device from the horizontal splitting that occurs with repression of fantasy content. Every percept is shaped by the mode of registration and by prior experience. Whether conscious or preconscious, human perception is a construct of both mind and stimulus and can be defensively distorted or split off as is true of all other mental content. The original stimulus can be an external one or it may be an internal one. This view sustains our awareness that there are important psychological differences between experience with the external world and experience with the internal world.

In sum, I do not consider a psychological trauma to be an automatic injury to the mind by an outside force through a process analogous to physical trauma. *Psychological trauma* is the name we give to the experience of helplessness and hopelessness which accompanies an event whose meaning is felt as overwhelming.

During infancy, experience is integral to the developing structures of the brain and to its functioning. There is a deep and instructive difference between maladaptive developmental shaping of infant mentation by untoward experience on the one hand and psychological trauma in older children or adults on the other. In the infant, sensory input outside the optimal range may permanently alter neuroanatomical and neurochemical development. If too low, the level of sensory input may not be sufficiently stimulating to neuronal development and "pruning" or, if excessive, incoming impressions may not be adequately processed or regulated by the immature nervous system. The resulting functional limitation may be endangering to mental development for the infant but is not a state of psychological trauma. For the older child and adult, over- or understimulation may also be stressful, even disorganizing, as in sensory deprivation experiments. However, the physiological impingement of sensory overload or insufficiency, analogous to an insufficiency or an excess of oxygen, is not a psychological trauma. Beyond early infancy, when psychology in the usual sense of consistent functioning begins, it is the experience of helplessness, a felt sense of psychological disorganization, which deserves the designation *psychological trauma.* Again, I am removing the locus of trauma from what is outside to the inward environment of experienced psychological life.

Let me illustrate with an example. Many years ago I was asked to see a 9-year-old boy who was terrified, speechless, trembling, and unresponsive to the explanations and consolation of others. His father was an abusive, alcoholic Air Force sergeant who frequently relieved his frustrations by attacking the little boy's mother. The previous evening there had been a rousing argument between the sergeant and his wife that the boy observed from the relative safety of his bedroom. The battle ended with his father stomping from the house and off to the local bar for an evening of drinking. At 3 A.M. the boy woke from a distressing dream, got up, and walked from his room to a balcony overlooking the living room below. From there he saw, by the light of the moon, the spreadeagled figure of his father, face up, motionless. As it happened, the sergeant had come home drunk and had passed out on the floor. Within moments the child was screaming uncontrollably that his father was dead; a short time later he became—and remained—terrified, speechless, and dissociated from the explanations and consolation of his parents. As I learned in succeeding days, the trauma lay in the perceived realization of the boy's wish for his father's death. The origin and the impact of the trauma lay within the child's mind, in the *meaning* to him of that spreadeagled figure—his father. He had wished him dead, and he had died. The trauma lay in his individually determined experience, which was the terrible realization of a dreadful wish and his personal guilt for the realized wish, his father's death.

Must a traumatic overwhelming be rooted in an actual event or may it be rooted in a fantasied event? A brief case history will illustrate this issue. Ms. D entered analysis with a conviction that an event of her eighth year had traumatically determined all of her subsequent life. Ms. D and her mother, an often angry, wildly inconsistent bipolar woman, were visiting relatives and slept in the same room. Mother and daughter undressed together, and Ms. D recalls the image of her mother's pendulous breasts before her. A sudden thought occurred to her, to take her mother's breast into her mouth and swallow it. Simultaneously she felt a shock wave of warmth, reducing her to imagined helplessness as it coursed through her body. That image and that sensation have come to mind repeatedly in the years since. They have remained the reference point for many of her later thoughts, beliefs, and activities. She recalls feeling disorganized and shaken. She elevated the event to the position of "the central trauma of my life." It became "the focus of my existence," the wellspring for a luxuriant fantasy life that was vertically split off from much of the rest of her daily life. In the lonely isolation of her room, to which she would retreat from family arguments, she would fantasize encounters with teachers and friends in which she would become helpful and important to them, exciting them and gaining control over them. They were bound to her by the exciting pleasure they found with her. At age 18 she eloped from home and a successful academic life, marrying a man who provided an ideal life of security, affection, and energetic engagement in life. Alongside her appreciation and comfort with him, she burned with jealousy of his attention to others and felt diminished by others' appreciation of him. When this combination of feelings—appreciation and attachment on the one hand and jealousy and rage on the other—became intense, as they often did with family members, managers, or others, Ms. D would retreat to a familiar pattern of eliciting sexual excitement from an unfamiliar woman, often in a setting where sexual advances could be anticipated, and then rejecting her. Following these encounters she would be filled with feelings of triumph and exaltation, freed from the despair which she felt in the relative helplessness of angry confrontations with authorities and when envying others in her work or home life. After a brief time, feelings of guilt would assail her, starting another cycle that regularly included a new seduction and rejection. Ms. D established herself in a rewarding occupation. She had a husband and children whom she loved and cared for. It was only in her analysis that she felt the contradiction of this dual existence, which she was helpless to change. A striking difference between these two areas of her life was that the hidden life of her seductive sexual encounters never resulted in a personal relationship with the women whom she met. She finally came to treatment when, for the first time, she found herself in an affectionate relationship with one of these women that "threatened to ruin my life."

What was the event that set off this chain of events and attitudes? There was little that was overt, simply a woman and a young girl undressing. She felt that the trauma of this event had determined all that followed. There was, of course, a background of the young girl being frightened of her mother's psychotic rages. And there was the internal state of the girl who longed for the attention and the affection of her erratic and sometimes cruel mother. There was the anger and the competition the little girl felt toward her mother and a desire to gain for herself and reduce the status of the mother. These many aims were achieved in the fantasy of swallowing her. Later we learned about the little girl's awareness of her mother's feelings of social inferiority and of anxiety about herself as a mentally ill woman. In the background was the child's distressed relationship with her father, a depressed man who became chronically ill, requiring care by his daughter because of mother's unavailability. These facts were denied by the recollection of the "central event." These expressive and defensive meanings were gathered together at the dramatic moment when the fantasy of swallowing her mother's breast sprang into consciousness.

Was the event of undressing with her mother traumatic as she believed? And if so, in what does the trauma lie? It seems evident that the extreme feeling of helplessness lay in the intense meaning ascribed by the girl to this experience. The overload came from the convergence of emotionally charged meaning that seeing her mother's breasts in these circumstances evoked in her and which acquired the literal quality of "a hot wave running through my body." The meaning (and the defense against it) was encoded in the fantasized act of taking her mother's breast into her mouth and keeping it inside herself. The wish to contain the breast without awareness of the accompanying aggression was well served by this fantasy in which biting or tearing apart had no place. A similar pattern of intense feeling can be found whenever a psychological trauma occurs in an older child or adult.

I have had the opportunity to see many psychologically traumatized children over the period of my professional life. One little girl whom I remember with particular clarity illustrates my view that an external happening triggers an inner sequence leading to the overwhelmed and helpless feeling we call psychological trauma; the external happening's traumatogenic power is provided by the intense unconscious meaning of that event rather than by the apparent severity of the event self. This 10-year-old child was hospitalized for urological examination under anesthesia. She responded to the hospitalization with unremitting nightmares, hypervigilance, and tearfulness. She readily involved herself in psychotherapy for these symptoms. What was striking was that it was not the anesthesia, not the surgery, and not the discomfort associated with those events that was most distressing to her. It was the preoperative preparation, where her genital area was "painted red," that evoked the experience of helplessness, the traumatic experience. We found furthermore that a whole series of memories, relating to a genital cancer of her grandfather, to mother's menstruation, to her concerns about her own menarche, and to religious–masturbatory conflicts were represented by the preop preparation.

Some readers may recall a slim volume by Douglas Bond, *The Love and Fear of Flying* (1952), in which the same point is made—but more dramatically. Bond wrote about the psychologically traumatized aviators of the U.S. Eighth Air Force during World War II. Returning from their bombing missions over Germany, these aviators were exposed to terrible events—shrapnel and bullets tearing through the plane, killing one or more crew members; fire trapping screaming, disabled friends; and, in at least one instance, a comrade from another plane free falling through the air into the windshield of the patient's aircraft. In his interviews with these traumatized aviators, Bond found, in every instance, that conflict laden events from childhood had shaped the meaning of those events, fueling their traumatogenic power.

There is another and very important sense of the term *traumas of everyday life*, one which is distant from the analytic couch. I refer to the life experience of millions of this earth's inhabitants, those who daily live with terror, uncertainty, death, and loss. This morning I listened on the radio to a young man in Kinchasa, vowing to defeat Tutsi rebels in his country, screaming that he would massacre them all, men, women, and children. That threat has been carried out against millions within the past few years, as also occurred during the Holocaust, at a terrible psychological cost to the survivors. The young man I heard on the radio was almost certainly such a survivor. Similar traumas of everyday life are rampant in this country as well. Like others who work with economically disadvantaged families, I see many youngsters injured by the murder, maiming, or incarceration of their parents or other family members, by domestic violence, by sexual and physical assault, by drug or alcohol related impairment of their families, by chaotic conditions of family disorganization. In many of the youngest children, the injury results from a lack of the physical or emotional requirements for neurological–psychological growth. In others it results from psychological trauma, from events with overwhelming, disabling psychological meaning to the child—gross physical or sexual stimulation and pain; witnessing brutality between others; psychological fragmentation or psychotic behavior of their loved ones; living in conditions of unpredictability, disinterest or despair. These constitute the traumas of everyday life in our society and usually require a different attitude, set of skills, and therapeutic approach than are utilized with an analytic or psychotherapy patient. First and foremost (and often beyond our capabilities to achieve as individuals), we must work toward the reduction or elimination of the ongoing disorganized and hurtful aspects of these children's lives. We must embrace the imperative of social change if we are to make any head-way in countering the most frequent psychological traumas of everyday life. In some instances we can effect the reduction of continuing trauma and, when achieved to a significant degree, psychotherapy or analytic work to deal with the residual traumatic meaning of these experiences can be undertaken. Our literature contains a few heartrending, cautiously optimistic, and impressive reports of this kind of work; for example, the writings of Moses and M. Egle Laufer (1984), Marjorie McDonald (1970), Muriel Gardiner (1985), and Dale Meers (1995), to name a few. Anna Freud's (1973) report of wartime experiences at the Hampstead Nurseries is an early example of exemplary work among traumatized children. Although not often mentioned in the psychoanalytic literature, I believe there is still much to be learned from the experiences of those who have worked with these issues in residential treatment. I refer not to the short-term, medication dominated residential treatment defined by managed care but to long-term residential care as provided by psychoanalytically inspired therapists and administrators such as August Aichorn (1925), Fritz Redl (Redl and Wineman, 1951), and Fritz Mayer (Mayer and Blum, 1971) and the modern equivalents of those efforts, such as Mercy Home for Boys and Girls in Chicago, Bellefaire Residential Treatment Center in Cleveland, and The Christie School in Portland, Oregon. An underlying theme of much of this work is the pervasive influence of trauma (perceived helplessness) on all aspects of a child's life and the need for a therapeutic approach which can assess, acknowledge, and alter environmental impediments to overcoming a child's sense of helplessness (milieu therapy), provide education and emotional realities that can support psychological change (special education and specialized child care), and fashion therapeutic techniques to meet the requirements and capabilities of individual traumatized (chronically helpless) children.

In summary, I will return to Arnold Cooper's charge and respond to his question: Does it matter to me whether a trauma actually occurred or was a fantasy? If an individual is caught up in feelings of helplessness, a trauma occurred. The question really asks: Need there be an external event? My position is that there is always an external event or events, but its role varies from extreme importance to simple vehicle for the external realization of fantasy. Some events, such as the death of a child's psychological parent, remove a foundation of health, universally resulting in the psychological trauma of abandonment by a loved and loving caretaker. I would also add, somewhat paradoxically, that there are no fantasies without links to prior experience, which is to say, that I am not a believer in phylogenetic or inborn fantasies. So, in every instance of psychological trauma, there is both a link to the "outside" event and a foundation in previously existing fantasy. From these ingredients the individual constructs meaning with accompanying feelings of boundaries violated, of being overwhelmed and helpless.

Do I devote therapeutic effort to attempt to distinguish fantasy from actual trauma? I may very well devote therapeutic effort to define the nature of the external event to which the traumatic state is linked. With Ms. D, it was crucial to distinguish the aggressive, feared mother from the weak, inadequate, preoccupied mother we later discovered; it was the latter who had, in fact, been the more fundamental basis of the external link.

If I am convinced a trauma was real, is it important to me to confirm it to the patient? Taken literally, the question is meaningless; trauma exists if and only if the patient experiences helplessness. The patient knows the sense of helplessness without my announcing it to him or her; they may require my help in dissolving defenses against that awareness (as is often the case with chronically helpless children). It is often important to me to engage the patient in defining the meaningful interaction of external event with their inner life; it is that interaction which provoked a traumatic state of helplessness. These interactions are often represented in the transference. It is never important to me to "confirm" something to the patient, which implies an omniscience concerning "truth" that is both false and antitherapeutic; it *is* important to me to facilitate the process of discovery.

REFERENCES

Aichorn, A. (1925), *Wayward Youth.* New York: Viking Press.
Bond, D. (1952), *The Love and Fear of Flying.* New York: International Universities Press.
Freud, A. (1973), *The Writings of Anna Freud,* Vol. 3. New York: International Universities Press.

Gardiner, M. (1985), *The Deadly Innocents.* New Haven, CT: Yale University Press.

Laufer, M., & Laufer, M. E. (1984), *Adolescence and Developmental Breakdown.* New Haven, CT: Yale University Press.

Mayer, F., & Blum, A. (1971), *Healing Through Living.* Springfield, IL: Charles C. Thomas.

McDonald, M. (1970), *Not by the Color of Their Skins.* New York: International Universities Press.

Meers, D. (1995), A child analyst looks at addictive behavior. In: *The Psychology and Treatment of Addictive Behavior,* ed. S. Dowling. Madison, CT: International Universities Press, pp. 147–162.

Person, E., & Klar, H. (1994), Establishing trauma: The difficulty distinguishing between memories and fantasies. *J. Amer. Psychoanal. Assn.,* 42:1055–1081.

Redl, F., & Wineman, D. (1951), *Children Who Hate.* Glencoe, IL: Free Press.

5

What Happened Matters, and What Really Happened Really Matters

Marylou Lionells, Ph.D.

Generations of analysts, following Freud's lead, dismissed the idea of widespread seduction of children and consequently relegated all forms of external experience to secondary status in understanding psychopathology. But if we broadly include all psychic disturbance resulting from relational encounters under the mantle of the seduction hypothesis, we address (and need to reexamine) every fundamental question in contemporary analysis: experience and fantasy, past and present, sexuality and relatedness, repression and dissociation, reality and imagination, external and internal, damage and deficit, cognition and passion, and transference and countertransference.

After a century of debate concerning the centrality of intrapsychic forces versus relational experience, it seems that the wars of competing paradigms may be nearing an end. We are all, from every analytic school and tradition, engaged in dealing with these same issues. To paraphrase Sullivan's[1] famous aphorism, perhaps we will soon agree that we are all more simply psychoanalytic than otherwise. But of course, we each approach these questions having become embedded in our various organizational cultures and have developed very different ways of looking at things. Each perspective has amassed a body of theory and technique, often leading us to confuse metapsychology with fact. So we come to believe that such terms as *libido*, the *self, oedipal conflict,* or even the *unconscious* are real entities rather than hypothetical constructs. And each analytic theory prioritizes its own core concepts, assuming that other psychic functions are necessarily derivative.

New doors have opened in the walls that separated classical analysts from the Interpersonal–Relational school, but there are still barriers to a fully interactive dialogue. Although we have achieved some consensus that relational issues are crucial in analytic effectiveness, there is little agreement about how these same factors operate throughout life. All analysts recognize that real life events are always of central importance, and that the meanings of such events are always idiosyncratic.

But Interpersonal analysts argue that whether or not an experience is technically traumatic, relational issues are as central at the initiation of psychopathological tensions as they are in the analysis. And, to the Interpersonal analyst, the personal meanings of all real events are relationally defined. I believe that the psychoanalysis of the twenty-first century must be forged out of a new conviction, one based on the recognition that there is no natural or necessary priority appropriately bestowed on either the intrapsychic or the interpersonal. We await a paradigm that fully incorporates the interpenetration of these dimensions.

In preparing for this symposium, and thinking about the eroding barricades in our analytic milieu, I found myself reminded of a particular man whose difficulties reflect some of the challenges analysts face in crossing the boundaries that separate us. I will describe portions of my work with this patient to illustrate how internally and externally

---

[1] Harry Stack Sullivan (1953) based his views of psychological treatment on the principle that what is common among human beings is far more important than what is different. He summarized this view in his "One Genus Postulate," which is generally paraphrased as "We are all more simply human than otherwise."

derived psychic elements are interwoven as constituents of character, and how his analysis necessarily included emphasis on both determinants. For the purpose of this discussion, I will basically ignore postmodern questions of the relativity of historical truth, and the intersubjectivity of reconstruction, asking readers to accept the events I will describe in my patient's life as factual. And while I will omit attribution, my account draws heavily on the work of many writers from the Interpersonal–Relational school.

THE DOOR IS OPEN

For many years my consulting room was at the far end of a large suite, with a long, narrow waiting area. The outer door was unlocked, so patients came in unannounced. From within the double doors of my office, I could not hear when someone entered, even if they rang the outside doorbell. I began to leave my office doors open between sessions so a late arrival could simply walk in. Eventually, my open door became the signal that I was ready for the next session. It was my habit to go to the waiting room to greet the patient if I had closed the door during my break, but typically patients entered on their own. By and large the system worked well until I met the man I will call Al B. Al was a middle-aged businessman, motivated to seek analysis by an impending divorce. One day, after waiting a while, I discovered he was seated in the waiting room. When asked, he said he vaguely recalled my saying that he might come in unannounced, but he couldn't imagine that I meant this as a regular practice.

In time I realized that Al never took the initiative in entering my office. He sat, or sometimes stood, near my door, apparently ensuring I would see him when a previous appointment ended. On the rare occasion that he arrived late, he called from the waiting area to bring me out to meet him. He would not, could not, spontaneously talk about his expectations at beginning sessions any more than he could freely enter the room. I tried to spark his curiosity with detailed inquiry (Sullivan's [1954] technique for exploring selectively inattended meanings), but Al insisted there was really nothing to discuss. It was my problem if I chose to neglect the civility of greeting him and expected him to barge in unannounced. He denied there was a power struggle going on between us, and suggested that I was hypocritical, pretending to be open but demanding he follow my rules. He was not angry at my emphasizing the issue but expressed sorrow that he seemed to be causing me to be uncomfortable. He also felt trapped since, despite wishing to relieve my concerns, he simply could not comply with the socially unacceptable behavior of entering unannounced. Soon he began to hear my ongoing questions as criticism and my interpretations as blame. The relational stage was set.

My ostensible openness escalated Al's anxiety. My sense of being easily available created a barrier to his treatment. My wish to convey mutuality and respect felt like a test, measuring courage he could not achieve. Eventually his reactions took on a paranoid cast. Al feared I would lure him into trusting me only to close the door in his face.

Al's approach to sessions, like his approach to my office, was evidence of his character style, seen in interpersonal terms as a patterning of relatedness. While he was intelligent and attractive, his virility was muffled. He evoked parental rather than competitive or erotic responses. In obsessional fashion, he controlled his inner world to control his reactions to others as well as the other way around. Always taking the temperature of relationships, he constantly made assumptions about my emotional state, often too accurate to be comfortable, then carefully attuned his behavior to temper my response. I felt controlled by his watchfulness and sometimes countered by contriving reactions. It became unclear who was monitoring, seducing, caring for, or indeed manipulating, whom. I felt by turns guilty for creating such a difficult threshold for him to cross, and irritated that it had become so difficult for me as well. What he wanted from me was presented as a simple concession to etiquette, but it felt to me a demand for special consideration.

Eventually we settled into a tacit compromise. I would greet him if he was waiting at the end of a prior session. Otherwise, when he arrived he called out and I would respond from inside. We met halfway so to speak, so the analysis of other matters could proceed.

BEGINNING THE TREATMENT

In the early sessions Al described the pivotal experience of his life. As a young teenager, Al returned from school one day to find his mother on the basement floor. Seeing her body upon opening the door, he thought she was dead. Al called for help, managed the hysterical reactions of his father and siblings, and arranged for hospitalization. For an extended period, it seemed unclear whether she would survive. The eventual diagnosis was multiple sclerosis, a weakened leg having caused her fall. The prognosis seemed hopeful. But, on her return from the hospital, dismissive of medical opinion, Mrs. B's vanity precluded any sort of rehabilitation. She took to her bed and never resumed caring for herself or her family. It fell to Al to manage the household as well as to cater to his mother's needs. In secret, from time to time he would curl up in a corner of the cellar where he cried, ashamed of his lingering self-pity. The same door, which he had opened to reveal the end of his childhood, now shielded him from his siblings' scorn, his mother's demands, his father's inadequacy, and his own grief. Clearly Al had reason to fear what he might encounter behind a new door.

Despite conscious recall of this dramatic period in his life, affective meanings were suppressed. Al believed that working through this event would release his feelings and allow him to become capable of the intimacy he longed for but could not experience. Slowly he began to acknowledge the horror of having discovered his mother's body, his sorrow over her disability, and his self-pity for becoming martyred. He expressed pride in having learned to control his family, felt pleasure in being able to satisfy his mother's needs, and recognized the thrill of oedipal victory. He also uncovered disgust for the vanity that rendered his mother unable to bear appearing crippled (and therefore refusing to learn to use a cane or walker), rage at his family's dependency on him, and his deep sense of inadequacy concerning his forced and premature maturity.

In the aftermath of tragedy, there is often a desire to see the event itself as the source of all difficulties, and indeed, Al traced all his problems to his mother's illness. But we slowly learned that Al's troubles did not begin when the cellar door opened. That moment crystallized relational patterns that predated his adolescence. Al's mother, Mrs. B, had been orphaned at an early age. She had little interest in parenting and no tolerance for childishness. She had made her way through life on the basis of her striking looks and elegant manner. Narcissistic and inconsistent, she was sometimes seductive and alluring, more often cruel and demanding. If Al raised his voice in argument, she saw his loss of control as evidence of his failings. Reason left her unmoved, and her emotions always registered a notch above his, so he never felt he had any impact. He retreated into himself, stifling his responses. When unable to contain himself, he would run off and slam his bedroom door, a futile gesture of forbidden defiance. Later she would appear in his room, not to console but because she was ready to accept an apology. Indeed, his guilt and shame were wrenching. By disagreeing he caused her to suffer, and revealed intolerable selfish neediness. Mrs. B had always dominated her family with imperious expectations, scathing criticism, and piteous complaint. Al's father spent little time at home, leaving the children to fend for themselves, with neither a role model nor protector.

A PARADIGMATIC DREAM

During this period of the analysis, Al had the following dream:

> He was in a large room with his wife. A murderous gang seemed to be organizing outside the house and threatened to enter. The couple discussed how to protect themselves. They quickly began to disagree and started to fight, which escalated until they were wrestling on the floor. Al awoke in terror, feeling locked in battle, unsure with whom he was fighting or why.

For Al, internal threat and external damage are indistinguishable. Al wars against himself, subverting effective action. At another level, Al also turns against those who might help him. The struggle in his dream represents his inability to trust, obtain support, feel respected by others, or to expose his vulnerability. Chronic strife dominates his attention, obscuring the nature of the menace and his ability to face it. He has no idea why he is under attack and no way of finding out. He experiences himself as the victim, unclear about his own role in creating the conflict.

Is Al sabotaging his survival in the real world by attending only to his struggle with internal demons? Or does he externalize threat to defuse the fury of his unconscious? Is his difficulty with my open door generated by fears of what is inside the room or inside himself? Must he reject my invitation because he cannot tolerate the kindness of others, or is my offer misattuned? Does he distance to protect himself or me, to protect us from ourselves or each other? Is it engagement that is dreaded, or exposure of his inner states? Indeed, what distinguishes what he brings to the situation, what I have brought, and what we create together?

THE ANALYTIC RELATIONSHIP

Al's characteristic way of interacting was intriguing. He talked about a wide range of emotions, insisting that he was certainly able to differentiate feelings internally but simply could not display them. His voice was flat and his demeanor subdued. While exceedingly sensitive to others, he never seemed to share their feelings. He imputed emotions, certain that someone felt lust, desire, or rage that he could envision but never share. My attempts to interpret unconscious emotions had little effect. Generally he rejected even the possibility of having such reactions. Even when he could imagine that he might have wished to be rid of his dominating mother, for example, or that he was proud of the power he had usurped from both his parents, or was conflicted about his mother's seductions and rejections, he obtained neither relief nor change from such speculation. Such discussions seemed to become empty intellectualizations, interesting but wholly disconnected from his experience.

This period of treatment was characterized by repetitious working through of my misattunements, Al's misperceptions, and our mutual enmeshments. The rituals at the beginning of sessions, waiting for a polite welcome, testing my mood, denying conflicts, ridiculing my suggestions of feelings or fantasies, began to yield as certain patterns came into focus. For example, Al had a way of responding to attempts to explore, explain, or empathize that left me feeling I had failed to reach him. He didn't disagree or say that I didn't understand, but nothing I did was affirmed. If I was silent, he became worried that I was ill or distracted. When I tried to retrace our interactions to understand what triggered his concerns about me, he couldn't quite recall the sequence, or agree to my account, or imagine the implied feelings, for which he would then apologize. Always concerned about causing any possible rupture between us, but simultaneously oblivious to how his behavior could possibly be anything but helpful and cooperative. Time and again I was left holding the emotional bag, confused, frustrated, isolated, and lonely in the relationship.

Analysts have many explanations for this sort of obsessional control, but in this case I was reminded of Oscar Wilde's caution that it is sometimes superficial to look beneath the surface. The fact was, Al really never felt understood or that his feelings were acceptable. He did not believe he existed in another's imagination, was not contained within another's cognitive embrace. Conversely, he constricted his psychic world, his own feelings, wishes, and fantasies, out of the certainty that they would be rejected and would cause him to lose even his tenuous connections to others.

Eventually, Al's relational expectations were recognized through the countertransference rather than through explicit transferential messages. In rapidly shifting transitions, Al oscillated between portraying his contemptuous, cynical mother and presenting himself as desperate and placating. I, in turn, would feel furious yet trapped, then moved by his poignant vulnerability. Al resembled a battered child, struggling with an internalized sense of badness, unable to identify the source of his tortured self-blame or to strike out against it. Despite recounting tales of his mother's verbal savagery, Mrs. B remained the idealized, tragic victim, while he was the one who seemed traumatized. Describing his inner world through reflections of my own presumed identifications with his reactions allowed us to speculate about his experience, but did not open the door to his actually embracing the feelings as his own.

AN "ACCIDENTAL" DISCOVERY

One day Al showed up on crutches. He had fallen out of bed during a playful encounter while on a weekend reconciliation with his wife. While the accident was richly symbolic, his physical disability was seemingly minor; however, it eventually required surgery and triggered another level of analytic reconstruction. Al became even more keenly focused on my reactions, worried that he was too great a burden, and that I would tire of him. He was certain I was disgusted with his inadequacy, made evident by his vulnerability to injury. And of course, Al was oblivious to the possibility that he was projecting, transferentially, from the period of his mother's illness, and he vehemently denied any possible acting out. A sense of retribution for lustful pleasure colored the incident, although to Al, guilt about sexuality took second place to his dismay about the consequences of being less constricted. Spontaneity, so hard won through his treatment, was now seen as too dangerous. His goal was expressed as the wish that I would help curb rather than release his appetites.

Viewing his pain, I felt increasingly solicitous, while he became preoccupied with the feeling that he was dying. At this point, Al recalled that as a small child he had been hospitalized for an extended period. His memories of being in the hospital were sketchy, but he clearly remembered that he had regressively lost the ability to walk upon his return home, and that he was cruelly ridiculed for playing the baby. His dreams during this period of analysis included images of being looked at from afar, alone in empty rooms with no one responding to his call. He recovered the sense of profound abandonment associated with the hospitalization, as well as feelings of being a specimen, a curiosity. His initial resistance to using the analytic couch could now be seen as related to feeling monitored by an unresponsive authority. Eventually, the persistent feeling that he was dying was connected to images of his mother crying at his bedside.

Al considered this a breakthrough. He was electrified by the idea that his mother had nursed him through a near fatal illness. He now believed that his chronic guilt was his quite appropriate fate for causing his mother's despair. While unable to recover his own feelings during the period of his illness, he readily accepted responsibility for her reactions. This was a pivotal experience. Sullivan (1953) taught that anxiety avoidance is central to personality development, and that the child's early encounters with anxiety are generated by an anxious parent. It seemed that Al's repressive style could be connected to a need to avoid damaging others and a belief that his pain must be suppressed lest others suffer. Recounting his mother's distress brought Al's first tears in treatment. He grieved for causing her anguish and was terrified of witnessing her unhappiness. Although he had no memories of his own feelings, we reconstructed the experience of stifling expression of his own pain so she might suffer less.

Controlling himself to modify others' reactions had became central to his psychic development. Al's character embodied the conviction that his needs were the source of Mrs. B's lifelong unhappiness. He equated his flawed body with a corrupt soul, causing suffering in others. He constricted his emotionality to deny need and desire and avoid their damaging impact. He despised vulnerability because it signaled lack of control as well as a potential plea for help and support. He felt inextricably tied to the mother, who, he believed, suffered so deeply for his sake. Anger, lust, power, vitality, all must be buried lest they reveal the wish to separate from her. He deserved penitent servitude. He saw his fate as the struggle between attachment and independence, either one inevitably causing pain to the other person.

But Al's loving connection to an idealized maternal image was countered by his deeply discordant behavior. He was not simply servile or deeply attached and attentive. Instead he was withdrawn and withholding, incapable of loving closeness or unconflicted generosity. In addition, his descriptions of his mother's self-absorption, currently as well as throughout his childhood, hardly meshed with the Madonna pictured in his fantasy. Lengthy analysis of his guilt, fear, paranoia, despair, and gratitude did little to resolve his emotional constriction. As before, little seemed to sink in. Nor did his pervasive isolation and sense of dread abate during his period. The apparent unconscious explanation of his problems seemed to offer little resolution of his symptoms. The analytic relationship remained distant, intellectualized and subtly edged with hostility. Eventually, motivated by conflicts and contradictions that became evident in the analysis, Al sought more information about his early illness.

THE "FACTS"

Al's hospitalization had occurred at a tumultuous time for the family. It turned out that Mrs. B had discovered evidence of her husband's philandering, initiating the marital war that became chronic. His mother confirmed the speculation that her tears at his hospital bedside represented the fear that it was her marriage, not her child, that was dying. It also appeared that for some time, preoccupied with jealousy,

Mrs. B had neglected her children, likely compounding the severity of Al's condition. Further, unable to tolerate the demands of nursing care, her visits to his hospital room were inconsistent, punctuating long periods of isolation.

The sick child believed that his mother's vigilance saved his life. He maintained the fantasy that despite her coldness and inability to be a nurturing parent, she nonetheless had some special secret affection for him. When she later became incapacitated, Al sacrificed his future to repay an unconscious debt. Despite her characteristic hostility and bitterness, Al assumed a covert bond between them. He dismissed her self-absorption, attributing her attitudes to his failings. His interpretation of his biological and psychological state, his pain, fear, and need for attention, affection, and reassurance, was predicated upon integrating the relational situation as he understood it at the time. Narcissistically focused as the center of his mother's world, the child's explanation never reflected, or included, his mother's emotional perspective. Al's sense of deadness, reenacted in the analysis, did not emanate from bodily experience of his illness so much as from identifying with his mother's pain. A sense of internal corruption organized his response to viewing her anguish. It was his fault. In later life, forsaking emotional certainty was the only way to be free of responsibility for another's suffering. He deadened desire to retain attachment. His character bore the imprint of those early encounters.

However, the residues of that illness in Al's memory also included his unconscious recognition of Mrs. B's emotional unavailability. She did not comfort. She was always unattuned. Her despair didn't fill his inner emptiness. Her tears did not touch his lonely soul. At one level, his physical pain, terror, loneliness, and confusion were interpreted through her apparent concern. At another level, regardless of how his guilt served to bind him to her feelings, there remained an unformulated awareness that she was present in body but incapable of emotionally entering his psychic world. Al could not label his mother's unavailability nor open the door to his own rage and despair. Unwelcome since birth, the child accepted responsibility for destroying the possibility of affection and security, and incorporated that guilt into his character. Al believed he hid his feelings to avoid causing others pain, but in truth, he could not know how to distinguish the nuances of feeling states. He had no capacity for articulating discrete reactions out of the chaos of affective turmoil.

In the analysis, my ability to recall details of Al's history was as important as any interpretation. What mattered was that I developed an image of Al in my mind, that he was seen and accepted as possessing his own attitudes, needs, and reactions. He needed me to describe my sense of him as well as my reactions to him, to offer what Sullivan (1953) called "reflected appraisals," as well as countertransferential hypotheses about his inner states. He assessed my respect for his boundaries as closely as my attempts to understand his psychology. He needed me to acknowledge and tolerate his deadness but ultimately refuse to accept it as his fate. His emergence into the world of the living required my welcome. He could not articulate his inner states until I was willing to relatedly renegotiate the complex developmental path toward emotional fluency. All this was the symbolic message of his difficulty in approaching my open door, entering my world, interacting in the analytic space.

AN INTERPERSONAL PERSPECTIVE

Let me offer a conceptual context for this work. Interpersonal theory considers the environment a relational field through which all experience is filtered. From conception, the fetus is contained within and responsive to the mother. Physiology becomes psychology as experiential residues coalesce into what eventually becomes consciousness and mind. Self-experience is initially indistinguishable from environmental tension. The earliest impingements are expressions of the mother's moods and movements, her psychic as well as physical states. Psychoanalysis rests on the assumption that bodily processes constrain experience. However, pressures within the fetal organism, such as nutritional deficit, pain, agitation, and the like—conceived of as need, drive, or impulse—are given shape and meaning by the nurturing environment. Such pressures, sometimes called *drives,* require cognitive interpretation in order to participate in mental activities (Sullivan, 1953; Mitchell, 1988; Lionells, Fiscalini, Mann, and Stern, 1995; Stern, 1997), and such interpretation does not accurately discriminate tensions originating within the organism from those stimulated from outside. The origins, meanings, and motivations governing experiences are learned. Internally and externally generated experiences may be equally salient. They are also, at the core, interpenetrating and indivisible. Neither is manifestly more primary, nor are they reducible one into the other. But to become psychically integrated, whatever their source, they necessarily require and involve experiential input.

Al's dream, mentioned earlier, resembles a paradigm that has received a good deal of attention from Interpersonal analysts (Eisold, 1995). Children are unable even to acknowledge, much less to validate, parental interactions that are mystifying, double binding, or potentially destructive. Relational adaptations offer a compromise between personal satisfactions and interpersonal requirements in a particular family. Character is defined by these patterns of reaction, without consciousness of the parental input that has influenced them. Children internalize responsibility to create the illusion of control, and, at the same time, unconsciously explain psychic damage.

Al believed he was traumatized by discovering his mother's body, and indeed that event did shape much of his subsequent experience. But this incident doesn't fit recent definitions of trauma. His near fatal illness in infancy, long ignored by the family, was pivotal in crystallizing the cognitive and affective patterns that restricted his emotional development and were so impervious to change, resembling the impact of trauma. However, it is critical to consider that the familial context which made that event so severe existed before and after his illness, reinforcing and perpetuating his pathogenic character trends. The relational paradigm of his illness continued through his life. In Al's family, emotional trauma was an everyday experience.

Al's rituals of approach and avoidance involved interlocking and sometimes contradictory assumptions. Fearing rejection, terrified of being toxic, he required elaborate repayment or, at the very least, appreciation for his suffering. Women seemed enticing and seductive, but needy, vulnerable, and demanding—danger lying in either direction. While desperate to convey respect and avoid intrusion, appearing the martyred caretaker, Al secretly pursued his own interests. Managing such relational conflicts formed the basis of repeated complex enactments. From the Interpersonal perspective, transference is neither simply symbolic of the past nor a reenactment of a prior situation; it is a contemporary reliving of familiar adaptive patterns. Patients, indeed all people, create a "tolerable (interpersonal) distance," balancing need and fear, fusion and separation, maintaining fantasied assumptions and expectations of self and other (Shapiro, 1985). Recreating and repositioning this equilibration may be seen as the foundation of what has been called the *repetition compulsion*. So, Al's inner truths surfaced as he approached my door, embedded in his interpersonal style. Given his unformulated scenario, the emotional door to relatedness was never open. The encounter at the threshold of our relationship incorporated condensations of every level of developmental experience. The perpetual outsider, he eternally sought permission to enter, always needing to fend off whatever surprises might be found inside and assuring that the door would not close as he approached. Over time, we played innumerable variations on this relational theme, returning again and again to examine how we might engage each other.

CONCLUSIONS

Did Al "know" of his parents' marital discord during his illness? Of course not. Could the analysis have succeeded by uncovering only the psychic reality of fear, rage, and guilt, the internal elaborations of Al's infantile cognitions and experience? I think not. Is the analytic task to reveal buried facts? Only in part. The Interpersonal perspective involves coming to terms with a wider sense of truth to unravel and defuse the impact of early experiences. To exhume intrapsychic components without examining the relational milieu in which they emerge renders a unidimensional image, devoid of context, flat and insipid. Victims of trauma often require validation, be it factual or through consensual affirmation. So, too, perhaps all analytic patients require implicit, if not explicit, support for their psychic constructions.

In this case, Al actually sought corroboration of analytic hypotheses through discussions with family members and even uncovering hospital records. But, just as insight alone is never enough, merely discovering historical fact carries little psychic weight. Emotional salience is found through the immediacy of the analytic relationship. I would argue further that analytic success requires anchoring understanding of psychic life in the contextual realities of the interpersonal matrix. I believe that the twenty-first-century psychoanalytic paradigm must revisit the question of analytic reconstruction from a new perspective, recognizing the interpenetration of relational factors with internally generated experiences.

The reader may have guessed that Al and I never fully agreed concerning whether my door was open or simply ajar. We reached a stand-off that involved mutual acceptance of our subjective differences, forever in disagreement although no longer in dispute. But this seems an appropriate resolution: two individuals, able to articulate alternative perspectives and respect each other's. Wolstein (1974) says that authenticity can only be achieved through relation and, conversely, that true intimacy requires separateness. The resolution of psychological discomfort is not to be found in openness or closure; it is rather about being able to live with ambiguity and differentness.

Most contemporary analysts agree that mutative treatment requires unraveling transference, and that this necessarily involves countertransference. Analysts across the theoretical spectrum have realized that intrapsychic and interpersonal, self and other, fantasy and reality, past and present are inextricably intertwined in the transference–countertransference interplay. However, few seem ready for what seems to me the next step. I suggest that the factors that are analytically effective parallel those initially responsible for the patient's disturbance, distortion, and distress. Psychoanalysis of interaction is the medium for transforming personality. So too, the interactions of early experience, whether or not we label them traumatic, are formative of personality and psychopathology. Cure is located in, as well as through, the relationship. So, too, is cause.

In my introduction I mentioned that this patient came to mind as I thought about recent changes in the psychoanalytic landscape, new doors that seem to be opening in the fortresses that we have historically built to protect our theoretical sovereignty. But walking through those openings is not so easy. Many question whether current friendly overtures are substantial or manipulative. Political agendas merge with conceptual differences in complex ways, clouding expectations and supporting suspicion. As was true with my patient, historical reconstruction has become important in allowing us to reconsider the paths that took us so far apart and now bring us back together. Ferenczi has been rehabilitated. Horney is no longer considered a heretic. And Sullivan has finally become appreciated for his seminal and revolutionary ideas about the ubiquity of interaction. Similarly, our organizational structures have been studied to illustrate the policies of exclusion that stifled creativity and created warring mentalities. Our historical schisms led us to develop wholly different traditions, separate analytic cultures supported by entrenched bureaucratic mechanisms and corroborating belief systems. Conceptually and organizationally, psychoanalysis will require long, thorough, penetrating self-examination and a new willingness to expand, adapt, and change if we are to establish a more unified public and professional persona. As was true in my work with Al, psychoanalysts will need to continue meeting in forums which allow us to air and compare our perspectives, respect our differences, and take from each other new insights that may prove valuable in our mutual quest toward greater understanding of human experience.

REFERENCES

Eisold, K. (1995), Dreams. In: *Handbook of Interpersonal Psychoanalysis,* ed. M. Lionells, J. Fiscalini, O. Mann, & D. B. Stern. Hillsdale, NJ: Analytic Press.

Lionells, M., Fiscalini, J., Mann, C., & Stern, D. B. (1995), *Handbook of Interpersonal Psychoanalysis.* Hillsdale, NJ: Analytic Press.

Mitchell, S. (1988), *Relational Concepts in Psychoanalysis.* Cambridge, MA: Harvard University Press.

Shapiro, R. (1985), Separation-individuation and the compulsion to repeat. *Contemp. Psychoanal.,* 21:297–308.

Stern, D. (1997), *Unfortunate Experience.* Hillsdale, NJ: Analytic Press.

Sullivan, H. S. (1953), *The Interpersonal Theory of Psychiatry,* ed. H. S. Perry & M. L. Gawel. New York: W. W. Norton.

———— (1954), *The Psychiatric Interview,* ed. H. S. Perry & M. L. Gawel. New York: W. W. Norton.

Wolstein, B. (1974), "I" processes and "me" patterns: Two aspects of the psychic self in transference and countertransference. *Contemp. Psychoanal.,* 10:347–357.

6

Traumas of Everyday Life: A Self Psychological Perspective on the Neuroses

Anna Ornstein, M.D.

INTRODUCTION

Over the years, the increasing acceptance of "post-Freudian" psycho-analytic theories has slowly and imperceptibly affected the practice of psychoanalysis. For example, Greenacre (1975) observed that instead of periodic, comprehensive reconstructions, which were once consid-ered to be essential aspects of psychoanalysis, analysts had been simply including reconstructions in the interpretive process. She asked whether this change in psychoanalytic technique indicated a neglect of the genetic point of view, or whether it was due to the fact that there was a lack of certainty as to what was genetically significant and, therefore, what ought to be included in a comprehensive recon-struction.

Greenacre's observation about the uncertainty as to what may be genetically significant has even more relevance today than it had thirty years ago. Since the 1970s, the practice of psychoanalysis has become even more diverse, and the question of what may be considered genetically significant is likely to be answered with a greater variety of views today than it would have been in Greenacre's time.

In reexamining the seduction hypothesis and asking ourselves about the significance of trauma, fantasy, and reality in relation to neurosogenesis, I shall focus in this paper on the questions that Greenacre had asked: Is the genetic point of view still relevant in our thinking, and if so, what do we think constitutes the childhood trauma that is responsible for the emergence of an adult neurosis? Do we consider the trauma to be based on drive-related infantile fantasies of the Oedipus complex, or do we consider the cause of a neurosis to have been an actual, lived experience? Is it fantasy or reality that would have to be reconstructed in the course of a psychoanalysis?

These questions could be more readily answered in the 1960s and 1970s, because patients who were accepted for analysis at that time were expected to reproduce the infantile neurosis (the unresolved Oedipus complex) in their transference neuroses. In an analysis that was conducted according to the "standard technique," the transference neurosis was considered to be the adult version of the infantile neurosis, the product of an unresolved Oedipus complex. In this manner a direct link could be established between the Oedipus complex and the manifestations of the adult neurosis. Since that time, however, this direct link between the infantile and the adult neurosis has been lost. Increasingly, analysts have been unable to identify the presence of a true transference neurosis because preoedipal issues would be mobilized that would drastically change the configuration of the neurotic ("oedipal") transferences.

I am introducing my paper with these reflections on the theory of neurosogenesis and the relationship of this to reconstruction because, I believe, these were the questions we were asked to address when we were charged with the task of discussing our views on trauma in relation to patients whose lives are characterized by the traumas of everyday life. As an analyst guided by the theory of psychoanalytic self psychology, I shall focus on issues that self psychology considers to be potentially traumatic in the childhood of patients whose adult psychopathology is "neurotic" in nature.

THE CONCEPT OF TRAUMA AND
NEUROSOGENESIS

The abandonment of the seduction theory and his growing interest in the pathogenicity of infantile sexual and aggressive fantasies did not constitute the end of Freud's interest in traumas that were externally inflicted on the psyche. His interest in this was reawakened with the war neuroses that reaffirmed his *economic* perspective on mental processes in general and on trauma in particular (Freud, 1916–1917). But it was the exploration of the cause of the neurotic disturbances, the neurosogenesis, that constituted the backbone of Freud's theoretical edifice, and it was this that had moved the development of psychoanalysis in the direction of the exploration of infantile sexual and aggressive fantasies. In subsequent years a great deal of disagreement surfaced between practicing psychoanalysts as to the significance of potentially traumatic experiences in the development of a psychoneurosis. The views ranged from considering developmental experiences themselves (such as separation-individuation and the Oedipus complex) as potentially traumatic, to conceptualizing psychic trauma to be analogous to a physical assault, an external force that disrupts and overwhelms the psyche irrespective of the maturity and resiliency of the preexisting psychic structures (Rothstein, 1986).

In contrast to major differences as to whether it was fantasy or reality that proved to be traumatic and therefore responsible for the development of adult forms of psychoneuroses, there has been a general agreement that the consequences of trauma inflicted on an immature, infantile psyche had to be differentiated from trauma that was experienced by a relatively mature mind. Specifically, traumas experienced by the infant and young child were supposed to be responsible for creating structural *defects* or *deficits*, while at a later point in development, especially during the oedipal phase, traumas of everyday life (birth of a sibling, death of a grandparent or pet) may alter the structure of a neurosis, but these were not considered to be causally related.

The cause of a psychoneurosis had to be sought in the *conflicts* related to sexual and aggressive *oedipal fantasies*. In other words, regarding their respective pathological consequences, environmentally inflicted traumas that create "deficiency illnesses" were relatively sharply delineated from intrapsychically determined traumatic experiences related to libidinal fixation, regression, and compromise formation (A. Freud, 1968).

The question of whether or not the trauma was inflicted by the environment or created by internal conflicts, whether what the analyst was observing was related to a structural deficit or an oedipal conflict, has been of particular interest to child analysts and created an ongoing debate regarding the technique of child analysis. Anthony (1980, p. 25), in an effort to separate the internally from the externally created forms of trauma, suggested that child analysts ought to recognize that children "construct" three forms of families—the intrapsychic oedipal one, the idealized representational one, and the actual interpersonal one. He suggested that the analyst's task was to "disentangle these various families and to appraise the family *realistically*" (1980, p. 25, emphasis added). The reality of the family and its impact on the child, said Anthony, become "superimposed" on the unconscious oedipal fantasies, which once exposed, become the legitimate subject of the analyst's interpretations. The question this suggestion raises is this: Who is to appraise the family *realistically*, and how is it to be delineated from instinctually generated intrapsychic experiences?

Ernst Kris (1956) was another child analyst who concerned himself with the question of the way in which *endopsychic* and *environmental* factors interact in neurosogenesis. Such an interaction would be in keeping with Freud's theory of the "complemental series" (Freud, 1918). It was in this spirit that Kris reported the case of Dorothy, who suffered a series of potentially traumatic events between the ages of 2 and 3: A brother was born, her grandfather died, and a beloved dog was accidentally killed. These were all traumas of everyday life. Kris also shared with the reader observations regarding the parents' personalities, their relationship with each other, and with their little girl. Kris tells us that Dorothy's parents had a stormy marriage and that, while the little girl behaviorally remained attached to her mother, she did not follow her mother "into her phobic tendencies" but rather shared her father's love for animals and for the outdoors.

Kris also recorded the mother's intense jealousy of Dorothy. In a somewhat paranoid vein, the mother experienced the child's close attachment to her father as if the two of them were "ganging up on her."

In reporting the case, Kris challenged the reader to predict how twenty years later Dorothy's analyst might go about reconstructing the potentially traumatic events in the child's life. In case Dorothy developed a psychoneurosis in her adult life, the *meaning* that would have to be given to the child's experiences by her future analyst, says Kris, would have to include the oedipal–sexual elements: "the wish for a child from the father, the death wish against the mother, the fear about both sexual and destructive impulses, and finally the fear of castration which seems adequately added and superimposed" (pp. 75–76). This strictly instinctual view of the neurosogenesis, however, would have to ignore the reality of the child's *actual, lived experiences* with her parents, experiences which Kris himself observed. As a child analyst and careful observer, Kris did not discount "the peculiarities of the parents' personality." However, in keeping with the theory of the neuroses at that time, Kris could consider the parents' personalities to be important in the child's development only in general terms but not as a *specific cause* of her later neurosis. Should Dorothy develop an analyzable condition, that is, a psychoneurosis, this would have to be explained in terms of sexual and aggressive fantasies related to the Oedipus complex.

A SELF-PSYCHOLOGICAL PERSPECTIVE ON THE PSYCHONEUROSIS

What significance would a self psychologist give to Kris's observation regarding the parents' personalities? A psychoanalytic self psychologist would say that whatever significance the mother's jealousy had in the early years of the child's life, it would acquire *special pathogenic significance* at the time when the little girl became flirtatious with her father, when her sexuality was in the ascendancy. The mother's inability to delight in her daughter's budding sexuality (especially during puberty) would be considered to be an *active ingredient* in the genesis of any difficulty Dorothy may develop later in life, be this in the form of a psychoneurosis or in some form of sexual disturbance. From a self-psychological perspective, failure on the part of the same-sex parent to respond to the child's developmentally appropriate competitiveness and sexual flirtatiousness can still create discrete deficits in the psyche. Such a view would affect the content and wording of reconstructions which would have to include the child's experiences of her mother's jealousy and inability to validate her budding femininity.

The reconstruction that includes the potentially pathogenic aspects of parents' personalities presents special problems. The concern is related to the fear of "parent blaming" and that patients will externalize their difficulties. Parent blaming can be (and has to be) avoided by recognizing that constitutional givens and the traumatic effect of absent or faulty caretaker responses have symptomatic and behavioral consequences already early in the child's life. These "mismatches" may be related to differences in infant–mother temperament or the infant's inability to organize experiences due to subtle neurological difficulties. Whatever the source of the incompatibility, not being able to affirm the mother's ministrations may easily and imperceptibly establish a negative feedback system between caretaker and infant.

But the reconstruction of the parents' personalities (or peculiarities) is not the central aspect of the interpretive–reconstructive process as this is informed by psychoanalytic self psychology. Rather, the central aspect of this process is the reconstruction of *childhood emotional states*, such as a profound sense of loneliness, compulsive daydreaming, and grandiose or revengeful fantasies. Kohut (1971) considered these childhood emotional states to be "early precursors of adult disturbance" (p. 195). In recovering these memories (which may or may not be preserved in visual images), the traumatic aspects of the caretakers' personalities become progressively clarified. These constructions do not aim at the recovery of actual pathogenic events. Rather, the aim is to recover intrapsychic experiences of childhood which, in the context of the original child–caretaker relationships, give meaning to the analysand's current symptoms and transferences.

Issues related to external versus internal, oedipal versus preoedipal were most fervently discussed in the psychoanalytic community when Kohut (1971) first described the transferences he observed in patients with developmental arrests and structural deficits. For many of us, his description of these selfobject transferences opened up a new horizon for analytic practice. The recognition of these transferences permitted an interpretive, analytic approach to patients who, according to traditional theory, were unanalyzable because they suffered from structural defects.

In his first description of the selfobject transferences,[1] Kohut (1971) also maintained the distinction between the oedipal and preoedipal forms of psychopathology and considered caretaker responsiveness to have structure-building properties only in infancy and early childhood. However, he changed his views when, in 1977, he distinguished between an oedipal *phase*[2] and an Oedipus *complex*. The normal oedipal phase, he said, was a silent phase in development that did not give rise to psychopathology unless the child's interest in sexual matters and his increased self-assertion were responded to with seduction, overstimulation, and counteraggression. Under these conditions, the oedipal phase becomes an Oedipus complex, which ought to be considered pathological already in childhood. (In this respect, it is particularly instructive to reread the case of Little Hans [Ornstein, 1993]). This was a conceptual giant step that had undone the artificial distinction between oedipal and preoedipal, external and internal, and between intrapsychic and interpersonal in relation to potentially neurosogenic factors in a child's life. Recognizing the neurosogenic significance of parental attitudes and responses not only during the preoedipal but also during the oedipal phase of development, opened the door to new perspectives on the analytic investigation of issues such as sexual identification, sexual object choice, sexual conflicts and inhibitions regardless of the time a child may have been traumatized.

The discussion of the following case demonstrates that an externally inflicted trauma, regardless of how subtle and imperceptible this may be to an external observer, ought to be considered potentially neurosogenic at a time in development when the patient's sexuality and self-assertion are in ascendancy.

---

[1] The concept of the selfobject transference constitutes the foundational content of self psychology. The method of empathy led to the recognition that, on an experiential level, patient and analyst do not relate to each other as two separate individuals. Rather, the patient experiences the analyst as being part of himself or experiences himself as being part of the analyst.

[2] Kohut's reference here to an oedipal phase has to be modified since we no longer conceptualize development in terms of phases. Rather, we conceptualize it as occurring along developmental lines, which shifts the emphasis from specific drive-related contents (oral, anal, phallic or oedipal) to the harmony between the lines (A. Freud, 1963).

CLINICAL EXAMPLE[3]

Mr. S, a 30-year-old single man, came to see me with the explicit wish for an analysis. At his age, he had to make some important decisions that involved his wish to get married and settle down. So far, however, he had not been able to establish a satisfactory relationship with a woman. He could not commit himself to a long-term relationship because he feared that he would be first exploited and then abandoned by the woman. Mr. S also suffered from a discrete form of sexual dysfunction: In the course of foreplay, he would suddenly become distracted by some kind of a blemish on the woman's body (a mole or a hair in the areola) which would disgust him, and he would suddenly lose interest in lovemaking. He had chosen a female analyst because he believed that his difficulty was related to a highly conflictual relationship with his mother. The fear of being exploited by a woman had a specific content: He feared that as his love for her would deepen and he would become increasingly dependent on her, she would become ill and die. This would leave him mourning for the rest of his life, which he envisioned as being brief because most men in his family—including his father—died at an early age. This fear was an undisguised expectation that he would repeat his father's life. Mr. S's mother died when he was in his early teens, and his father, a long-suffering man by nature, never recovered from the loss. At the time when the patient was seeking analysis, he called himself an orphan, his father having died a year earlier. He considered it "abnormal" that, at the age of 30, he was still attached to his dead parents.

Mr. S was a handsome young man whose regular facial features were buried in a sad and troubled facial expression. The sadness was also expressed in his posture: He was slightly stooped, shoulders thrust forward, his gaze directed downward as if he did not want to take in his environment fully. He dressed casually, and as he told me later, he had difficulty buying himself attractive, well-fitting clothes.

I shall describe the course of the analysis in two parts. The first part demonstrates that the patient's manifest symptoms were sexual

---

[3] This clinical example was first presented at a self-psychology conference in 1980 with a different emphasis.

in nature, and the transference he developed indicated that these symptoms arose in the context of a triangular (oedipal) relationship. The second part of the analysis revealed a deeper, more disturbing aspect of his difficulties related to an inability to idealize his weak and ineffectual father.

In the course of the analysis, the image of the mother emerged as an energetic, intense, and volatile woman who had musical ambitions for herself before her marriage. The patient was a professional musician, and many of his childhood memories were related to his interactions with his mother at the piano. "She was a teacher and an inhibitor of great magnitude," he would say. "She always criticized when I played. Then I would make more mistakes, she would get angrier, and I would play still worse. She would scream, and her saliva would spray all over me—I hated that. Then she would slap me, and we would both cry." As he spoke of this much repeated interaction with his mother, he stopped, took a deep breath and commented on the fragrance of my perfume, remembering how much he used to enjoy the smell of his mother's dressing drawer. On the one hand, he experienced his mother as a source of fascination and excitement but also a source of rage and humiliation; he feared that my interest in him could also cause him inhibition. Mr. S experienced his mother's death as if he had been "set free." His grades had improved, and the quality of his musical performance had improved.

The analysis of the sexual inhibition was facilitated by a "transference symptom" that developed in the first phase of the analysis, a symptom that could be traced to the memory of a childhood experience. As a young child, until his early adolescence, Mr. S would get into bed with his parents in the morning. Just as soon as he got into the parental bed, his father would get up. He hated him for that. Father insisted that he stay in bed with his mother, who had a chronic, progressive illness. Though the patient could not recover the memory of sexual excitement at these times, he recalled the disgust he felt whenever his leg would touch his mother's pubic hair. The transference symptom became the representation of the reactivated affects associated with this memory: Mr. S developed a strong aversion to my voice; whenever I spoke, even a simple "hmm," it would irritate him. The irritation barely concealed his rage, which was mixed with a sense of helplessness. At one time when he was particularly keen in describing his reaction to my voice, he said that it felt as if his penis would be cut off. I wondered whether his irritation with me and his disgust in his parents' bed could have been related to the sexual excitement he experienced whenever his leg would touch his mother's pubic hair. It seemed that the aversion and disgust successfully protected him from states of sexual overstimulation.

My acceptance of the intensity and the reality of his affects in the transference and my relatively few and brief interpretive comments facilitated the working through of this transference symptom and introduced a period of genuine mourning for his mother. He decided that the best would be for him to terminate his analysis at this time. "In order for me to separate from mother, she had to die. I have the fantasy that I have to leave the analysis to be free of you." He reflected on what he said and added that maybe his "real reason" for selecting a female analyst was that, at this time, he wanted a different ending to the relationship. He wanted the termination to provide him with a new experience: to feel free without thinking that for him to achieve this, the analyst would have to die. But he did not think that he could do this alone; he needed a man to "free" him from the fear of women. He also found—to his great regret—that he felt more alive and more enhanced in the company of men and that he still felt small and insignificant in the company of women. He now set new goals for his analysis: to experience himself as a strong and competent male in the presence of, and in relationship to, his female analyst.

It is at junctures like these that theoretical biases are decisive in the wording and phrasing of interpretations (Ornstein, 1983). Was the screen memory of his getting angry when his father would get out of bed a reaction formation covering up his wish to get rid of his father? Was the feeling of disgust when he touched the mother's pubic hair representing Mr. S's castration anxiety because he experienced sexual excitement on these occasions? In other words, was the sexual inhibition secondary to an unresolved Oedipus complex related to his drive-related unconscious sexual and aggressive fantasies? Had I considered the anger and disappointment in his parents and the reexperiencing of these affects in the transference to represent his unconscious sexual and aggressive fantasies, I would have had to interpret the patient's childhood perceptions of his father as a distortion. I would have had to help Mr. S recognize that his current sexual inhibition was the expression of castration anxiety, the symptomatic legacy of his wish to get rid of his father because of his incestuous sexual wishes toward his mother. The importance of reconstructing these pathogenic unconscious fantasies was most clearly stated by Arlow (1963): "In clinical practice, it is most important to be able to uncover the unconscious instinctual wish which is given form in the fantasy" (p. 21).

In traditional psychoanalytic theory, these interpretations would be in keeping with the theory of cure: Helping the patient accept his murderous wishes toward his father would facilitate identification with him and would make repression of incestuous wishes toward his mother possible. In my theoretical frame of reference, however, I considered the anger and irritation in the transference to be a response to the parents' failure to protect him from sexual overstimulation. And, as we shall see in the second half of the analysis, the identification with his depressed father was not a felicitous resolution of his Oedipus complex. Rather it constituted a major problem in Mr. S's life.

The transference affects related to his father emerged against a great deal more resistance than those related to the mother. The emerging anger and disappointment not only threatened the patient's tender and loving feelings toward the man who was his primary caretaker, but it also threatened the vital connection to his father that he established through a massive and gross identification with him. The content of this identification was a chronic, futureless depression, a deep conviction that, in every way, he would repeat his father's life. As the father-related transferences evolved, the patient was determined to experience his female analyst "as if she were a strong man." I could appreciate the patient's fear that, having chosen a female analyst, he might again be deprived of the opportunity to acquire those personality features which, in our Western civilization, are associated with masculinity.

The second part of the analysis was introduced with a dream in which Mr. S easily removed a man from a couch sitting next to a woman. He thought that the dream exposed features of his father's personality that he now recognized in himself. When the children were younger, they always turned to father; he was more responsive and more dependable than mother, but as they grew older, the boys realized that he was not a man who could help them face the hardships of life: "He shielded us from the world, but he could not shield us from his anxieties." The patient had a clear vision of what he wished his father would have been like. Once someone gave him a massage; the man had strong hands but did not hurt him. This was the feeling he yearned for in his analysis, but my "femaleness" was a handicap he wasn't sure he could overcome. He had a dream in which he wanted to fly; the pilot was brilliant but was physically unable to handle the plane.

Many of Mr. S's dreams dealt with his wish to experience me as if I were a strong man. In one of his dreams he engaged in a boxing match with me. He thought that the importance of the experience related to the level of interaction between us rather than on winning or losing. In the dream, he felt free to hit hard without having to concern himself with my ability to withstand his blows or that I might retaliate against him. I considered the dream to express a deeply felt *need* to experience me as someone who was able to withstand (and delight!) in his assertiveness and competitiveness. To have had a dream in which he actually felt that way excited him because he could feel his strength in relationship to me. This was in sharp contrast to the way he behaved toward his parents. Whenever he had an argument with them, especially with his mother and grandmother, he always gave in. Now, he could conceive of a different ending, one that could be a creative moment for him. There was a definite change in the ambience of the hours: from readily feeling intruded upon, which culminated in his feeling angry and irritated by my voice, to wishing that I would actively interact with him.

I shall finish the report on this case vignette with a story that indicates the patient's curative fantasy. The story beautifully captures his expectations of the analysis and the degree to which he felt these expectations were met.

Mr. S observed 3-year-old Joshua in interaction with his two parents. He observed the child pulling away from his mother, who, he felt, was "imposing" her hugs and kisses on the child. "I can't watch her kissing him. These kisses are not for him, they are for her." He also sensed that, at the same time, the child desperately wanted to be with his mother. Mr. S, too, wanted to be close to his mother, but "that's how she treated me . . . how I was reaching for Dad . . . but he wasn't quite strong enough." Mr. S once observed the same child being caught by his father as he was about to fall off the swing. "What perfect timing!" he exclaimed. He thought that the child must have experienced two marvelous feelings simultaneously: He could feel the *exhilaration* of swinging all by himself and the *safety* of his father's firm arms as he was caught in midair just in time. "What rejoicing!" —referring to the joy he observed on the faces of the father and the son as the child safely landed in the father's arms. He thought that he experienced something akin to this when he interpreted his own dreams in the secure knowledge of my attentiveness and added, "But I can also catch myself when you are not there." He again reflected on his relationship with his parents: "I must have been caught by them many times, but I had to learn to swing by myself." We agreed that my acceptance and understanding of his rages in the early part of the analysis made it possible for him to experience me as someone he could spar with without fear of destroying me and without the fear of retaliation.

DISCUSSION OF THE CLINICAL EXAMPLE

One of the most intriguing questions raised by this case is the patient's determination to experience his female analyst as if she were a male and a deeply felt desire to experience himself as a strong, freely competitive, and self-assertive man in relation to her. I considered these wishes to represent Mr. S's curative fantasy and the essence of his oedipal selfobject transference. My reason for this assumption is the following: The screen memory of his experiences in the parental bed not only helped to trace the origin of Mr. S's sexual dysfunction (his inhibitions in lovemaking when he noticed a blemish on the woman's body), but the screen memory also represented a *traumatic disappointment* in his father on a broader scale. The patient was particularly distressed whenever he witnessed his father's fearful, almost cowardly responses to his wife's demands on him. Mr. S's need to idealize his analyst as if she were a strong male was this legitimate developmental need now expressed in the transference. In development, too, it is the oedipal child's idealization of the strong, self-assertive father that aids in the consolidation of the male child's gender identity; it is through idealization that boys acquire the characteristics (competitiveness and self-assertion) that, in our Western society, are considered to be male attributes.

The essential difference in the conceptualization is this: Traditional psychoanalytic theory would consider the need to idealize the analyst as if she were a strong male a defense against oedipal rivalry and hostility. Psychoanalytic self psychology considers the need to idealize the analyst as a legitimate developmental need that in developmental terms was traumatically interfered with. Similarly, there is a difference in the way that anger would be understood: In self psychology, anger at the father would be related to a *traumatic disillusionment* in the father, while in traditional theory, anger would be considered to represent the poorly sublimated aggressive drive.

One could argue that there is no need to postulate the presence of an oedipal selfobject transference and consider that what the patient hoped to achieve in his analysis was to "exchange" his identification with his passive and depressed father to an identification with a strong, self-assertive analyst. However, identification as a psychoanalytic concept has been a problematic one. Analysts speak of "negative" and "positive" identifications and say that identifications can be with one or more characteristics of the object; they can be total or partial and can achieve different levels and involve various motives (Schafer, 1968). But what determines the aspects of the other that the child will identify with? What are the genetic–developmental roots of the pathological, negative identifications? And, most importantly, could such "negative identifications" interfere with the free expressions of sexuality and self-assertion?

Some of the answers to these questions can be found in the transferences patients develop in the course of a psychoanalysis. As the case of Mr. S demonstrates, because of the opportunity to idealize certain developmentally needed psychological functions in his female analyst (such as strength, as if she were a male, her vigor and aliveness), Mr. S was able to relinquish his identification with his depressed and passive father. In the developmental theory of self psychology, the acquisition of gender-related attributes are not conceptualized to occur via identification but through transmuting internalization.[4] Gross identification is likely to serve defensive purposes: It assures connection to the homogenital parent whom the child

---

[4] Transmuting internalization means the slow, bit by bit internalization of features of the idealized parent imago. In cases of sudden or repeated (traumatic) disappointment in the idealized parent, this normal developmental process is interfered with.

is unable to idealize in relation to his or her gender-specific attributes. Ideally, empathic, age-appropriate selfobject responses are "tailored" to specific, idiosyncratic features of the child's talents, intellectual and artistic endowment, as well as to his or her gender. Since such responses become transmutedly internalized, they facilitate the emergence of the child's own constitutionally and gender-determined capacities.

CONCLUDING REMARKS

I have described selected aspects of an analysis to illustrate the development of a neurosis on the basis of everyday microtraumas (strain traumas) which, in my theoretical perspective, constitute the traumas of everyday life. In the case discussed, the trauma was related to the disillusionment in the father's "manliness," resulting in a massive and gross identification with him. This is what Kohut meant when he said:

> [A]fter an eighty-year-long detour, we are returning to Freud's original seduction theory—though, of course, now not in the form in which Freud had entertained it. The seduction that we have in mind now relates not to overt sexual activities of the adult selfobjects—although such behavior would, of course, be included—but the selfobjects' unempathic responses to fragments (sexual and aggressive) of the child's oedipal self, instead of empathic ones to its totality (the child's affection and assertiveness) [Kohut, 1991, p. 721].

REFERENCES

Anthony, E. J. (1980), The family and the psychoanalytic process in children. *The Psychoanalytic Study of the Child,* 35:3–34. New Haven, CT: Yale University Press.

Arlow, J. (1963), Conflict, regression and symptom formation. *Internat. J. Psycho-Anal.,* 44:12–22.

Freud, A. (1963), The concept of the developmental lines. *The Psychoanalytic Study of the Child,* 18:245–265. New York: International Universities Press.

————— (1968), Indications and contraindications for child analysis. *The Psychoanalytic Study of the Child,* 23:37–46. New York: International Universities Press.

Freud, S. (1916–1917), Introductory Lectures on Psycho-Analysis. *Standard Edition,* 16. London: Hogarth Press, 1961.

————— (1918), From the history of an infantile neurosis. *Standard Edition,* 17:1–122. London: Hogarth Press, 1955.

Greenacre, P. H. (1975), On reconstruction. *J. Amer. Psychoanal. Assn.,* 23:693–712.

Kohut, H. (1971), *The Analysis of the Self.* New York: International Universities Press.

————— (1977), *The Restoration of the Self.* New York: International Universities Press.

————— (1991), Letters 1981. In: *The Search for the Self,* ed. P. H. Ornstein. New York: International Universities Press, pp. 681–729.

Kris, E. (1956), The recovery of childhood memories in psychoanalysis. *The Psychoanalytic Study of the Child,* 11:54–88. New York: International Universities Press.

Ornstein, A. (1983), Fantasy or reality? The unsettled question in pathogenesis and reconstruction. In: *Psychoanalysis: The Future of Psychoanalysis,* ed. A. Goldberg, New York: International Universities Press, pp. 381–395.

————— (1993), Little Hans: his phobia and his Oedipus complex. In: *Freud's Case Studies: Self Psychological Perspectives,* ed. B. Magid. Hillsdale, NJ: Analytic Press, pp. 87–106.

Rothstein, A. (1986), *The Reconstruction of Trauma: Its Significance in Clinical Work.* Madison, CT: International Universities Press.

Schafer, R. (1968), *Aspects of Internalization.* New York: International Universities Press.

Discussion: Analysts at Work with Patients Whose Lives Are Characterized by the Traumas of Everyday Life

Robert Michels, M.D.

I have two clear understandings of what happened in 1897: one, that Freud rejected the seduction hypothesis; two, that at least in part he did so for a psychoanalytic methodological reason, namely, that he found that he could not reliably know what had happened in the past on the basis of clinical data. Although there seems to be broad agreement that we should reject the specific seduction hypothesis of the etiology of hysteria, at times we still seem to think that we know what happened in the past based on clinical data from the present. I will return to this later.

I will begin by noting the nonequivalence of two pairs of concepts: First, the terms *seduction* and *trauma* are not synonymous. *Trauma* sounds bad and *seduction* is at least a little more ambiguous. *Seduction* implies another person. A person alone in the forest cannot be seduced. *Trauma* envisions a person alone, and the other, if present, can be a vague, fearsome, foreboding, and not clearly represented other. Some traumas don't even require an other at all. Trauma is negative. Traumatic seduction can occur, although seduction is in general more complex. *Trauma* refers to an event that for some reason or other cannot be fully integrated or metabolized. It doesn't fit easily into potential or preexisting meanings. We don't have trauma receptors in our minds. When we develop receptors for an experience, then it is no longer traumatic. A trauma is something for which the organism is not adequately preadapted. Seduction always relates to some potential for response in the organism. There are receptors, although the seduction may precede the normal maturation of the receptor (i.e., it may occur when there is only a protoreceptor), and thus the seduction may precipitate the premature development of the capacity to respond. However, at least potentially it is possible to integrate an experience of seduction. In summary, trauma disrupts, and seduction influences the course of development.

Seductions occur all the time—we know this from the media, if from nowhere else. Trauma is usually thought of as a less frequent occurrence. Therefore, the notion of traumas of everyday life is discordant. If there are everyday occurrences, we should have adapted to them so that they are no longer traumatic. If they are truly traumatic, they cannot be everyday. For some psychoanalytic thinkers, all traumas can be reduced to the failure of the caretaker to shield or protect the individual from the trauma—Anna Freud in her wartime studies; Anna Ornstein in her paper; or Marylou Lionells, somewhat indirectly, in her paper.

There is a special problem in considering traumatic seduction. The victim of traumatic seduction is both the victim of trauma and the seduced. Traumatic seductions may be particularly disruptive because of the ambiguity of whether one is a victim of trauma or a participant in a seduction.

A second pair of concepts that are not synonyms are *trauma* and *environment.* Not all environmental theories of pathogenesis are theories of trauma. The environment is the substrate for all growth and development. It facilitates, it nurtures, it supports, and at times it traumatizes. Everyday traumas are really everyday environmental events that have, to varying degrees, both traumatic and positive or growth facilitating aspects. Without any environment we could not exist. The very events that provide the microtraumas of everyday life also provide the opportunities for growth, development, and character formation. The *traumas of everyday life* is an oxymoronic phrase; as one moves away from extraordinary trauma, one moves into the environment of everyday life.

Scott Dowling questions whether the distinction between an event and a fantasy makes sense. For him all experiences are event-fantasies; you can't have one without the other. The case he presents raises the question of how we can separate a trauma that leads to splitting and the formation of pathologic symptoms (the formulation he offers) from what is in effect a screen memory. He conceptualizes a vivid recollection of a scene that encapsulates a dynamic theme in a patient's life, a theme that preceded that scene, then continued after it, has become symbolized by it, and that represents a complex, unconscious fantasy. His discussion suggests that he would find any trauma a symbolic encapsulation of important unconscious fantasies.

This point will come up again in Jacob Arlow's presentation, but an even more fundamental question concerns whether we are dealing with factors in the etiology and pathogenesis of neurosis, or rather with symbolic elaborations that provide clues for our understanding of dynamic constellations but offer no explanation of causation. In other words, was the memory from age 7 of the man Dowling describes the cause of his later pathology and character formation, as the term *trauma* would suggest, or was it an image that became a symbol, similar to a manifest dream, and that might provide a Rosetta Stone for unraveling the complex determinants of this unconscious fantasy, the cause of which cannot be uncovered from this sort of data?

Scott Dowling suggests that all traumas are memories that represent unresolved dynamic constellations. A traumatic memory is one that is associated with a sense of helplessness, that is projected or attached to the memories of events in the real world.

As a footnote he adds that much of what we used to call *trauma*, including the kinds of traumas for which his own research has made him famous, infantile experiences, such as those secondary to esophageal atresia, that occur to the prementalizing, prefantasizing child—that these are really prepsychic events. They are organismic traumas rather than psychic traumas, events that impact on the developing nervous system rather than on minds capable of fantasy. The latter is prerequisite for Dowling's definition of trauma. As I understand him, psychic trauma would not be possible at birth or in the first weeks or months of life but would only occur with the achievement of the capacity to mentalize. This is in sharp contrast with Anna Ornstein, for whom the formation of psychic structure continues well into postmentalizing phases of life and for whom trauma is understood as something that interferes with structure formation well after the age of active fantasy life. Scott Dowling's model of development suggests that first we form our psychic structures, and then we develop both the capacity to fantasize and with it the capacity to experience psychic trauma. Incidentally, he has a neurobiologic problem in his model, because he considers "pruning" to be something that can interfere at a prepsychic level, but pruning is a neurophysiologic phenomenon that occurs well into the second decade of life, after language, after the development of primary relationships, after fantasy, and after the event that he describes as psychic trauma in the patient whose case he recounts to us. This would mean that in his model, psychic trauma and prepsychic traumas can occur in either sequence.

Marylou Lionells identifies all trauma as occurring in the context of relationship-related events and goes on to say that all treatment works through the process of relationship-related transactions. She, more explicitly than any of the other panelists, recognizes that this theoretical stance is a choice that she has made. She makes clear that she knows that others with alternative theories have made alternative choices. She indicates that such terms as *libido*, the *self, oedipal conflict*, or even the *unconscious* are not real entities, but rather are hypothetical constructs (p. 142). I had hoped that she would include the point that relationships aren't real either, but are also hypothetical constructs that she has selected to organize her data. If she is willing to accept that modification, I join her totally in recognizing that all of us bring theories with us. However, most of us are more comfortable explaining the theories of others as being based on hypothetical constructs.

Why should we join her in assuming that the cause and the cure of her patients' problems must be related? Many treatments operate by mechanisms that have nothing to do with the causes of the disorders that they treat. Certainly there are disorders of temperament or biological disposition that can be treated effectively by psychological interventions, and as we have learned in modern psychopharmacology, the reverse is true as well.

Lionells also, more than any of the other panelists, relates the question of etiology to the clinical question of validation. She asks us to accept the events of her patient's life as fact. Interestingly, she does not ask him to do that. She supports him in seeking confirmation and corroboration of reconstructions in the analytic process by talking to his mother, by implication accepting his mother's current memory of those events as validation of what has been reconstructed in the analytic process, a mother, incidentally, whom she did not view as a reliable validator at the time that events transpired. She explains that victims require validation.

I would ask why. How do we know? And if they do require validation, aren't we in trouble because our method cannot possibly provide it? How do we respond to their ''need''? In the case that she reports, she works back through a series of developmental experiences: the discovery of the mother on the basement floor; the earlier experience of the mother as narcissistic, inconsistent, seductive, and cruel (I assume that it was not those characteristics that the mother herself validated); the patient's guilt about the distress that he felt he caused his crying mother at his hospital bedside; and ultimately his need to make sense of his unavailable mother during his development.

In her initial account of his behavior at her office door, Lionells told us that, unable to resolve or understand what was going on in this complex transference–countertransference enactment, they met half way ''so the analysis could proceed.'' I wondered about her choice to proceed by leaving the transference question unresolved and instead exploring the patient's memories of his past and reconstructing his childhood, using the psychodynamic pattern identified in the account of childhood as a template to be applied to the unresolved transference enactment, rather than continuing to explore the transference enactment itself. Would the exploration of their relationship have reached the same or a different endpoint as the application of the model based on their developmental reconstruction?

Anna Ornstein, in agreement with Freud of 1896 and with Heinz Kohut, believes that trauma is real, that is, real in the everyday sense of out there in the real world. She differs from Freud in that she does not think the most common critical pathogenic traumas are sexual, but rather the empathic failures of parents. She is confident that she can reconstruct the empathic failures of parents based on the data of memory and transference reenactment, and that from these data she can trace the cases of those empathic failures to the "real" behavior of parents. She sees the treatment as a means of repairing the consequences of those empathic failures, importantly facilitated by the availability of an adequately empathic analyst, a kind of countertraumatic reality.

She says that "reconstruction that includes the potentially pathogenic aspects of parents' personalities presents special problems" (p. 162). Here I agree, but she identifies that special problem as parent blaming, and here I differ. I believe that parent blaming is a surmountable problem. The much more difficult one is the same problem that led Freud to modify his thinking in 1897. After we have reconstructed a patient's memory or fantasy of childhood, we still do not know what "really" happened. It is hard enough to know whether parents really abused a child, but as we move from abuse to the sexualization of everyday experiences it gets harder. And as we move from the sexualization of everyday experiences to unempathic parenting, I believe it becomes impossible. It is not blaming parents that most disturbs me; it is presuming that we know them when the only data available are the memories and transferences of their children many years later.

Of course, one can say that we are only interested in reconstructing the intrapsychic experiences of childhood, not the actual events. Here we should have a better chance, but Anna Ornstein herself will not settle for this. She tells us: "In recovering these memories, . . . the traumatic aspects of the caretakers' personalities become progressively clarified" (p. 162). Her thinking in this is similar to that of Lionells. The issue arises again for Ornstein in discussing alternative approaches to her patient. She tells us, "Had I considered the anger and disappointment in his parents and the reexperiencing of these affects in the transference to represent his unconscious sexual and aggressive fantasies, I would have had to interpret his childhood perception of his father as a distortion" (p. 166). Once again the assumption is the same, that it is possible to move from the unconscious fantasies of the present to knowledge about the external reality of the past. I don't know how to make that move.

If I understand Ornstein, she sees the curative aspects of a self-psychological analysis as importantly requiring the inverse of the pathogenic aspects of traumatically unempathetic parenting. The analyst must have certain empathic capabilities and behaviors that are the reverse of the pathogenic ones experienced in the original parenting relationship. If this is true, an unempathic analyst (and here she would include a classical analyst treating a patient who had the kinds of pathology that she is describing) would be retraumatizing an already traumatized patient rather than facilitating healing. As a corollary, other schools of psychoanalysis would be unable to treat these patients, but would be retraumatizing them because of their failure to resonate to the core needs of the patient. I think that is an important, courageous, but rather controversial position.

I was distracted by a detail of Arlow's presentation. It is difficult for me to imagine that scene where the patient came to Arlow and was unhappy to be stuck with him after having been referred by a preferred senior colleague. I kept wondering how long ago that must have been. Arlow tells us that the seduction hypothesis was itself both a trauma and a screen memory in the history of psychoanalysis. It was a trauma in that we as a field have remained fixated on the search for a specific etiology in the pathology of our patients, and a screen memory in that it served to obscure the centrality of infantile sexual wishes in our patients' lives. He points out that we have long since recognized the importance of infantile sexuality and that there is little disagreement on that issue today.

But what about the question of etiology? If it isn't seduction, should we search for some other specific etiology? He warns us against doing so in the clinical setting, but what about in our theory of pathogenesis? Should we settle for a complex, multifactorial model which recognizes so many causes and so many factors that there is no possibility of testing or validating any of them? We have reached the point where we have formulated a comprehensive theory of meteorology that is not quite as good as looking out the window in predicting the weather an hour from now. Should we discard the notion that psychoanalysis is a method of learning about etiology or pathogenesis, accepting rather that it is some other kind of discourse than that which

Freud himself believed it to be, that what we are calling traumas here
are symbolically encoded memories, which may help us to unravel
dynamic meanings and unconscious fantasies, but which cannot even
in theory point to causes and etiologies?

His clinical presentation addressed the distinction between dramatic and shocking, as contrasted to everyday, traumas. He presented
a woman who experienced severe trauma as a result of everyday
events, in contrast to a man whose character and transference, although
not strikingly pathologic, were clearly organized by an unconscious
fantasy that could be traced back to an extraordinary and traumatic
childhood scene. Like Dowling, in contrast to Ornstein or Lionells, he
emphasizes that trauma is determined more by the state of the receiver
at the time of the event than by the nature of the event itself. Yet, he
holds onto an etiologic model. "Nonetheless, the injurious effects of
the woman patient's early experiences were far more deleterious and
incapacitating than the dramatic, devastating nature of the trauma that
the little $3\frac{1}{2}$ year-old boy experienced" (pp. 125–126). He prefers that
formulation to an alternative that might, for example, state, "Isn't
it interesting that the woman patient selected such trivial events to
encapsulate and present her central, dynamic conflicts, whereas the
man, although far healthier, selected a far more dramatic and singularly
traumatic story with which to convey the key that unraveled his unconscious conflicts and dynamics?"

Finally, let me return to the panel as a whole. If trauma is an
event that overwhelms the organism, I must conclude that everyday
trauma would be an evolutionary paradox. Through evolution we develop the capacity to deal with everyday events; when they impinge
upon us, we can respond to them. The only events for which we do
not develop such capacities are extraordinary rather than everyday.
These are the events that can overwhelm us and result in trauma.
Seduction may be everyday, but then it cannot be traumatic. Seduction
can be traumatic, but then it cannot be everyday.

General Discussion

Scott Dowling: In responding to Bob Michels, I think that we as analysts have failed to find an effective language for describing the interaction of the individual with his relational and nonrelational environment. We do not have a good language for describing what goes on between the individual's inner life and the outer life around us. We have utilized a language that uses such terms as *trauma* and what I think is the very unfortunate term *strain trauma,* in an effort to describe some of those interactions. We also get hung up on physicalistic analogies, and we become overly simplistic in our efforts to describe these phenomena. I believe that we as psychoanalysts need to emphasize the psychological side of life. We are dealing with the psychology of people, not with a psychology of something else. We are dealing with what things mean to us. A central term in my view of things is *meaning to the individual person.* Yes, I do think that all of trauma involves a symbolic encapsulation of unconscious fantasy themes, as Michels elucidated in reviewing what Arlow had to say. I think all those instances that we have called *trauma* are memories, or fantasies in some instances, with a sense of helplessness attached to them. But

181

again these are only a variety of potential interactions with the surround that require more specific description and enunciation.

Now this brings us to what I describe as the *organismic trauma.* Again, it is a central part of my way of looking at things that we not confuse the early life of the infant with a later and evolving psychology. I think that there is an ontogeny of the psychology. Rather than seeing a very small infant as having psychological equipment that is similar to that of older children and adults, we tend to lose the potential for a more complex and more detailed understanding. So, yes, I do think there are events that can occur to young children that specifically direct their development and limit or encourage it in a very organismic sense. I'm quite willing to extend that possibility into certain kinds of events later in life. I'm not saying where one begins and the other ends. If pruning happens later, and if it results from some specific event, then so be it. But I don't think that should be confused with the coexisting psychology of the same era.

It is inherent in what I am saying that we do have to embrace a multifactorial etiology of psychological disturbance. I don't take a negative view of that. I don't think it is like looking out the window and trying to judge the weather by what we see in one small sample. In fact, I would hope that in time we would try to develop a true science of meaning rather than psychoanalysis being a natural science analog. We need to embrace the basic psychological nature of it and develop a more detailed and elucidated psychology of meaning, which is what I think psychoanalysis is all about.

Arnold Cooper: Let me take you one step further. I think there's agreement among some of us on the panel that the term *trauma* doesn't serve us as well as it might and that we should have a series of terms for the kinds of things that we are talking about. But in Dowling's case presentation he implied that if this little boy had not hated his father, finding him spread-eagled on the floor might not have been so traumatic. Is that so?

Scott Dowling: That's true.

Arnold Cooper: Tell us why the loss of a father, or in this case the apparent death of a parent, would not be traumatic for a child who loved the parent. For a child who loved the father, would finding his parent apparently dead be a shocking traumatic event?

Scott Dowling: That also could be a shocking and traumatic event. In this instance, what was not an entirely unexpectable view was lent a particular force for him and a particular intensity of meaning because of the unconscious ambivalence toward his father and the negative feelings. In fact, when he found his father was alive and was reassured, this did not immediately resolve the issue. He remained in this state for some time after.

Robert Michels: It was the live father that traumatized him.

Scott Dowling: Is was the live father.

Marylou Lionells: Well, in the spirit of my Woodstockian metaphor, I certainly would agree with Michels about the nature of what is real and what is constructed, perhaps not in terms of *relationship* but certainly in terms of the *relational matrix* and the *interpersonal field* (which are terms that come up a lot in my literature). They certainly are not real but are constructs. On the other hand, relationships, such as in a marriage, are real, which, I think, has a different quality. The other thing I want to comment on is validation. It has to do with the real experience of the event regardless of the facts of the event, regardless of the facts of the original trauma. The issue is not that reconstruction is veridical but rather that it is accepted and affirmed. As a side issue in my own patient, the historical reconstruction that he attempted did not simply include mother but also interviewing people in his family and actually getting hospital records in order to understand something of the nature of the illness, which had not been discussed in the family and which the mother had originally refused to discuss. And, as Robert Michels has described, the mother was a very unreliable witness. It was only when he was able to talk with her about her experience during this time that she was willing to talk with him.

Arnold Cooper: The case material that Lionells presented represents the primary impingement of a frame issue upon the analytic process. Such matters have been described by theorists from many different schools as the primary nodal points around which an issue of the analyst's care would play out. One could argue that the patient was responding to specific failures by the analyst to maintain a safe environment. Was the way Lionells handled her office specifically designed to induce a neurotic reaction in this patient?

Marylou Lionells: I tried to address briefly some of those points in the introduction to my paper in the sense that the frame I felt I was constructing was obviously very misattuned to this patient's sense of frame.

Anna Ornstein: I was trying to organize my thinking because I think Bob Michels had saved up all his questions about self psychology for his discussion after many years of arguments between him and Paul Ornstein. So let me give it a try. I am going to start backwards with the questions that he raised about what I had to say. I think he implied—although he never said it, since these are dirty words, really—that I referred to a "corrective emotional experience." I don't know if he had exactly that in mind, but something of that nature.

But what I do think is that we do need some kind of relationship between our theory of pathogenesis and what we say, when we say it, how we say it, how we behave. These things are a unit in my mind. In other words, the technique or the theory of treatment and the theory of pathogenesis must have some relationship. This does not mean a direct one-to-one relationship. Just as we do not know what has really caused the problem, we cannot therefore say we have the answers in terms of how we will reverse it. But we do have something that is specifically psychoanalytic, and we have discovered that what is similar among us is that we are all psychoanalysts.

Marylou Lionells: That we discovered that we are all more simply psychoanalytic than anyone thinks.

Anna Ornstein: What makes us all psychoanalytic to me is that we are all using the transference as the "royal road" to understanding what was activated and what is distressing to a patient—what became activated in this particular dyad, with this particular analyst. The way

I understand the patient is going to determine not only the psychopathology but also my reaction. I would like to mention Ernst Kris's remark (he was one of my favorites) to the effect that we don't know what happens to a patient in the twenty-four-hour period in a day. We see them for forty-five, fifty minutes. A lot of life experiences get integrated into the psyche with a patient in psychoanalysis. Being in psychoanalysis is not restricted to what is happening and what we can encompass with our understanding. No, we don't know what is curative, just as we don't know what is pathogenic. But we do have transferences, things become activated between two people, and we want to be interpretive of what we see. So, in the case that I had presented in terms of the specific issues about self psychology, the question I was raising is: How do I understand the patient's need (this was the transference) to experience me as a strong male? What was the significance of that, and how will I respond to it? That had to be informed by my understanding of the need—I don't say wish—in developmental terms as a legitimate developmental need. I understood his dreams of sparring with me and experiencing himself, not me, as strong—that he could feel free now to be competitive and self-assertive. You asked me whether empathy was necessary. Again, I do believe that it is central. It simply means, as Michels knows very well, that we are making an effort to take the *patient's* view of himself and of the world. This is really a tremendous change from many of the other things that we have had to deal with in psychoanalysis. It is not only patterns and this question about what gets reconstructed. I do emphasize the importance of childhood emotional experiences, so that we can jointly articulate what it was like. And you are absolutely right, Bob Michels: I don't know the parents. I should never say that this is how it was, because I don't know that.

What the transference brings into the process will be what the patient can articulate in terms of certain outstanding memories. I have to go with that just because it is important to the patient, and this is what he or she is emphasizing. What I find so very helpful in these reconstructions of childhood emotional experiences is that it brings with it a sense of "that's me, you got me"—this feeling of being understood. We can make the effort to find words that can describe that state of mind so that the patient can feel understood and therefore can "detoxify" his own memories if they have been burdened with particular traumas and sadness and losses.

You said that I don't consider the state of the self to be crucial. I would disagree with that. I think the state of the self is very important because a fragmentation-prone or fragmented self has a very different experience from somebody who is in the possession of all his faculties. This also applies developmentally, and it is why Dowling and I disagree on the importance of the timing of trauma. I do believe that the childhood traumas are much more destructive in the long run than are those where people can defend themselves because they have developed certain defenses and adaptive measures.

Arnold Cooper: Thank you, Anna Ornstein. Jack Arlow, we also have a question for you from the audience. Sending a patient for testing after consultation could be experienced by the patient as traumatic. In effect, are you responsible for the patient's panic?

Jacob Arlow: Well, I could say it didn't happen. There was a question about what makes these fantasy structures that we described as pathogenic. I am not quite sure that I know the answer. People differ to a very great extent on how they respond to the unconscious fantasies that they have and even in the process of treatment how they respond when these fantasies are slowly and laboriously brought to the surface. Here we would have to fall back upon a complemental series. But I think if we take the fundamental elements that Brenner described in compromise formation, we would have to judge the interplay of these various elements that go into any compromise formation: the intensity of the wish, the guilt association with it, the adaptive consequences or maladaptive consequences that have to be taken into account, and so on. These are many factors which differ vastly from person to person, and they differ vastly about specific conflicts in any one particular individual.

As I said in the paper, there are certain situations where the outcome has a conflictual wish, expressed as a fantasy which is itself a compromise formation. The outcome may be at the same time paradoxically constructive and maladaptive. It depends upon the range of compromise formations that the individual is able to effect. Certain experiences in life may be helpful, depending upon specific contacts with individuals or specific identifications or specific problems that have been resolved in the past. On the other hand, one may be weakened by previously deleterious influences, failed experiences, and the like. I have to fall back on the idea that we have multiple determination of these factors so far as a solution of the various elements in conflict and compromise formation are concerned. And we can only judge it restrospectively—in part—from some of the background associations that we get about the nature of the mechanisms instituted to control the potential pain, anxiety, guilt, and so on, generated by the conflict.

Marylou Lionells: I would just like to add a point. In the interest of trying to understand the differential impact of experiences in the patient's fantasies, what I find omitted is the relational qualities of the parents and the relationship in the family.

Arnold Cooper: While I can understand that the analyst cannot provide validation for historical events or memories, is it not possible for the analyst to provide validation in the reenactment or transference–countertransference within the treatment situation?

Robert Michels: It changes the meaning of validation. The analyst can say, "I think you are feeling such and such." So long as we don't suggest that we are saying, "I think such and such happened before we met." The analyst doesn't know what happened before they met. But validation doesn't usually mean recognizing the patient's experience; it means agreeing with the patient's conjecture about the events that led up to that experience. The danger of doing that is that you might be wrong. Even more important, the patient may become realistic enough to recognize that you couldn't possibly know what you just assured them was so. You are assuming an antitherapeutic authoritarian stance, therefore, rather than exploring their desire to have you validate something that they and you both know cannot be validated in treatment.

Arnold Cooper: Can there be psychopathology without the occurrence or experience of either specific trauma or long-term traumatic processes or relationships? Do we require a trauma in order to explain psychopathology? There is another question here along similar lines, asking in effect whether we can have traumas which are growth enhancing rather than growth inhibiting. And if we do mean growth enhancing, should it still be called a *trauma*?

Anna Ornstein: I think that people call it *stress* nowadays. And when you call it stress, you think that it can go either way. When you call it *trauma*, the implication is that it has pathological consequences. Depending on the prior psychological organization and what that experience meant, it might be growth producing.

Scott Dowling: Part of my answer would be that I would just as soon do away with the trauma language entirely. As an example, I think that what is being questioned is the same thing that I was trying to point out: There are other kinds of experiences that we need to delincate and understand that we don't see as being traumatic, yet that are also significant and regular in their effects upon personality development. We do have a language for some of these. There is one that occurs to me at the moment. Children at various points have experiences that are particularly satisfying and where the accretion of pleasure is particularly forceful. These experiences in the same way can be organizing and lead to a whole direction of movement and life to reproduce, to elaborate on, or to reexperience that type of pleasurable experience. Clearly, these are not traumatic.

I also think there are many instances of what might be viewed in some instances as being traumatic that can be growth enhancing. Arlow has referred to that already.

Jacob Arlow: That question begs the question: How can you define trauma except in relationship to damage? It doesn't make sense to ask whether you can have trauma without damage.

Arnold Cooper: I think there has been general agreement that you can have trauma that is damaging which then leads to compensatory processes that are even more strengthening than the original character structure. But that's a different story.

Jacob Arlow: We shouldn't say *trauma;* we should say *painful experiences.*

Arnold Cooper: Exactly.

Part III

Analysts at Work with Severely Traumatized Patients

Introduction: The Analytic Aims in the Treatment of Severely Traumatized Patients

Chair: Leon Hoffman
Panelists: Peter Fonagy, Leonard Shengold
Discussant: Glen O. Gabbard

Leon Hoffman: The readers of this volume, like the participants in the original symposium, are at an historic crossroad in psychoanalysis. Until recently, various groups of psychoanalytic theoreticians and clinicians have ignored the formulations and theoretical developments of others rather than challenge and debate. The organization of this symposium symbolizes the extent to which analysts with divergent views of mental life and treatment have begun talking *with* each other rather than either talking *at* each other or not talking at all. As analysts from different orientations interact with each other, perhaps they may even find that, despite different outward affiliations and orientations, the understanding of good and therapeutic clinical work may not be so far apart. Volumes such as this one can help overcome the impact of the lack of cross-fertilization that occurred for many decades. As there is greater interaction among analysts of different theoretical perspectives, one hopes that a fuller clinical and theoretical development will ensue, with a resultant greater clarity in the psychoanalytic understanding of a variety of issues.

How can the work of this panel, in the exploration of difficult clinical situations, help other analysts apply the successes (and failures) of the presenters to their own clinical work? As moderator I hope not only to provide a brief introduction to the papers, but also to place these papers in a context so that the clinical work presented can be compared and contrasted with readers' own clinical work. Whenever one reads or listens to clinical material, there is an inevitable (conscious and unconscious) influence on one's own clinical work. Furthermore, as one reads a variety of clinical approaches, one compares and contrasts them. Are they consonant with each other or divergent from each other? Which is most consonant with my own work? This introduction will help place the ideas presented in a general context as well as in a selective historical context.

In 1927 Freud wrote: "For me, the explanation of fetishism had another point of theoretical interest as well. I arrived at the proposition that the essential difference between neurosis and psychosis was that in the former, the ego, in the service of reality, suppresses a piece of the id, whereas in a psychosis it lets itself be induced by the id to detach itself from a piece of reality" (pp. 155–156). Freud then realized that he was mistaken. He remarks that in the analysis of two young men, he learned that in childhood (one at the age of 2 years and the other at 10 years of age) both had lost their fathers and "scotomized" the deaths but did not develop a psychosis. As in fetishism, these young men disavowed a piece of reality. Such a disavowal of reality, Freud maintained, is common in childhood. In the cases of the two young men, this disavowal persisted into adulthood: There were two mental states that existed side by side, one which fitted in with the wish and the other with reality.

In his posthumously published *An Outline of Psycho-Analysis,* Freud (1940) discussed further the idea that splitting, as a mechanism, was ubiquitous in childhood. Children, he stated, in addition to coping with undesirable instinctual demands by repressions, often find themselves in positions needing to fend off distressing demands from the external world. They do this by means of disavowal of the perceptions from reality. "The disavowal is always supplemented by an acknowledgement; two contrary and independent attitudes always arise and result in the situation of there being a splitting of the ego" (pp. 203–204).

The papers presented in this panel refer to patients who have been traumatized by the external world and whose lives have been dominated by the kinds of splits alluded to by Freud. The impact of severe trauma on people, in fact, has been an ongoing interest for psychoanalysts, psychotherapists, and psychiatrists. A review of the literature of this topic would be so vast that it would require many volumes. However, I would like to note one other author, in addition to Freud, who makes a connection between severe early trauma, continuing sexual dysfunction, and severe impairment in object relations.

Greenacre (1969) discusses fetishism, which develops in patients who have a variety of experiences during the first two years of life: illness, illness in the mother which may have made her less reliable as a mother, or a deprived or violent family atmosphere. In addition there may be exposure during the first two or three years to the genitals of the opposite sex and the acute experience of witnessing an injury (usually bloody) to the self or, even more importantly, to another, more often the mother, another child, or pet. Thus, in these children's development, vision, looking, is a central factor (pp. 330–331). Greenacre maintains that during analytic treatment of these adults there is an unusual degree of primary identification and a diffuse and rather simple type of envy, jealousy, and projection. There may be some impairment of object relationship and evidence of magical expectations and apprehensions. Greenacre (1970) emphasizes further that fetishism becomes most manifest during latency and adolescence. Though less common in women than in men, she says that in women, when it appears, it is less obvious but in a very persistent form and represents an extremely severe form of the deviation (p. 335). Although none of the authors in this panel refer to fetishism, they do refer to issues in the transference–countertransference in which the analysts are almost forced to engage in sadomasochistic interactions with their patients.

Greenacre (1969) stresses that, although fetishism relates particularly to the genital, these patients often have intense anger with sadomasochistic fantasies and practices. As a result, many of these patients are incapable of tender object-related love (pp. 333–334). Although Greenacre uses a language that is different from that used by the authors herein, the patients described by Fonagy and Shengold have many of the characteristics described by Greenacre, such as an unusual degree of primary identification, impairments of object relationships, magical expectations, and projections. I cite this example to exemplify the notion that, as we engage in a mutual discourse, one has to differentiate between different ideas and different vocabularies. Are different vocabularies indicative of essential differences, or are they merely different labels for very similar clinical phenomena and their theoretical underpinnings?

In his paper, "Living the Experience of Childhood Seduction: A Brief Account of an Unusual Psychoanalysis," Peter Fonagy writes that a fairly standard psychoanalytic technique can be judiciously applied in cases normally regarded as beyond the scope of psychoanalysis. As one reads Fonagy, it is very valuable to compare his technique with the technique one uses with one's own patients and, furthermore, to ask whether he has demonstrated a perspective that one can usefully add to one's own day-to-day work, especially with traumatized patients.

As Fonagy introduces us to his patient, who was seduced as a child by both father and teacher and later in life murdered her boyfriend, what quickly becomes clear are the terror in the transference and countertransference and, as Fonagy states, "the remarkable pervasiveness of the wish to be heard and recognized." This patient preferred being empty because only if people knew you were *somebody* would they attack you. In Fonagy's formulation he began to understand that the patient's self-representation was distorted by containing within it a representation of the other. This is common to other traumatized borderline individuals so that the patient finds other people to become the vehicle for this torturing part of the self-representation, which, of course, comes to be enacted in the transference-countertransference, as described by Fonagy. By the fourth year of this analysis, the histrionic outbursts receded and the tragic quality of the patient's life came to be reenacted in the transference-countertransference.

Fonagy asks an important question: Why are these patients considered to be difficult? These patients, he explains, behave in such a way so they find how to get the analyst to react; and, of course, the analyst is forced to act. Analysts react despite their attempts not to react. The aim of the treatment for Fonagy is to help the patient recover the reflective function (but not to achieve insight as in classical analysis). In this way there is a clarification of the moment-to-moment changes in the patient's mental state. There is a gradual transformation of a nonreflective mode of experiencing the internal world so that it is treated with more circumspection and respect, as separate and qualitatively different from physical reality. One would think that, as a patient is able to shift from a nonreflective mode of experiencing the internal world, the patient could then engage in a collaboration with the analyst rather than simply persist in a sadomasochistic interaction. Within Greenacre's frame of reference, one could consider that with the patient's improvement, there is less primary identification and a diminution of magical expectations and apprehensions.

In the second paper, "A View of Severely Traumatized Patients—Soul Murder Victims," Leonard Shengold, like Fonagy, talks about his most severely disturbed patients: those with primal affects (overwhelming primitive and compelling feelings) but inadequate and excessive defenses against them. Some of these patients have been traumatized or neglected as children and some have not, but had been born chronically traumatizable. As adults these patients have catastrophic expectations often covered by denial and splitting. Like Fonagy, Shengold reports that in the traumatically abused there is a deadness, a compulsive deadness, plus breakthroughs of uncontrollable feelings and behavior. Unlike Fonagy, who uses the term *borderline,* Shengold feels that diagnostic categories are of little value. He prefers the descriptive term *very disturbed.*

Shengold states that the conviction that something traumatic has happened should originate with the patient and not with the therapist. He discusses the brainwashing of these children, the pathological doubting that exists side-by-side with conviction, a kind of Orwellian doublethink. In treatment, analysts know what to do; the mystery lies in how to do it. Shengold states that if the therapist or analyst can get the traumatized person to care about the analyst, bearing in mind that the patient is generally too full of sadomasochism to care about the analyst as a separate person and to tolerate that caring, the control over violence can at least be partially achieved or restored. Like Fonagy, Shengold stresses how these children learn to keep themselves emotionally closed, especially to positive feelings. As with concentration camp victims, it is safer for them to suppress emotions or to stay on the level of regarding others primarily as fulfillers of need (while concomitantly, consciously or unconsciously, keeping the abusers as part of the self). For these patients, closeness and caring for another person has been crushed because it made the child feel so vulnerable. (Shengold described a patient treated by McLaughlin: " 'I love him. He's real, and he's mine! He's me!' [The patient's] voice dropped in vigour and insistence. 'Even as I say this I'm fading.' ") If caring can be established with the analyst as another person, the patient can begin to establish such relationships with other people.

Shengold stresses that the analyst has to be guided by empathic understanding: tact, patience, reliability, the honesty to admit one's mistakes and failures, and a good deal of technical flexibility. Above all, Shengold, like Fonagy, stresses that in one way or other the analyst has to tolerate the onslaught of hatred that has to emerge in the treatment setting.

CONCLUSION

In this brief introduction I have stressed the similarities in the work of the two panelists as they attempt to engage in the treatment of severely traumatized individuals. Fonagy stresses that one hopes that there will be a gradual transformation of a nonreflective mode of experiencing the internal world so that the internal world is treated with more circumspection and respect, as separate and qualitatively different from physical reality. For Shengold, if caring can be established with the analyst as another person, the patient can begin to establish such relationships with other people.

REFERENCES

Freud, S. (1927), Fetishism. *Standard Edition,* 21:147–157. London: Hogarth Press, 1961.

———— (1940), An Outline of Psychoanalysis. *Standard Edition,* 23:139–207. London: Hogarth Press, 1964.

Greenacre, P. (1969), The fetish and the transitional object. In: *Emotional Growth: Psychoanalytic Studies of the Gifted and a Great Variety of Other Individuals,* Vol. 1. New York: International Universities Press, 1971.

———— (1970), The transitional object and the fetish: With special reference to the role of illusion. In: *Emotional Growth: Psychoanalytic Studies of the Gifted and a Great Variety of Other Individuals,* Vol. 1. New York: International Universities Press, 1971.

7

Living the Experience of Childhood Seduction: A Brief Account of an Unusual Psychoanalysis

Peter Fonagy, Ph.D.

This is an illustration of fairly standard analytic technique. It needs illustrating just to show that it can be judiciously applied in cases normally regarded as beyond the scope of psychoanalysis.

Henrietta was in her middle thirties, eleven years ago, when she referred herself to a forensic psychiatrist colleague for "counseling." Stangely, the referral to me mentioned nothing about a forensic history, nor did it prepare me adequately for the paranoid, almost psychotic, but ultimately dissociated episodes with hallucinations and some thought disorder which were to become a feature of my ongoing work with her since that time.

This paper was included in a previously published article coauthored with Mary Target entitled "Playing with Reality: III. The Persistence of Dual Psychic Reality in Borderline Patients" (*International Journal of Psycho-Analysis*, 81:853–873, 2000).

There are a couple of "facts" that make Henrietta's case unusual from a psychoanalytic standpoint; as these also make the case highly recognizable, given a certain amount of publicity associated with them, readers must forgive the unusually heavy disguise. The first fact is that Henrietta is a murderer, not of her internal objects, her self-representation, or other parts of her mind, although she is undoubtedly guilty on all these counts—but of her boyfriend. She stabbed him in the course of a violent quarrel, pleaded self-defense, and claimed the stabbing was accidental. She was charged with manslaughter and was freed with a suspended sentence. About four years into the analysis she, for the first time, confessed to me that the stabbing was not an accident, and, while not premeditated, the act was certainly intentional, even if driven by violent, blinding rage. As, by that time, I was well familiar with Henrietta's violent tendencies, her vicious explosive attacks of rage, I was remarkably unperturbed by her revelation.

The second fact is her experience of "seduction," initially by her alcoholic father and subsequently by the teacher in the boarding school to which she was sent following her parents' separation. Neither experience was, so far as I know, ever "forgotten." While the former remained a secret between her and her father, who died shortly before the start of her treatment, the latter became public after the arrest and prosecution of the man concerned. Both experiences involved penetration as well as the threat of physical violence, which was never carried through by the teacher but was a routine part of her father's relating to her. Father beat Henrietta for various misdemeanors at least once a week, and *severely*, usually for "answering back," at least once a month.

Why *should* someone like Henrietta seek analytic help? She had no discernible experience of an understanding relationship. Her aim in coming to see me was to obtain assistance with the terrifying dreams that had started with the death of her father. She came to the first interview in a strident mood, demanding a brief period of counseling. She did not know that I was a psychoanalyst and, on noticing the couch some time into the interview, she said "So, this is where you fuck your patients?" A feeling of fear washed over me, helping me to see her vulnerability and enormous anxiety. I said, aiming to be reassuring, "You must feel quite brave that you dared to come and see me." She said, continuing her contemptuous tone, "You shrinks are abusers. It's just a power trip." I said, now more confident of my countertransference response, "I think it is your *own* power to destroy and abuse that frightens you about therapy. You feel much more confident about being able to cope with me." She stopped short and asked me what I meant by therapy. So this was how it began.

She started once a week, then twice a week, then three times a week and, after about eighteen months, four times a week. She would have come five times, except her work is no longer in London, so she comes Monday and Tuesday mornings and Thursday and Friday evenings, pays a low fee, and misses almost no sessions. Her commitment to the analytic process has been humbling. It has strengthened my belief in the remarkable pervasiveness of the wish to be heard and recognized.

Having said that the paper is an illustration of standard technique, I should add that I am not sure if many analysts would call what has happened between Henrietta and me over the last years, analysis. I am not sure if my interventions were ever experienced as interpretations, and I am certain that she experienced little (at least during the early years) of what most analysts would recognize as insight. Let me illustrate what happened between us at this time.

She arrived on time to the session, sat in a chair, and said she felt upset. I said, "I don't understand. You need to tell me what upset *is* for you at the moment." She said that she had had another dream about her father that had upset her. He had asked her to put her head up his backside, and she did not want to do it. She was ready to follow through with a string of obscene images depicting the sexual life between her father and her. I interrupted: "I think you are upset because you are frightened that I will make you bury your head in messy thoughts here." She stopped in her tracks, told me in a rapid sequence I could not follow, that she was lost, that her mother didn't understand, she wasn't trying to hurt anybody, that the death was an accident, that she tried to resuscitate him, to give him the kiss of life, but failed, and now I was trying to kill her. There was a gradual acceleration of tempo and intensification of affect, so by the end I was in the room with an apparently angry yet basically terrified person. It was unclear what these feelings were about. She seemed terrified by violence, her own or mine, and expected to be killed by a raging jealous object or to kill an invading, threatening one. I said, trying to calm her by stepping outside the fray, "It seems that you feel driven by a terror that you might lose me in this violence, that you have to constantly resuscitate me, to breathe life into me to keep me alive for yourself." She was silent. Eventually, somewhat calmer, she responded that she was frightened of being a person. She preferred being empty because people only attacked you if they knew you were somebody. I said, "I agree. I think you feel safer with me when you feel empty and it feels even safer if you have emptied me too." Her terror that I might kill her and even greater fear that she would kill me, intentionally or accidentally, overrode all other concerns.

It took me some time to realize that in these conversations with Henrietta there was always a third person present, a voice inside her head, someone she felt was her, but not her at the same time, an aspect of her dissociated state. Her "free associations" at these times were responses to what she "heard" as much as a dialogue with me. This put an interesting spin on my work in the transference. Eventually, I learned to address this voice more directly.

For example, in one session she came in confused, obviously more so than usual. She sat down on the couch and looked at me quizzically, as if asking, "What is going to happen next?" I said, equally puzzled, "You don't know what to say to me, and I don't know what to say to you." This prompted her to launch into a long and puzzling narrative about dancers who "gave their blood" in training and practice but found no work. She claimed to be upset about the injustice of it all. But then, as if she was aware of the transference meaning of what she had been saying, in quite a different voice, she said, "You are going to have to stop this treatment, aren't you?" Thinking of the internal conversation that must be taking place in her mind, trying to spell out her thoughts, I said, "I think that you are being *told* that I will reject you, no matter how hard you try here. Yet, you *want* me to understand your distress but perhaps also that you are not allowed to tell me about it. And this makes you feel confused." She buried her head in the pillow and started to sob violently: "I am so confused. I feel so bad. I am told I am fine, but I feel hopeless. Please tell me what is wrong with me." I replied, "You feel that, because I ask you to come here for only fifty minutes on a particular day, I can't possibly understand what your needs really are. I think you have a voice inside your head telling you you are fine. And it sometimes sounds like my voice." She calmed down a bit, and then she said, as if unaware of the contradiction, "I don't need help. I am fine. I am sick. I want to throw up." Then a pause: "I want to throw up when people get too close. You get taken over. You must understand me. You don't understand me. Do you understand me?" I said, attempting to identify the source of anxiety, "You are terrified of what I *would* understand. I would find you so sickening that I would have to throw you out." She said, still sobbing, "It's the sex. It's so wrong. I am so frightened you might *mis*understand. I am trying so hard to make something happen this time." I said, as usual regarding the reference to sex as defensive, aiming to distract us from the immediate source of her anxiety: "You hope for something good to happen here, but you are also frightened because you hear a voice telling you to spoil it by confusing and misleading me."

There are many analytic understandings to "explain" what was happening between us—the wish to create a perverted analytic intercourse, filled with sexual excitement that hid her guilt and vulnerability; the wish to make me into a pathetic dancer to her tune and observe me "giving my blood" in a futile attempt to save her; the regressive infantile omnipotence of the triumph of chaos over understanding; and so on. All these and more are true. The understanding that I had to hold onto over these early years was somewhat different. She desperately fought the truth, not for its specific contents, but the intolerable sickness that the closeness of two human minds created. There was something that felt sickening and disgusting about genuine feelings and ideas, an abhorrence of mere communication, a terror of reflection and mentalizing. Analysis was obscene seduction because thinking about mental states was *an incestuous act*, experienced as the intrusion of an object into a space too small to contain it.

In these sessions the actual affect was intense. The terror and the distress were real. The desperate hunger for understanding was matched only by her desire to empty her mind of all contents. The countertransference was brimming with discomfort and confusion. She acted dangerously, regularly threatened to take her life, and got into violent quarrels with both friends and strangers for which I was made to feel culpable. She frightened me with the threat of litigation for negligence and gave me a letter of complaint which she drafted for my professional association where my "incompetence" was carefully documented (changes of appointments, cancelations, lateness, confusions about times, even occasions when I misremembered names—all listed and dated). I was criticized for speaking and then ridiculed for my silences. At other times I was made to feel I was her savior. Much of the time I simply did not know what I was doing. Any clarity and coherence that this account possesses, I assure you, was fleeting over the first years of my work with Henrietta.

Dreams were like small oases in a cruel desert of enactments and manipulations that all but destroyed the possibility of reflectiveness. The dreams were vivid and varied, but I gradually noticed a consistent theme. There was always something within something else—and the thing within was absolutely dependent—almost parasitic—upon the thing without. For example, there was a dream about a lizard with a fly buzzing inside its stomach. Another about a skyscraper which had a yard with a semidetached (little) house with its own tiny yard. An abstract dream about a kaleidoscope where she was struck by the symmetry of shapes. A whole series of dreams where she dreamt that she was dreaming another dream. Transference dreams of the analysis where she and I, as patient and analyst, discussed another patient within another analysis. I came to feel, as I strongly feel now, that in patients incapable of reflectiveness, dreams provide a valuable special window. Perhaps dreams are, in part, residues of a nascent reflective capacity where the dreamer tries unconsciously, as best as he or she is able, to depict the structural constellation within his or her mind (the state which precludes verbalization).

In my understanding, in these Russian doll constellations Henrietta represented an experiential inner world depicting a self which, in its turn, contained a self. I began to understand her problem as one, in common with many traumatized borderline individuals, of a self-representation distorted by containing within it a representation of the other. It is internalized in early infancy when the mother's reflective function at least partially failed the infant, who in her attempt to find herself in the mother's mind found, as Winnicott (1967, p. 32) so accurately put it, the mother instead. This residue of maternal nonresponsiveness, this alien other, probably exists in seed form in all our self-representations, but it comes into its own when later trauma calls it forth as a defensive maneuver.

Let me illustrate what I mean by elaborating on the two "facts" of Henrietta's life. First, Henrietta's experience of having been abused.

Henrietta's mother, probably herself a "survivor," had a second child from another man when Henrietta was 4 years old. At this stage she began seriously to neglect both Henrietta and Henrietta's father. This probably exacerbated his already considerable drinking problems, and he began to seek solace from at first cuddling, then rubbing against, and finally vaginally and then anally penetrating his daughter. I suspect this happened when she was about 7 and went on for at least four years. Henrietta recalls initially welcoming his attention (even encouraging it) and gradually, when "the pain" started, going blank, and this helped him get inside her. She describes imagining herself as one of her lifeless dolls. The essential part of this description is the lack of attribution of mental states to the self and other representations. The strategy of inhibiting her mentalizing, and thus creating a dissociated state, is critical. It was impossible for her to understand how her father could contemplate hurting her as part of what grew out of an act of affection. As she turned away from mental states in him, and in herself, she simultaneously activated the nonreflective organization within the self—the alien other.

The alien other is not entirely a creation of trauma. It is an infantile structure internalized in place of, yet also as part of, the self. Henrietta's mother of infancy was incapable of satisfying her infant's essential need for reflecting her distress and nascent states of intentionality. I would guess that her infant's dependency was an unbearable reminder of her own experience of helplessness (by all accounts she did better with her son). Normally, the internalization of the mother's mirroring becomes the core of the representation of the psychological self. Henrietta, neglected or unrecognized as a child, internalized an image of absence or vacuousness as the representation of her state of distress. Not surprisingly, it was this state which was reactivated in moments of the acute distress of seduction since it was a corresponding experience of feeling unrecognized. Reflectiveness temporarily abandoned, the self–other boundary destroyed, the abusing father's cruelty was internalized into the alien self-representation through a process which may be related to the mechanism whereby the victim identifies with the aggressor. Thus, the alien part of the self became torturing as well as vacuous. Her experience of abuse at boarding school, after the age of 11, simply reinforced this deeply pathological self-organization. Her real, or what may be called constitutional, self was experienced as tiny in relation to the monstrous other (the tiny house in the backyard of the skyscraper). Yet, she also felt herself a monstrous lizard because this other was also her self.

Finding others to be a vehicle for this torturing part of her self-representation became a matter of life and death. Her experience of self-coherence depended on finding someone willing to torture her. The teacher was perhaps the first. A line of severely sadomasochistic relationships testified to the fact that he was certainly not the last. The transference was a lived instance. Let me give a very mild example of a category of experience that was far more frequent than I feel comfortable in admitting.

One day she came in late, complaining that she could no longer park her car for free. The change in parking regulations was somehow my fault. It was also my fault that she could not afford the parking fees, *and* I was going to be away again the next week. In fact, her lack of progress was entirely due to me. She had heard of a senior Kleinian colleague who was renowned for her abilities to deal with difficult patients. She wished she had been referred to *her*. I was a disaster. She would have gone on but, as far as I was concerned, she had said enough. I said, perhaps attempting to imitate the colleague whose reputation I envy, and failing to recognize the obvious manipulativeness: ''You are trying to destroy my ability to help you, to think about you clearly.'' This was a misunderstanding. I think she had no intention to destroy me but rather a wish to bring forth a critical, irritated reaction. She was silent for a while and then said, ''You see. *I* was right. You can't cope. You are too young, too inexperienced.'' I found myself saying, ''You see, you *are* frightened! You may have destroyed me, but without me you can't cope and you feel lost.'' She got up and said, ''For me, you and this analysis is dead'' and walked out of the session.

Of course, as soon as she left I knew I had been had. I had become the vehicle for her alien self and abandoned my analytic self with its albeit limited capacity to communicate understanding. This was confirmed in the next session when she came in, feeling a lot better, full of apologies, hoping that I was not too angry with her, reassuring me left, right, and center about how helpful I was being and that she would surely have killed herself by now were it not for my remarkable commitment and skills. I said, ''I think you hope that I will believe you, because that will confirm your picture of me as conceited and stupid. What you said yesterday was far closer to what you need to feel about me.'' She said contemptuously, ''Don't you realize it makes no difference what you think? You mean nothing to me. Nothing!'' I said, ''I think you are right. But being able to make me into someone who means nothing to you makes you feel in control, and that makes all the difference.'' She thought for a moment and then said, ''You are just clever with words like my teacher X (the abuser). You are evil. You care nothing about your patients.'' I said, ''If you can make it so that you can see me as evil, then you can kill me, and then you will be free.'' She fell silent, but the sense was that we both knew that this was the truth. Not that I think that stating the truth was ever necessarily therapeutic for Henrietta—it made her sad and sometimes suicidal. What seemed to be helpful were those few precious moments (like this last session) when I could become what she needed me to be, yet retain my capacity to hold her in mind with her fears and anxieties, and enable her to see this in my words and actions. Her ''confession'' of murder may be a helpful illustration.

Over its fourth year, her analysis began to take on a tragic quality, and the dramatic outbursts receded. She was functioning somewhat better, but the sessions came to be dominated by expressions of bitterness. Hatred for her father began to emerge, together with a genuine and deep dislike of me. The transference could now become sexualized and, at times, she explicitly asked me to molest her whilst she was angry with me. She came in one Thursday evening and recounted a particularly ghastly episode of allowing herself to be used and abused by ''an old friend'' who regularly visited her as his needs dictated. My mind was filled with bizarre and perverse associations. I said that I suspected that, for some reason, it was particularly important to feel that she could control me by exciting me or worrying me, and I suspected that she had felt the same vital sense of control in relation to her ''old friend.''

She responded that she hadn't been going to tell me, but she had had a dream about me where I had offered her my penis, suggesting that she should take it in her mouth. She was revolted by it because it was smelly and dirty. She was frightened because she knew I was going to beat her unless she submitted. She paused, waiting for me to say something. I remained silent. She said that she thought that I was probably extremely clean since I always wore well-ironed white shirts.

But in the dream my shirt was deep red. She added, speaking particularly calmly, that red was the color of anger.

I said that I understood very well how important it was for her to feel that she was in control because she was terrified that I would be angry and displeased with her for what she had done with her friend. The dream was like an offering—an appeasement—because she could not really bear me thinking badly of her. If she sensed that I was, it was almost better for me to be dead. I added that red was also the color of blood.

Her body shook as if an electric current had passed through it. "I think that is why I had to kill him," she said. "I couldn't bear him thinking I was disgusting." The story which unfolded in that session, and in many others that followed, was a tragic one. She regularly had allowed herself to be maltreated by her boyfriend. Normally, she somehow felt "cleansed" by the experience, particularly by his sense of shame about his own actions. But this time she saw contempt in his eyes. This she could not tolerate. She screamed and shouted at him. He ridiculed and disparaged her. She picked up the knife, and as he moved toward her, still mocking and sneering, she stabbed him. And with it she hoped to have killed her self-hatred and humiliation.

My work with Henrietta continues. She has improved enormously in terms of both structural and symptomatic criteria—yet horror and despair are never far away. It is hard for me to talk about this treatment because by knowing about the murder she has made me an accomplice in her crime.

Paradoxically, I also often feel grateful to Henrietta, who I feel has taught me more about violence, borderline functioning, and the unconscious than most other patients. It was from her that I learned that the mere remembering of experience, however horrific, could only have therapeutic value if the experience was lived in the here and now. The experiences that permeated her personality were encoded in her ways of relating, in her procedural memory; the mere remembering of the events, of the seduction or of the murder, was the consequence of the lived experience in the transference, and incidental to any therapeutic effect.

CONCLUSIONS

Why are patients like Henrietta designated as difficult? Part of the difficulty undoubtedly arises out of the obligation we quickly feel as clinicians to enact that which is projected onto us. We are forced to be as our patients wish us to be because we sense that without this, prolonged contact with us might be intolerable. Unless I could become the tormenting teacher, I was of little use to Henrietta. She behaved "unreasonably" toward me to elicit the reaction that she required, which confirmed for her that she had successfully externalized the alien part of her self. Because, as analysts, we try our damnedest not to react in the directions we are being forced to in response to mild provocation, we unwittingly force our patients to become "even more difficult." I certainly was somewhat guilty of this with Henrietta. But all personality disordered patients with histories of seduction get under our skin and eventually discover what will make us react with anger, what will cause us to neglect or reject them, or to feel excited by them, in all instances forgoing our therapeutic identity.

Once they see in us the hated alien other, once we have become who they need us to be, they are calm and safe and experience the coherence of self-representation, which was their goal in this projective identification. This was noticeable in Henrietta's reaction to my loss of temper. Unfortunately, in such states we are usually no longer able to offer therapeutic help. This is why these patients *are* difficult; their treatment involves a paradox (Fonagy and Target, 1995). In order for them to enter a therapeutic dialogue, to make their genuine or constitutional self accessible to us, they have to shed the alien self-representation, which dates back to failed moments of mother–infant interchange, and is powerfully reinforced by later trauma. Once the projection has been successful, they have in all probability destroyed the interpersonal situation that might have helped them.

So, what to do? Many recent approaches to borderline personality disorder (BPD) patients with a history of abuse, for example that of Marsha Linehan (1993), make use of a dual therapeutic context, simultaneously offering group and individual therapy. Others "split the transference" by simultaneously offering the help of a psychopharmacologist and a psychotherapist. Yet others attempt to contain the projections but make the therapy contractually dependent on the patient forgoing major enactments (Kernberg, Selzer, Koenigsberg, Carr, and Appelbaum, 1989). All these approaches are partly successful at tackling the problem but also have various shortcomings. Dual therapies may permit effective work, but it cannot be ensured that the externalization occurs in the context which is best able to cope with this. Contracts may help maintain the frame but at times they are as binding and as limiting for the therapist as they are for the patient, and so on. Contracts are easy to make; the problems start when the patient breaks them.

Our approach is to forgo the temptation to impose major modifications or parameters and to adjust technique (Fonagy and Moran, 1991). My work with Henrietta is as close to textbook psychoanalysis as I am able to keep it. We believe that such patients are treatable in the context of ordinary psychoanalysis, so long as the *aims* of the analysis are modified from ones which aspire to the achievement of insight to the less ambitious aim of the recovery of reflective function (Fonagy and Target, 1998). Interpretations in the classical sense have no place in the treatment of such patients. Clarification of moment-to-moment changes in the patient's mental state is a reasonable goal. Enactment on the part of the therapist is inevitable. The realistic aim is for the therapist to retain sufficient insight to be able to continue to reflect on his experience to the patient. The patient's enactments cannot be ''interpreted,'' since they simply do not have symbolic meaning beyond wishing to create a specific reaction in the therapist. It should suffice for the therapist simply to elaborate on the emotional state in the patient that might have triggered the enactment, in other words, the patient's current feelings at the time. The therapist should aim to retain in a part of his mind the patient's mental state and enable the patient to perceive his understanding, notwithstanding the concurrent massive projective processes that he must also accept (Target and Fonagy, 1996).

This kind of dual function is not easy, yet within it lies the patient's salvation. The psychotherapist's mentalistic elaborative stance ultimately enables the patient to find himself in the therapist's mind and integrate this image as part of his sense of himself. In successful therapy, the patient gradually comes to accept that feelings can safely be felt and ideas may safely be thought about. There is a gradual transformation of a nonreflective mode of experiencing the internal world that forces an equation of internal and external to one where the internal world is treated with more circumspection and respect, as separate and qualitatively different from physical reality (Fonagy and Target, 1996). This is part of a maturational process that was defensively abandoned in a futile attempt to avoid painful conflict. The biological pathway, the potential for reflective functioning, remains intact in probably all but the most severely deprived and handicapped patients. For these individuals, the experience of intimate contact with another mind capable of recognizing the patient's turmoil may be all that is needed for the recovery of a way of being, which is essential to adequate functioning in the human world. These patients do not make it easy for us to help them. Better understanding of their and our experience in this process is of considerable assistance in meeting this challenge. I hope that the present contribution may be of some assistance for those who are engaged in the, at times thankless, task of ameliorating the distress of these difficult patients.

REFERENCES

Fonagy, P., & Moran, G. S. (1991), Understanding psychic change in child analysis. *Internat. J. Psycho-Anal.,* 72:15–22.
———— Target, M. (1995), Towards understanding violence: The use of the body and the role of the father. *Internat. J. Psycho-Anal.,* 76:487–502.
———— ———— (1996), Playing with reality: I. Theory of mind and the normal development of psychic reality. *Internat. J. Psycho-Anal.,* 77:217–233.
———— ———— (1998), Mentalization and the changing aims of child psychoanalysis. *Psychoanal. Dial.,* 8:87–114.
Kernberg, O. F., Selzer, M. A., Koenigsberg, H. W., Carr, A. C., & Appelbaum, A. H. (1989), *Psychodynamic Psychotherapy of Borderline Patients.* New York: Basic Books.
Linehan, M. M. (1993), *Cognitive–Behavioral Treatment of Borderline Personality Disorder.* New York: Guilford.
Target, M., & Fonagy, P. (1996), Playing with reality II: The development of psychic reality from a theoretical perspective. *Internat. J. Psycho-Anal.,* 77:459–479.
Winnicott, D. W. (1967), Mirror-role of the mother and family in child development. In: *The Predicament of the Family: A Psycho-Analytical Symposium,* ed. P. Lomas. London: Hogarth Press, pp. 26–33.

8

A View of Severely Traumatized Patients—Soul Murder Victims

Leonard Shengold, M.D.

I have found that my most disturbed patients, whatever their history
and diagnosis, suffer from a mixture of primal affects: overwhelming
primitive and compelling *feelings* (emotions, body sensations, and impulses)—and inadequate and excessive defenses against them. These
primal affects are derived from instinctual drives that are too intense,
either because that is the way they start out (inborn excess of drive
or deficiency of defense) or become, due to traumatic or deficient
environmental reinforcement. The environmental psychopathological
factor often derives from some kind of bad early parenting, different
combinations of trauma and neglect. Sometimes there appears to have
been initial good enough maturation, followed by regression after loss

The latter part of this paper about therapy is taken from the book *Soul Murder Revisited:
Thoughts about Therapy, Hate, Love, and Memory.* New Haven, CT: Yale University Press (1999).

or trauma that prevented modulation and proper developmental transformation. Too much infantile or primitive mental functioning remains; and psychic structure either never develops properly or is too easily erased with regression. Primal mental functioning is laden with aggression-murder and cannibalism, alongside the seeds of caring and love magnified by idealization. Hell and Paradise coexist for the infant. And the attachment to others—the (at first) absolute dependence that makes for the inevitability of neurosis—is based both on hatred (innate and later reactive sadomasochism) and love.

Some of these disturbed people, all with their individual differences, have been massively traumatized or neglected as children, and some have not—some seem simply to have been born chronically traumatizable. (We are all neglected and traumatized to some extent, complicating the difficulties of being certain about pathogenesis.) But I have found the severely disturbed different from most of us who have suffered the traumas of everyday life.

The differences are basically economic, in Freud's metapsychological sense; too much is wrong, and therefore something fundamental in the mental apparatus doesn't work right. Pathology here has an exigent quality—severe, prolonged, relatively unmodifiable, repetitive—as against transient, flexible, and at least relatively modifiable by will. The chronically disturbed I have seen as adults also seem especially subject to regression to traumatic anxiety from any of the subsequent psychological danger situations that Freud outlines in his 1926 book on anxiety. They have not only characteristically bad, but also catastrophic, expectations. Sometimes these lurk largely outside of consciousness, having been more-or-less covered over by massive primal defensive combinations involving denial and psychic splitting that make for predominantly permanent islands—isolated compartments—of diminished and regressive psychic performance. Sometimes the mass and rigidity of primitive defenses result in as-if functioning (absence of spontaneity and authenticity) or even some kind of dehumanization. One patient stated: ''I can get away with it not being noticed, but sometimes I feel and act like a machine.'' To return to the traumas of everyday life, it is chastening to remember that there is some of this obsessive deadening in all of us. Consciousness is constantly shifting between sleep and full awareness. (Allen Ginsberg is quoted as saying, "Every once in a while you become aware that you're alive" [Pacernick, 1997, p. 23].)

For the chronically disturbed, there is an endless variety of combinations of primitive and massive defenses, working differently for every individual, which can fail and allow anxiety and even panic to break through, with loss of impulse control that can result in compulsive sexual and destructive action. In both the congenitally deficient and the traumatically abused (or deprived) there can be a reduction of full human experience toward caricatured simplification: predictable, individually different combinations of compulsive deadness and uncontrollable feelings and behavior. There is always a significant detrimental effect on psychic development—especially on the all-important function of unconscious and conscious fantasy (Grossman, 1991), compromising the mind's capacity for playfulness; this threatens to rob the subject of joy in life. And yet, alongside the devastation, the victim's need to survive can compensatorily push adaptive and even creative functioning.

I want to stress the difficulty of being certain about traumatic pathogenesis. The signs I have described in my generalizations over thirty years of writing about soul murder victims (people who have been criminally traumatized as children under conditions of what amounts to family concentration camps) appear in myriad individual, different variations. There are so many differences and a great range of severity of pathology. Diagnosis is of little value here—except for the most disturbed. There are a few psychotic or characterologic diagnoses which denote the caricaturelike reduction of humanity that some unfortunate individuals are reduced to: severe obsessive–compulsive character; paranoid personality and psychosis; some forms of schizophrenia; even so, individual variations abound. Soul murder victims show varying amounts of psychic health. Grab-bag terms like *borderline states* don't help, serving only to hide our ignorance. (If one looks closely enough, to paraphrase John Kennedy, *Wir sind alle* borderlines.) I prefer a descriptive term with no scientific connotations, like "very disturbed."[1]

I don't think one can derive pathological signs and symptoms from trauma without a convincing history of trauma. The differentiation from what might be the result (or also the result) of inborn or

---

[1] Fonagy (p. 211, this volume) says "these difficult patients."

environmental deficiencies is not possible starting from the pathology. Linkage can work in reverse. If trauma has taken place, certain general pathological results can be anticipated—yet there are always variations and surprises. One should be modest and look for signs and symptoms that might be the result of massive and chronic trauma in the patient's past.

I want to focus on the therapy of chronically disturbed people, including the chronically traumatized. The conviction that something traumatic has happened, right or wrong, optimally should originate with the patient, not with the therapist. Trauma should neither be denied nor assumed. One should suspend disbelief in the possibility. Patients who have been tortured and seduced as children, especially if at the hands of parents, usually have had their ability to register what was done to them impaired; this can amount to brainwashing: self-imposed, demanded by the parent, or both. Therefore, even if the trauma has been unmistakably registered—remembered, confessed to by the perpetrator, confirmed by or performed on others—there remains some pathological doubting in the former child victim, unable to hate a parent felt as necessary for survival.[2] Doubt exists alongside conviction, in a kind of Orwellian doublethink. There are also false convictions. Given the vagaries of memory (we can no longer believe in the simple psychic recording of historical truth), it can be difficult to impossible for the patient and therefore for the therapist to know what actually happened. And even when the trauma is clearly remembered or unequivocally established, uncovering the accompanying and obfuscating minimization and distortion is a large part of the work of the therapy.

For the therapist-analyst, working with patients who have been or may have been abused, takes skill, tact, flexibility, patience, and knowledge of the need to be nonjudgmental and empathic. One sees from clinical work that, whatever conscious hostility there may be, there is always a formidable resistance to the idea of a parent abusing a child; this contributes to the current trend toward denying child abuse. I have learned from my patients how important it is to an individual's sense of identity to establish some conviction of the reality

---

[2] Soul murder victims are caught in a particularly cruel form of the human burden stemming from feeling murderous hostility toward the parental figure one feels one cannot live without.

of the past. Yet what is crucial for psychological change is not primarily the patient's becoming able to answer the important question, "Did it really happen?" but rather acquiring the ability to acknowledge and to "own" the current psychic registrations of the past that continue to motivate the mind in the present. The ability to explore critically the mental registrations of relationships between the past and present with more freedom and flexibility is a major force for psychic change and increased mastery in psychoanalytic work and in life. This cannot be accomplished without considerable responsibility for what one feels, what one knows, *and what one does not know.* (This is true for all people, but especially for soul murder victims.) A perceptive patient once said to me, "Now I understand. You want me to be responsible for what is going on in my mind." This "understanding" was his first giant step toward acquiring that responsibility. The attainment of "owning" what one thinks and feels gives perspective; with it the patient can distance compulsion and reduce overwhelming emotions, as well as overwhelming defenses against the flow of passion.

In psychotherapeutic treatment, we know *what* to do; the mystery lies in *how* to do it. We cure by love. Love enables the patient to accept and make his or her own the insight the analyst offers and evokes. If—it is a big, sometimes an impossible, if—the therapist or analyst can get the traumatized person (so full of rage and sadomasochism, conscious and unconscious) to tolerate caring about him or her as a separate person, then the control over violence can be at least partially achieved or restored. Love for another person is needed to temper the overload of murderous hatred and its associated terrors in those abused as children. Soul murder victims are only some of the many who are severely inhibited in caring about other people, about themselves, even about causes, and who are condemned to regard others mainly as fulfillers of needs. Freud says that it is necessary to be able to love (here he means the Biblical *caritas*,[3] which connotes loving kindness, tenderness, sympathy and empathy—a nonsexual love) and to work in order to attain psychic health. Perhaps the most reliable index of that health is an individual's ability to care. Simone

---

[3] Mistranslated in the King James version as charity ("faith, hope, and charity. . . . And the greatest of these is charity"[1 Corinthians: 13:13]). *Caritas* can be defined in terms of tenderness and empathic contact; it does not refer to overt sexual love (which of course would always at least lurk in the unconscious) but to the sense of the dearness of another human being.

Weil said, "Belief in the existence of other human beings as such is love" (quoted in Auden and Kronenberger, 1962, p. 90).

In Primo Levi's *The Drowned and the Saved* (1986), the last book Levi completed, he tells of special squads of prisoners ("crematorium ravens") who were allowed to survive for a time because they were willing to perform the despicable tasks involved in the operation of the crematoria. He feels that conceiving and organizing such groups was "National Socialism's most demonic crime [which] represented an attempt to shift onto [the victims] the burden of guilt [as if to say], 'We, the master race, are your destroyers, but you are no better than we are; if we so wish, and we do so wish, we can destroy not only your bodies but also your souls, just as we have destroyed ours' " (1986, pp. 53–54): This is soul murder. The soul murderer's guilt is passed on to the faceless victims, who in turn become degraded enough to forget the humanity of the bodies from which they have to extract gold teeth and hair and whose ashes they have to dispose of. Since the squad members were witnesses to the crimes of the SS, they were eventually murdered themselves. Levi describes an unusual event:

> In the gas chamber have been jammed together and murdered the components of a recently arrived convoy, and the squad is performing its horrendous everyday work, sorting out the tangle of corpses, washing them with hoses and transporting them to the crematorium, but on the floor they find a young woman who is still alive. The event is exceptional, unique; perhaps the human bodies formed a barrier around her, sequestered a pocket of air that remained breathable. The men are perplexed. Death is their trade at all hours, death is a habit because, precisely, "one either goes mad the first day or gets accustomed to it," but this woman is alive. They hide her, warm her, bring her beef broth, question her: the girl is sixteen years old, she cannot orient herself in space or time, does not know where she is. [She] has gone through without understanding it the sequence of the sealed train, the brutal preliminary selection, the stripping, the entry into the chamber from which no one had ever come out alive. She has not understood, but she has seen; therefore she must die, and the men of the squad know it just as they know that they too must die for the same reason. But these slaves debased by alcohol and daily slaughter are transformed; they no longer have before them the anonymous mass, the flood of frightened, stunned people coming off the boxcars: they have a person [1986, pp. 55–56].

They revive her and try to save her. The anecdote shows the temporary and almost miraculous reversal of the defensive dehumanization that being mistreated and tormented imposes on the victims. I tell this story to show something about what is necessary (and how hard it is) for formerly abused children to be helped in therapy. They must become able again to *feel* for another human being and for themselves as human beings when their past experience has led them to defend themselves by divesting themselves of all feeling—even, with these concentration camp "ravens," to the extent of dehumanization. For those who have been abused, love as Weil defines it—the daily, potentially wonderful (although, alas, at best transient), empathic exchange with another person whose humanity is recognized—is so dangerous. Therefore, being able to care can be exceptional.

Victims of violence and soul murder don't find it easy to love others (a prerequisite for caring about and loving one's self optimally—for healthy self-esteem rather than defensive narcissism or masochistic abnegation). For those who have been seduced or beaten as children, it was usually the child's intense need to love, and the consequent emotional opening up for the parent, that led the child to the overstimulation, torment, and rage that ensued. The children learn to keep themselves emotionally closed, especially to positive feelings. As with concentration camp victims, it can be safer to suppress caring or emotions, to stay on the level of regarding others primarily as fulfillers of need (while concomitantly, consciously or unconsciously, identifying with the abusers).

If it is possible (with some degree of safety) to establish in relation to the analyst the sense of the dearness of another person that has been crushed because it made the child feel so vulnerable, the caring can become in the patient's mind a capacity for mutual dearness that can be extended to others. This allows for an interweaving of the newly acquired feelings toward the analyst with the important people in the patient's present as well as those from the past, even those who have been the abusers. Hate as well as love must be able to flow and, more difficult, to be contained in the mind at the same time. The inevitable murderous hatred of the parent who abuses or neglects (or for the parent held responsible for the abuse) is perhaps the hardest task for the patient, threatening the loss of the much needed internalized image which has become part of the self. (The analyst must be able to tolerate being the object of the rage.) If the external relationships with others are allowed to change, so can the inner mental pictures of the parents that have become part of the self. This can modify the primitive either/ or dimension that so often characterizes the stark emotions of the abused child, as well as the zombielike emptiness that can serve as defense against the too intense extremes. The inner pictures of the much hated and much idealized parental figures from childhood can, with the achievement of enough emotional moderation, be integrated sufficiently to justify the metaphor of change in psychic structure and functioning. The patient can attenuate identifications with abusers and relax the compulsion to repeat the abuse, can become able to love-and-hate (a mixture compatible with the conditions of life) rather than feel the unbearable primal intensity of *either* hating *or* loving that burns away ambivalence needed for human existence. If one feels that all must be perfect or nothing, one ends with nothing. There can be some relief from the comparative paralysis furnished by the double bind of feeling toward the internalized bad parent: I want to kill you, but I can't live without you.

With my patients I have found that the ability to care for another comes most often (and most easily, although it is never easy) in relation to children—if the patient is a parent. If not, they sometimes become able to tolerate the idea of, or even the wish to have, children. This goes along with increasing ability to care about oneself as a child. This is one path toward caring that begins with the kind of narcissism that is optimally invested in a child by a parent—a healthy transition between primitive narcissism and true ability to love.

The access to loving feelings toward others for patients in psychoanalysis and psychoanalytic psychotherapy depends on their gradual acquisition of tolerating, caring about, and accepting the analyst as a separate and predominantly benevolent person different from the internalized traumatizing parent. That would mean the acquisition of a considerable feeling of trust that caring will not lead to abuse and abandonment by the analyst. James McLaughlin (1996), with his characteristic bravery and honesty, furnishes a rare and moving documentation of an analytic patient, traumatized and deprived as a child, hesitantly allowing an emotional flow in transition from distrust toward caring about his analyst. McLaughlin shows his patient, Mr. Q., fighting to *own*[4] (I am using my word for it) his good and bad feelings. It

---

[4] *Owning* includes what Fonagy calls "the attainment of self-reflective functioning."

seems clear that good feelings—loving himself and loving others—have been most difficult for this characteristically distrustful man.
He is depicted as having been seesawing through a search for his
separate identity while also struggling to hold onto the bad internalized
images of his abusive parents in the context of a long period of con-
frontational repetitions of themes full of emotion and conflict between
patient and analyst. This material from the last year of the long analysis
comes after a period in which the patient was expressing (and fighting
off in the working through) the feeling that the analyst was trying to
rob him of his identity. Mr. Q. talks of

> his increasing grasp of "my basic self, my gutsy kid-self that would
> never give in, even if it meant I had to hide all of my life. I *love* him!
> He's real, and he's mine! He's me!" His voice dropped in vigour and
> insistence. "Even as I say this I'm fading, losing hold' (emphasis added)
> [Analyst]: "Such strength and conviction in your voice as you held him,
> and now [you] sound sad and meek giving him up?" [p. 221].

The patient then apparently reacts regressively to what appears
to me to have been an empathic intervention, by feeling that the analyst
(like his parents as he had registered them in his mind) was threatening
his shaky hold on his identity: "Mr. Q. (Half sits up as he replies):
'Are you putting me on? You know we've just again been talking
about how saying anything I really mean means I give it up. It's
not mine. It's yours. It's nothing!' (Sinks back into the couch)." His
emotions shift:

> But, I know that's not really so. I could hear your voice. No teasing in
> it. I *will* hold onto this [basic] self, regardless! . . . This is harder to say,
> to stick with. When I feel this me that seems real, I'm also feeling
> something about you that feels real. I'd like to say it feels good. But that
> would mean giving you something. And I can't give you anything that
> is real, that's worthwhile. Something goes wrong [p. 221].

The patient is threatened by loving feelings and impulses toward Dr.
McLaughlin, but the "owning" is being worked through in the transference. He continues: "[Once] when I was talking about how good
it felt between Little Ben [the patient's lovable young nephew] and
me, you said something about the generosity of loving back. I didn't

get it. I know it's time to go now. I'm going to hold onto this basic feeling. *That* I feel I'm getting!'' (p. 221).

In the next session the patient goes on to express his hatred toward the analyst, but now it has not taken away his feeling about his ''basic self''—''I've held onto me all this time'' (p. 222), and the hatred (''I'm hating you right now!'' [p. 222]) does not keep him from also feeling love:

> I can feel you've had a lot of caring for me, respect for me. And say! I think I've got it, about that generosity of loving back. I have felt it with Ben. I'm feeling it now with you. That my loving you for your loving me makes me feel I do have something good to give back! It feels safe here. Will it be safe out there? I've been slow to get there, but I'm going to give it my best try! [p. 222].

McLaughlin comments: ''And, as his own words say clearly enough, when he could trust me enough to feel I loved and believed him, he found in himself capacities to trust and claim his own positive as well as negative feelings toward himself and others'' (p. 223). (I usually find it difficult to tell whether the ability to own loving and hating the self or the other comes first for any given patient. This can be as moot and as inconsequential as discovering the primal priority of the chicken or the egg. In our work, the hatching and the separation are all.)

The analyst has to find individual and sometimes idiosyncratic ways to evoke and sustain caring in each patient. This takes the intuitive art of psychoanalytic therapy, guided by empathic understanding: tact, patience, reliability, the honesty to admit one's mistakes and failures, and a good deal of technical flexibility in relation to the patient's individual needs. Above all one must be able to take the onslaught of hatred that has to emerge. The soul murdered (or those who are similarly burdened by violent and murderous impulses) expect that either they or those they feel too close to will be killed. The therapist's comparative lack of alarm in the face of the patient's murderous wishes and feelings helps; perhaps it is most reassuring that no one dies, that the feeling and expression of rage doesn't result in catastrophe. These people are saddled with the worst expectations—terrifying anxiety, loss of control, feeling like killing and being killed, being alone and unable to survive in a murderous universe. (Primo Levi points out in relation to his experiences at Auschwitz that once one has been helpless and tortured one never really gets over it.) In many cases the former victims of God's concentration camps can, if caring for the analyst is allowed as a result of the comparative stability provided by the long (and, realistically speaking, predominantly benevolent) relationship with the analyst, attain the kind of emotional insight that grants strength and perspective. These achievements can ultimately reduce overwhelming intensities; new and more flexible defenses and strategies can be developed. There can be increased ability to use conscious will to fight for health and love. Did it really happen?—crucially important as the question can be to an increased feeling of identity, if it can be answered definitively or at least settled on as unanswerable, is less relevant to healing than being able to tolerate and own one's deficiencies sufficiently to allow love to triumph, predominantly or even occasionally. There is a kind of psychic economic determinism here that may become more malleable when and if we get to know about the sources of psychic health and strength and how to tap them. We cannot change the basic conditions for human life, but for some unfortunates, soul murder victims or not, it is possible, with therapy that can restore some authenticity of feeling for others and for oneself, to help release the capacity for joy and distance the need for sadomasochistic holding onto the past.

The gifted psychoanalytic essayist Adam Phillips, in his 1988 book, *Winnicott*, points to the evolution of psychoanalytic technique toward "an analytic setting in which the patient does not [simply] undergo authoritative translation—having his unconscious fed back to him, as it were—but is enabled by the analyst, as Winnicott wrote, 'to reveal himself to himself . . . not just a matter of interpreting the repressed unconscious [but] . . . the provision of a professional setting for trust in which such work may take place' " (p. 11). Psychoanalysis could really never have been exclusively based on interpretation, but early practitioners probably did caricature Freud's early and imperfect technique by magisterially "translating" the patient's associations to something like "You have an Oedipus complex." Interpretations of this kind are still made, one hopes more tactfully worded and at an appropriate time. They have to be followed by a working through which can enable the patient to accept emotionally, to *own* the interpretation. McLaughlin's clinical example shows how difficult it is to establish the "professional setting for trust" Winnicott mentions.

Does it matter if it really happened? The answer here is yes and no. In any individual case it really matters. It can shore up the sense of identity so regularly threatened in soul murder victims, to know with conviction that abuse occurred, that parents were predominantly or repeatedly brutal, or indifferent, or crazy, or psychopaths, or absent, or deficient psychologically and empathically. One can put the question in its complicated perspective by asking: Does it matter to its victims or the children of its victims if the Holocaust really occurred? It matters greatly for each individual who feels traumatized or neglected and asks, "Did it really happen?" to be able to be or become reasonably certain about the subsequent interplay between the offending or indifferent parent and child: What they did, what I did; what they were like; what I was and am like?[5] These questions need to be settled in relation to the past (very difficult to impossible to do with certainty) and in relation to how they are registered and active in the mind in the present (still difficult but possible).

But viewed from the point of view of the individuals with established pathology, one must be aware that it often cannot be ascertained how that pathology came into being. It can look to the observer as if it doesn't make much difference how the propensities for evil or the devastations of the capacity for loving and for joy came about. Ralph Greenson is reported to have said, "Parents who lie create children who deny," and he also could have reversed it to "Parents who deny create children who lie." These can be truths, but it doesn't always happen that way. We must also account for the children who lie and who deny, who are violent and evil, who cannot love, whose malignant and pathological qualities do not seem to stem simply or primarily from the depredations and deficiencies of their parents. There are also those whose qualities of strength and good character, even the crucial ability to care for others, seem not to have been derived from their criminal or defective parents. And sometimes the child who says with Milton's Devil, "Evil, be thou my good!" has not necessarily been criminally treated and can be the bad seed of good fruit. These are the mysteries of powers and handicaps that we are born with, for good and for bad.

---

[5] This is central to a feeling of identity: cf. Walt Whitman (1851): "I am the man. I suffered. I was there."

But acknowledging mystery does not mean abandoning what we can and do know (Simone Weil: "Evil is to love what mystery is to intelligence" [quoted in Auden, 1970, p. 344]). We must not forget, painful as it is to know it as a child and as a parent, that the helpless dependency and the overwhelming emotional needs of the infant and child make brutalizing them all too easy. Soul murder exists, and it does matter.

REFERENCES

Auden, W. H. (1970), *A Certain World: A Commonplace Book.* New York: Viking.

———— Kronenberger, L. (1962), *The Viking Book of Aphorisms.* New York: Viking Press.

Freud, S. (1926), Inhibitions, Symptoms and Anxiety. *Standard Edition,* 20:75–176. London: Hogarth Press, 1959.

Grossman, W. (1991), Pain, aggression, fantasy and concepts of sadomasochism. *Psychoanal. Quart.,* 60:22–52.

Levi, P. (1986), *The Drowned and the Saved.* New York: Simon & Schuster Adult Publishing Group, 1988.

McLaughlin, J. (1996), Through the patient's looking-glass: Reflections upon the analyst's self-inquiry. *Can. J. Psychoanal.,* 4:205–229.

Pacernick, G. (1997), Allen Ginsberg: An interview. *Amer. Poetry Rev.,* 4:23–27.

Phillips, A. (1988), *Winnicott.* Cambridge, MA: Harvard University Press.

Whitman, W. (1851), *Leaves of Grass.* New York: Modern Library, 1921.

Discussion of Papers by Fonagy and Shengold

Glen O. Gabbard, M.D.

I would like to begin my discussion with a story. One day the devil and his friend were walking down the road when they saw a man ahead bend over and pick up something, which he then placed in his pocket. The devil's friend asked Satan what it was the man had picked up. The devil replied that it was a piece of Truth. The devil's friend commented, "Oh, that's a bad bit of business for you then." The devil replied, "Oh, no not at all. I'm going to let him organize it."

Two experienced analysts have described their own struggles with organizing a piece of truth that they have obtained from their traumatized patients. The task of making sense and organizing that piece of truth often falls entirely to the analyst for long periods of time while the traumatized patient stands aside, perplexed at the prospect of finding meaning in his or her suffering.

Analysts only have access to a piece of the truth because, as Len Shengold stresses, we have a great deal of difficulty in ever knowing with certainty if the pathogenesis is traumatic or not. What we do have

227

access to is the psychological drama that unfolds in the consulting room.

Indeed, one common thread in these two superb and moving presentations is the emphasis on the transference–countertransference dimensions in the here and now, the essence of the psychoanalytic setting. Through the projective–introjective processes between analyst and analysand, the analyst gains a unique perspective on the internal world of the patient. As Fairbairn (1952) stressed, *"What are primarily repressed are neither intolerably guilty impulses nor intolerably unpleasant memories, but intolerably bad internalized objects"* (pp. 62). I would simply add that intolerably bad internalized object relations are what become reenacted with the analyst and what constitute the currency of the treatment of the severely traumatized patient.

I agree with Shengold's point that the crucial issue for psychological change is not a definitive answer to the question "Did it really happen?" Rather, it's a matter of owning the representations of the past that continue to be active in the present. Some of the most misguided treatments of patients who have experienced childhood trauma are those that take an archaeological approach emphasizing a search for buried relics that must be uncovered from the deep dark past. A version of what happened between the patient and the significant objects in that patient's past is unfolding in the transference–countertransference in front of the analyst's eyes, and no excavation is required to study it. Moreover, the archaeological search may be a form of countertransference collusion with the patient to avoid being the target of the patient's aggression or rage. The analyst must resist the temptation to form an alliance with the patient by directing all hatred and bitterness toward distant figures from the patient's past in the service of preserving the relationship with the analyst as an island of idealized and loving understanding (Gabbard, 1997b). In a recent paper on Freud's first case of hysteria, Phil Bromberg (1996) suggested that "we do not treat patients such as Emmy to cure them of something that was done to them in the past; rather, we are trying to cure them of what they still do to themselves and to others in order to cope with what was done to them in the past" (p. 70).

The most compelling piece of truth to which the analyst has access is what the patient is actively doing in the here and now and in the extratransference setting to perpetuate misery and unhappiness. Unfortunately, the patient may not wish to follow the analyst in systematically examining his or her contributions to that ongoing suffering. In my own work with severely traumatized patients, I have frequently felt myself sinking into despair after what I consider to be an important piece of work is seemingly erased from the patient's mind and appears unretrievable. Like Sisyphus, I must start from the beginning again, hoping that this time the boulder will not roll down the hill.

One of the principal reasons that the patient may not wish to follow the analyst in this exploration relates to the collapse of analytic space that Peter Fonagy describes. From the patient's perspective, there may be little meaning to reflect upon. These patients tend to experience themselves as "damaged goods." There is a conviction of being bad and beyond redemption, in many cases accompanied by a view that suicide is the only real option. The victim role is "bedrock" so far as the patient is concerned (Gabbard, 1997b). The patient is stuck. Yet the patient comes to treatment with some dim hope that a rescuer might be available. These patients live in a limbo described by Heidegger as "a double knot: the no more of the gods that have fled and the not yet of the god that is coming" (Robinson, 1969, p. 26). Hope is contaminated by a sense of dread that the abuse from the past will simply be repeated. Different is bad. If the patient collaborates with the therapist in attempting to form a new object experience, a certainty of further trauma must be dealt with. Patients like this learn to anticipate misfortune as a primary way to protect themselves. As Bromberg (1996) stresses, the patient always prepares herself for further trauma because at least it prevents unexpected abuse from ambushing the patient. A thin thread of mastery is preserved in this respect.

Fonagy poignantly describes how the patient cannot comprehend how her father could do what he did, so she inhibits her capacity to mentalize and becomes lifeless. One way to organize the chaos of early childhood trauma is simply to assume badness. The little girl assumes my father must do this because he loves me, so the most logical explanation is that I am bad and deserve this kind of treatment. In this kind of thinking, the child assigns responsibility to the self because it is preferable to the more terrifying view that violence is random in the universe and can occur at any time for no reason what-soever.

Both of our presenters note the difficulty that traumatized patients have in experiencing love or caring from the analyst. How can they assume that the analyst actually has the patient's best interest in mind? The childhood experience of a severely abused child is plagued by questions about who is doing what for whom.

Much of the abuse comes packaged as statements about what is good for the child, yet the child feels that she or he is doing something for the parent. Such ambiguity is brought into the transference, and the patient cannot trust that the analyst is genuinely interested in help-ing. There is always an assumption that the analyst is up to something, that there is a hidden agenda involving the analyst's needs.

In Shengold's paper he says that we know what to do, but the mystery lies in how to do it. He then says, "We cure by love." I would like to ask Shengold to clarify a bit further what he has in mind. When Freud wrote in his December 6, 1906, letter to Jung, "Essentially, one might say, the cure is effected by love" (McGuire, 1974, pp. 12–13), he clearly meant that transference love was the vehicle of cure. He was not implying that it was the force of the analyst's love that cured the patient. Influenced by his forays into hypnotic suggestion, Freud was more or less convinced that erotic attraction was the active ingredient in the treatment.

Shengold would appear to mean something similar in that he goes on to say that the therapist or analyst attempts to get the traumatized person to care about the analyst as a separate person and to tolerate that caring. The erotic tie in a sexually abused patient, however, may be inextricably bound up in malevolence and sadism so that many patients with this history will simply shut down their capacity for sexual excitement. The capacity to love seems to be the end result of the cure, not the cure itself.

On the other hand, if Shengold is referring to the analyst's love as curative, which could be implied by the use of the preposition *by*, then I think we are also on problematic ground. The notion of the analyst's love is a highly complex issue in the analysis of patients who have childhood histories of severe trauma. The word *love* may be infused with a constellation of painful physical sensations and mean-ings of betrayal and exploitation. Fonagy's patient feels like throwing up when she senses that the analyst might actually care about her. The notion of taking in love or caring, or internalizing a loving object, is concretized by these patients, who view it as an invasion and a taking over. We must be wary of filling the patient's evacuated space with our own experiences, however loving and caring they may be.

In my experience as a supervisor, consultant, and subsequent treater, I have found that various miscarriages of love have caused great harm to traumatized patients. The longing for a perfectly loving parent to make up for the horrific experiences of childhood pulls powerfully at the analyst's heartstrings. However, the analyst who attempts to provide this love, what Ferenczi considered as *all conquering love,* will find this to be a promise to the patient that cannot be kept (Dupont, 1989).

The patient must be able to evoke hatred to find peace, however temporary that peace may be. There is a powerful unconscious wish to be enslaved to the tormenting object. Freedom is terrifying. As Fonagy notes in his extraordinary case of Henrietta, coherence of the self depends on finding a torturer. Her goal, in fact, was to irritate him. Hence, the management of hatred, not love, may be the key to some degree of success with the severely abused patient. Shengold would appear to acknowledge this when he says that hate as well as love must be able to flow and be contained in the mind at the same time.

In essence, what I have suspected is that the patient who has experienced severe childhood abuse is seeking a bad enough object (Rosen, 1993; Gabbard, 1996). We must fail the patient. Fonagy appears to agree with this view when he notes the paradox that the patient must make the analyst into the bad object even though it destroys the analyst's ability to help. Disavowing the bad object role is a defensive stance that I have termed *disidentification with the aggressor* (Gabbard, 1997b). In the analyst's frantic efforts to avoid the role, he or she enacts the hatred by repeating the abusive situation under the guise of love. The analyst may take the patient in his arms and hold her, he may sit the patient on his lap and kiss her, and he may do all he can to provide the love that the patient did not receive in childhood. Ultimately, in the worse case scenario, the "love" escalates into a sexual relationship where the patient is retraumatized while the analyst is professing his love for her.

Although I've cautioned about the perils of using love defensively to disavow hate, I would nevertheless argue that Ferenczi was onto something critically important regarding certain modifications of Freud's technique in the treatment of traumatized patients. Kirshner (1994) has pointed out that the symbolic function of the internalized good object is damaged through the trauma of childhood so that more active measures of caring and concern may be necessary for the analytic setting to be experienced as sufficiently safe. Much of this approach involves an affirmative stance on the part of the analyst. This affirmation may depend as much on the tone of the analyst's voice as the content of the words (Killingmo, 1995). Affirmation may mean nothing more than validating that the patient has a right to feel whatever it is he or she feels. It may serve as a powerful antidote to the chronic experience of having one's reality invalidated.

I certainly don't think that love is irrelevant to the treatment of these patients, but I do think it is a particular kind of love, akin to what Loewald (1970) called analytic love. This is the idea that the analyst believes in the potential of the patient to grow through the process of analysis and safeguards the analysand's future. Loewald once noted, "In our work it can be truly said that in our best moments of dispassionate and objective analyzing we love our object, the patient, more than at any other time and are compassionate with his whole being" (1970, p. 297).

These are moments of love accompanied by many other moments of hatred, masochistic endurance, sadistic torment, boredom, anger, envy, and despair, to name only a few of the analyst's affect states. I think the therapeutic action of the analytic work with such patients is closely related to what Fonagy describes when he says, "What seemed to be helpful were those few precious moments . . . when I could become what she needed me to be, yet retain my capacity to hold her in mind with her fears and anxieties, and enable her to see this in my words and actions" (p. 207). In other words, the analyst desperately struggles to maintain that dual state of consciousness in which she allows herself to be transformed into the transference object while also observing that transformation and reflecting on it. As Fonagy suggests, this allows for a derailed developmental process to become reactivated.

The missing experience of having one's mental state reflected on by a parent or older child is provided by the analyst. Hence, in concert with what the British middle group would call *holding* or the Kleinians would call *containment* is the internalization by the patient of the thinking self of the containing object, namely, the analyst. Consequently, a major mode of therapeutic action with such patients is that the analyst gradually helps the patient learn that mental experience involves representations that can be played with in an analytic space and ultimately altered.

In my own work with abused patients, I make active efforts to get them to entertain the possibility that their perception of me may in some respects differ from the way that I actually am (Gabbard, 1997a). In this regard I have considerable agreement with Fonagy's formulation of the process. He and I work together as colleagues at Menninger, and we have been research collaborators for several years now. We have read each other's work and had a mutual influence on one another. My main area of disagreement is his recommendations regarding technique. He suggests:

> Our approach is to forgo the temptation to impose major modifications or parameters and to adjust technique. . . . We believe that such patients are treatable in the context of ordinary psychoanalysis, so long as the *aims* of the analysis are modified from ones which aspire to the achievement of insight to the less ambitious aim of the recovery of reflective function. Interpretations in the classical sense have no place in the treatment of such patients [p. 210].

My own view is that his recommendations apply to certain patients but not others. We are on tenuous ground when we generalize too much about patients who have been severely abused. I would also disagree with Shengold's view that diagnosis is unimportant. In my work over the years with abused patients who are seriously disturbed, I have found that a careful psychoanalytic diagnosis of the patient's strengths, weaknesses, characteristic modes of object relatedness, conscience, and motivation to understand has been of enormous value in tailoring a treatment that is specifically designed for the patient.

Some can tolerate analysis as Fonagy describes, while others require face-to-face modes of treatment with a heavy emphasis on support. A corollary of this point, of course, is that the impact of childhood trauma varies considerably from patient to patient. I realize that both presenters know this, but I am simply making note of it for the sake of completeness. Specific kinds of support, involving the encouragement of a reflective understanding of internal states, may offer protection from more severe outcomes. For example, Fonagy and I recently viewed a research video in which an adult woman recalled how her stepfather placed her in a room by herself for a week without food, water, or light. She recognized that her stepfather wanted her to feel as though she didn't exist, so she defied him by sitting calmly and contentedly whenever he checked in on her. Her capacity to imagine his internal state was crucial to her survival.

I also disagree that interpretations have no place in the treatment of such patients. In fact, I would make the case that some of Fonagy's interventions that he described were interpretive in nature and appeared to be helpful to the patient. In our study of audiotape transcripts of psychoanalytic psychotherapy with borderline patients (Gabbard and Wilkinson, 1994; Horwitz et al., 1996), we found that those with childhood trauma were able to use transference interpretations provided that the way was paved for them through a series of empathic and validating comments that made the patient feel held and understood. In his introduction, Fonagy said that he was not sure if some would call his treatment analysis. Frankly, I don't think we should be particularly worried about whether we call it analysis or something else. I am satisfied with Winnicott's definition that analysis is what analysts do. I think the endless debates about whether a particular treatment is analysis or analytic therapy have done very little to advance the field. The analyst must flexibly respond to the specific characteristics of the patient.

Having enumerated some areas of disagreement regarding technique, I must say that, on the other hand, I heartily endorse the overall strategy that Fonagy describes of trying to retain one's own analytic space in the face of the slings and arrows of outrageous projection and extraordinary attempts to transform the analyst. I think this relates very closely to Bion's notion that we must retain our capacity to think our own thoughts in the midst of extraordinary efforts by the patient to make us someone that we are not (Symington, 1990; Gabbard and Wilkinson, 1994). Freedom of thought may also be a reasonable goal for the patient.

It may be impossible for her to free herself completely from her enslavement, but she can loosen the shackles enough to play with ideas and perceptions in a realm of fantasy that is simultaneously real and not real. This state is beautifully described by Brian Friel in the closing lines of his play *Dancing at Lughnasa*:

> But there is one memory of that Lughnasa time that visits me most often; and what fascinates me most about that memory is that it owes nothing to fact. In that memory atmosphere is more real than incident and everything is simultaneously actual and illusory. In that memory, too, the air is nostalgic with the music of the thirties. It drifts in from somewhere far away—a mirage of sound—a dream music that is both heard and imagined; that seems to be both itself and its own echo; a sound so alluring and so mesmeric that the afternoon is bewitched, maybe haunted, by it [pp. 83–84].

REFERENCES

Bromberg, P. M. (1996), Hysteria, dissociation, and cure: Emmy von N revisited. *Psychoanal. Dial.,* 6:55–71.

Dupont, J. (1989), *The Clinical Diary of Sándor Ferenczi,* tr. M. Balint & N. Z. Jackson. Cambridge, MA: Harvard University Press.

Fairbairn, W. D. R. (1952), *Psychoanalytic Studies of the Personality.* London: Routledge.

Friel, B. (1993), *Dancing at Lughnasa.* New York: Dramatists Play Service.

Gabbard, G. O. (1996), *Love and Hate in the Analytic Setting.* Northvale, NJ: Jason Aronson.

——— (1997a), A reconsideration of objectivity in the analyst. *Internat. J. Psycho-Anal.,* 78:15–26.

——— (1997b), Challenges in the analysis of adult patients with histories of childhood sexual abuse. *Can. J. Psycho-Anal.,* 5:1–25.

——— Horwitz, L., Allen, J. G., Frieswyk, S., Newsom, G., Colson, D., & Coyne, L. (1994), Transference interpretation in the psychotherapy of borderline patients: A high-risk, high-gain phenomenon. *Harvard Rev. Psychiatry,* 2:59–69.

——— Wilkinson, S. M. (1994), *Management of Countertransference with Borderline Patients.* Washington, DC: American Psychiatric Press.

Horwitz, L., Gabbard, G. O., Allen, J. G., Frieswyk, S. H., Colson, D. B., Newsom, G. E., & Coyne, L. (1996), *Borderline Personality Disorder: Tailoring the Psychotherapy to the Patient.* Washington, DC: American Psychiatric Press.

Killingmo, B. (1995), Affirmation in psychoanalysis. *Internat. J. Psycho-Anal.,* 76:503–518.

Kirshner, L. (1994), Trauma, the good object, and the symbolic: A theoretical integration. *Internat. J. Psycho-Anal.,* 75:235–242.

Loewald, H. W. (1970), Psychoanalytic theory and psychoanalytic process. In: *Papers on Psychoanalysis.* New Haven, CT: Yale University Press, 1980, pp. 277–301.

McGuire, W., Ed. (1974), *The Freud/Jung Letters: The Correspondence between Sigmund Freud and C. G. Jung,* tr. R. Manheim & R. F. C. Hull. Princeton, NJ: Princeton University Press.

Robinson, M. (1969), *The Long Sonata of the Dead.* London: Routledge.

Rosen, I. R. (1993), Relational masochism: The search for a bad enough object. Presented to Topeka Psychoanalytic Society, January 21.

Symington, N. (1990), The possibility of human freedom and its transmission (with particular reference to the thought of Bion). *Internat. J. Psycho-Anal.,* 71:95–106.

General Discussion

Leonard Shengold: We have heard some impressions from these two presentations of patients who are not victims of the traumas of everyday life. There is much coherence between the papers because I have a feeling that we all know what we are dealing with. I have enormous admiration for Peter Fonagy and the way he works. But I also have differences of opinion in relation to his paper.

I don't think that all of these severely disturbed people that we are talking about are necessarily the victims of abuse. One can get the same devastating pictures without their necessarily having been soul murdered. *Soul murder*, in the way I have used the term, is not a diagnosis, it's a crime. Arlow, who was a most esteemed teacher of mine, used to devastate me by saying, "What you are saying is very poetic." That always made me think that something was wrong with what I was saying.

Arlow discussed crime and said quite rightly that we are not here to be detectives. We are not here to find out what happened. But of course he and we are fully aware that sometimes we are dealing with crimes, those that patients commit and those committed against the patients. There is a whole continuum. The traumas of everyday life and everyday patients have to remind us that every single patient is an adventure. Every single patient is different despite their similarities. We all have the same features, but we all look different. The Oedipus complex story itself is a detective story. It is the story of a crime. We are not to be the detectives. But Oedipus was both the criminal and the detective. It is perhaps the first great detective story, but he had to find his own way, as these people have to find their own way in order to be helped.

Freud told us that ours is an impossible profession. However, it is an impossible profession that we still work at, and we work at fairly successfully. It really is true that some of what we need to do is impossible in that some people whom we see appear impossible to help. Yet some of them can be helped.

Leon Hoffman: Regarding differences in approaches to patients, some analysts view the curative function of analysis as a function of "us," of facilitating relationships, whereas Fonagy views the curative function of "I," the development of a fuller and freer "I" in the patient, facilitated by the maintenance of an analytic "I" on the part of the analyst. Whereas some analysts focus on how to respectfully find their way into the relationship, others focus on how to lovingly stay outside of the relationship. Here is a related question: Shengold feels the therapist helps by not being alarmed, and Fonagy seems to use their "alarm" to help. Are these essential differences, or do they relate to style, theory, or gender?

Leonard Shengold: I think that's a misunderstanding. Nobody who is human cannot be alarmed. But you have to handle the madness. These things are therapeutically both inevitable and sometimes very useful. But you can't always be alarmed. If you're afraid all the time, you can't contain the patient's feelings. I feel misunderstood in the way that I was afraid I would be by Glen Gabbard in relation to the matter of love. I don't know whether it was my fault because I condensed things so heavily. I said, for example, that diagnosis is unimportant. How he went on to define diagnosis is exactly why I don't like to use diagnoses. I want to know what my patient's strengths, weaknesses, characteristics, modes of object relations, and so on are like. Knowing what the other person is like is the only thing approaching certainty that we can have in this field. That cannot, in my mind, be reduced to DSM-III or a number.

Peter Fonagy: To see what is essential, the analyst starts to focus on the mental state of the patient. Then you encounter enactment or the outrageous projections that we have talked about. But I would never say to the patient, "I think you are projecting something into me." That, as you said in your talk, would be intrusive and probably unpleasant even for neurotic patients. The important thing is to try to understand the patient's state of mind—what they are trying to do, what they are trying to be free of. It is that state—what we call the *constitutional state,* the part of the self that is genuinely reflective of the internal goings on—that needs to be amplified, called out, and understood. Then, the patient perceives this representation in your mind, not necessarily just in the things that you say, but also in the way that you behave. I really agree with Glen Gabbard's emphasis on that. As an infant internalizes in representation, what is perceived can become a core part of the self-representation. To me, that's really the therapeutic gain and what will get the patient better.

Leon Hoffman: Can any member of the panel say something about the kind of qualities that analysts must have to be able to do this kind of work, to be able to do what you just described?

Peter Fonagy: They have to be the kind of person, I think, who can hear a discussion without there being further brutality. It speaks to a lot of commitment. That is what it calls for in me. At the human level, there is no pay-off. There is nothing. At certain times there is very little that you get from the patients, as you would rightfully expect in many normal relationships. Glen Gabbard described it as very Sisyphean. You give and you give and nothing happens. You are there every day and you get abused and you have human mindlessness and intolerance really pushed into you and all over you and you feel by the end of the day completely and utterly dehumanized and exhausted, and then in the middle of the night you get the phone call. And then your wife has to ask: "Why did you give him your phone number? I told you.'' I think it calls for nothing exceptional, but it's just a little bit more than I think we have. That's why we are all here.

Leonard Shengold: In relation to this, I want to say something about mothers. You have to be able to approach the impossible goal with these people—no offense intended—with love, in the sense that Simone Weil put it: that I can see the human being here, and I am motivated to try to get to that human being. Of course, it takes a tremendously long journey. It takes years to be able to make the interpretations and make them meaningful, and to be able to expect that the person is going to be able to love. We all see the same thing, and we can see it clearly. Love is what they can't take. They have to change so completely by virtue of internalizations, by virtue of self-reflections, by virtue of a kind of bravery that was demonstrated in their clinical material. Like a good mother, you have to be tough as well as loving.

Part IV
Concluding Papers

Introduction

Chair: Arnold Rothstein
Discussants: Steven J. Ellman,
Stephen A. Mitchell
Discussion with the panelists

Arnold Rothstein: I see this meeting as a kind of nodal point in a process of development that has been going on over the past fifteen or twenty years in psychoanalysis, as things have been evolving such that institutional structures have loosened a bit and people have come together more to discuss issues related to the essence of psychoanalytic work. The present work reflects that evolutionary process.

9

Freud and the Seduction Hypothesis

Steven J. Ellman, Ph.D.

For both personal and external reasons Freud was anxious about the analyst as seducer. No one can doubt that Freud was concerned about his involvement in therapeutic encounters when he discussed sexuality with young women. He was constantly vigilant about how the community would view his forays into the world(s) of "hysterical young women." Although Freud was affected by the outside world, we know enough about him to understand that a good part of his elation in his work (not cocaine induced)[1] was his growing realization that he was on the verge of making a unique contribution that had eluded the authorities (medical, academic, and philosophic). In my view Masson (1984) got it exactly wrong; although Freud was concerned with public

---

[1] This is a reference to Swales's, in my opinion, absurd notion that Freud's theorizing is best understood as a reaction to his cocaine induced elation (Swales [1983] as cited in Gay [1988, p. 749]).

opinion, he was mostly delighted in showing up the hypocrisy of Viennese society in his announcement of the seduction hypothesis.[2] His change in the seduction hypothesis occurred partly because of a growing awareness of his anxiety about the analyst as a seducer. He was also beginning to acknowledge that the seductions that he feared were to some extent an inherent danger in the analytic situation. Thus, the value of the original seduction hypothesis is that it places the seduction in the external world and leaves the analytic relationship untouched and the analyst and analysand free to engage in mutual seductions.

While I would agree with Greenberg that the seduction hypothesis is certainly part of our psychoanalytic theory, it is part of it because it signals one of Freud's continuing struggles, that is, his struggle to allow transference to become a central issue in the "psychoanalytic playground" (Freud, 1914a). Freud ultimately lost this clinical struggle (which I believe was a contributory factor in his pessimistic attitude toward old age) but today is on the verge of winning the conceptual struggle. Let me now try to make what I am saying somewhat clearer: Freud never really had a definitive idea of countertransference, but he was continuously struggling with the implications of his private reactions to the material that patients put inside him. He was never certain where this material came from, the extent to which he contributed to it, or in a consistent way how he should deal with it clinically. What he became more and more certain about conceptually (until he started doing training analyses after the war) is that "the compulsion to repeat is rendered harmless . . . [by admitting it] into the transference as a playground" (Freud, 1914a, p. 154). He wrote this Winnicottian sentence at a time when he was actually doing clinical analyses.[3]

However, even during this period of time, when he was acknowledging the importance of transference, he maintained that he did not

---

[2] Jeffrey Masson has asserted that Freud abandoned the seduction hypothesis because he could not tolerate the isolation from the Vienna medical establishment. Gay correctly characterizes this assertion as preposterous and wonders why "if Freud had been made so anxious, he then proceeded to publicize even more unsettling theories, such as those on infantile sexuality . . ." (Gay, 1988, p. 751).

[3] It is my view that the many classical analysts have presented a myth about Freud, namely, that as he continued in his career and developed the structural model, clinically he began to develop in the manner that classical analysts in the United States eventually conceptualized as the analytic situation. In my view the reverse was true. After World War I, Freud stopped seeing analytic patients and became a world figure who would see patients from other countries for brief periods of time. These "training analyses" were often conducted in a loose manner, and at times Freud's main purpose was psychoanalytic propaganda. A close reading about his ideas regarding psychoanalytic

want to treat (severe) narcissistic disorders (Freud, 1916), nor did he want to treat patients who were "accessible only to 'the logic of soup, with dumplings for arguments' " (Freud, 1915, p. 167). These patients did not view their transferences in symbolic terms but only as referring to reality. They saw their love (or hate) as due only to qualities present in the external world. Freud advocated that such patients be terminated because the burden they placed on the analyst was intolerable. We can say that these nonsymbolizing patients are at times difficult to treat, particularly if one demands symbolizing verbalizations. Although we can sympathize with Freud when he stated that dealing with transference is the hardest clinical task (1905), we must realize that the creator of psychoanalysis was never at home analyzing the manifestations of transference. He had particular difficulties when the patient did not follow the optimal course in analysis. Thus, if a patient developed a negative transference or did not engage in free associations, Freud had difficulty in maintaining an analytic stance. It is only if we demand perfection from the creator of psychoanalysis that we should be surprised that in many ways his clinical difficulties were prototypic of the difficulties that many analysts have experienced in doing clinical work. His difficulties with transference are perhaps the best example of his travails in creating and attempting to master a theory and practice of treatment. I believe that his problems with transference are echoed in contemporary psychoanalysis. I have stated (Ellman and Moskowitz, 1998) that, much more frequently than we admit to and perhaps know about, the analysand's transference frequently leads to what I have called narcissistic disequilibrium[4] in the analyst. This happens most frequently with patients who have undergone traumatic circumstances.

Thus, the potential for this disequilibrium is present in many of the patient reports presented here. Certainly the patients talked about by Fonagy and Shengold bring up the issue of how the analyst should deal with a patient who does not want to follow the analyst's normal procedure, who wants the analyst to be someone else, or who is either deadened or so excited that the analyst is filled with the patient's dissociated self and objects (others). These papers are about how the

---

technique (Ellman, 1991) revealed that, if anything, Freud in the 1920s began to return to his earliest ideas about treatment, as opposed to becoming a "classical analyst."

[4] I have used this term to indicate that analyst's tendency to disrupt the transference by injecting an aspect of themselves into the treatment (Ellman and Moskowitz, 1998).

analyst deals with trauma and tries to keep the patient and the treatment alive during this process.

BEGINNING ASSUMPTIONS

My interpretation of the struggle that has been presented by Arlow, Dowling, Lionells, and Ornstein, and highlighted by Fonagy and Shengold, is around a question that Freud posed: "Why should the patient trust the analyst?" This question is especially relevant to patients who have had little to trust or to rely on in their lives. It is also pertinent, however, to anyone who is analytically beginning to explore aspects of their life. I will first begin my discussion by referring to patients who are considered difficult, who have been designated *nonclassical, very disturbed,* or Rothstein's term, *too difficult for me,* and who frequently have undergone notable traumatic circumstances in their lives.

In my definition, analytic trust begins with the analyst listening to, reflecting, and synthesizing the patient's conscious states. These states frequently are fluctuating, and it is often the case that defenses such as splitting make the patient's (at times dissociated) states difficult to read. Thus, when the analyst is able to provide integrative (or synthetic) statements (particularly across different states and circumstances), the patient begins to recognize that someone can enter their world in a way that they have never before systematically experienced. This entrance is not the establishment of full analytic trust because most frequently patients will not easily tolerate this entry and make attempts to remove the analyst overtly or covertly or to destroy the analyst's empathic capacities. Containing these attempts to immobilize the analyst is an essential aspect of the development of analytic trust. During the initial phases of treatment there may be frequent enactments, particularly if the analyst's narcissistic equilibrium is disrupted. How these enactments are endured (Winnicott, 1962) will be an important determinant of the establishment of analytic trust.

During this initial phase of treatment, interpretations are usually ineffective and most often disruptive to the analytic process. The patient does not want to tolerate another, and the analyst can be tolerated if there is a selfobject relationship established. When the analyst begins to sit back in her chair and feels that the other (she, the analyst) has gradually become another (lessening of selfobject tie), then in my view an interpretive field is established. The presence of another even slightly independent person implies the utilization of self-reflective capacities. I believe that Winnicott's concept of transitional space (Winnicott, 1971) is an optimal way of conceiving of the opening of an interpretive field. The object has become simultaneously real and not real, and either is, or is on the way to becoming, a protosymbol. The object can be played with in Winnicott's sense of the term (Winnicott, 1971). Most importantly, the analyst is seen to survive the play, even though in fantasy he or she may be destroyed many times.

O'Shaugnessy (1981) has presented a clinical illustration and Freedman evidence from research (1994) as to why an analysis is best thought of as occurring in transference cycles. These cycles are more easily discerned with patients who use splitting and projective identification as primary defenses. When a new transference cycle begins, patients often require that early forms of analytic trust be reestablished (in some ways a new aspect of transference is like a new object relationship). It is during these transitions (beginning the treatment or transitions between transference cycles) that enactments are most likely to occur. These transitions always imply a state of narcissistic disequilibrium in either analyst, patient, or both parties. Thus the analytic pair is likely to see the transference–countertransference sequence as real during this transitional period.

I have presented this condensed version of the concept of analytic trust since it seems to me to be relevant to all the patients who were discussed at the conference. Moreover, the survival of enactments is frequently a crucial aspect of an analytic treatment. Perhaps we should turn to some clinical examples of how several analytic pairs survived the type of experiences that I have schematically outlined.

PAPERS BY PETER FONAGY AND LEONARD SHENGOLD

The two papers that were presented describe, from different perspectives, the effects of trauma on both the patient and the analyst. It is an encouraging sign of our times that each analyst has written a paper that deals with his clinical response to the questions that have been posed by the organizers of the conference.

Peter Fonagy's paper is a good example: In his riveting account of Henrietta's analysis he is not concerned with differentiating the effects of trauma; he must feel reasonably certain that we can hear the effects from his case report. He tells us that patients like Henrietta "are treatable in the context of ordinary psychoanalysis, so long as the *aims* of the analysis are modified from ones which aspire to the achievement of insight to the less ambitious aim of the recovery of reflective function" (p. 210). He goes on to say that "I am certain that she experienced little (at least during the early years) of what most analysts would recognize as insight" (p. 201). I am less certain, and yet I can understand that Fonagy wants to emphasize the importance of the self-reflective function. Without this function interpretations would surely be meaningless to Henrietta. Rather, she would have continued to experience her fears and overwhelming excitation as real (in the moment) and not in addition as a psychic reality that she has brought with her during waking and sleeping hours. In places Fonagy's paper exemplifies what I mean by the development of analytic trust; in one sequence he continually attempts to untangle the contents of her conscious mind, and in doing this she becomes aware of her transference anxiety concerning termination (or more accurately, anxiety about the relationship being destroyed). Undoubtedly, termination for this woman has the meaning of annihilation, but Fonagy at this point in the treatment is relatively content to stay on the surface of her mind. He wants the analytic pair to survive and thus does not defensively interpret to the patient.

He also shares with us the difficulties of treating someone like Henrietta who must evacuate her mind of the horror she is experiencing, and does this by projecting the "hated alien other" (p. 209) onto the analyst. He tells us that when this happens and "we have become who they need us to be," they are calm, even though "they have in all probability destroyed the interpersonal situation that might have helped them" (p. 209). Thus, Fonagy is pointing out that often the therapist becomes the projected hated alien, and when this occurs (usually via an enactment) the patient is calm. Fonagy is stating this seeming paradox even though Henrietta has not destroyed their analytic situation. I believe he is letting us know that at many points in the analysis it felt as if the analysis were being destroyed. Even though Fonagy had to enact the role of the tormenting priest, his survival of this experience allowed her to reclaim what he calls the externalized alien part of her self. This is undoubtedly an example of containment, no matter how out of control he felt. We can now wonder about his admonition that we can perform standard treatment so long as we change our aims. Has he really changed his aims?

Interestingly, in the paper Fonagy talks about the patient's lack of insight, at least early in the treatment. Here we might say that perhaps he still is, in some sense of the term, early in the treatment, and this may help us to realize that with some patients the beginning of the treatment is the longest aspect of the treatment. I am reminded of a patient who only began to tell me about his core delusionary fantasies four to five years into the treatment. Important aspects of the treatment had not really begun up to that point in time. I would change what Fonagy tells us and reiterate that he has shown us that one cannot facilitate insight before analytic trust is established. One measure of analytic trust is the person's ability to withstand multiple perspectives (Bach, 1985).[5] Let us tentatively conclude that one clinical manifestation of severe trauma is the extreme inhibition of the capacity for self-reflection. This will lead to a patient who is prone to enactments and what I would call frequent projective–introjective oscillations.

We might note that Fonagy is using the term *insight* in a traditional manner, and perhaps it is time for us to broaden the concept of insight. One may view this question as similar to the issue of the self-analyzing function in analysis. In attempting to broaden the idea of the self-analyzing function (Ellman, 1991), I maintained that we can formulate the goals of analysis in terms of the analysand's ability to internalize, and then voluntarily call on those traits developed in the course of analysis that have been curative (or useful). These traits may not be capable of verbalization but are traits the patient has internalized and may involve a process that is a parallel (nonverbal) form of recognition and insight. The patient may be able to contain impulsive tendencies and soften them or present them in a less toxic more useful

---

[5] Here I mean the capacity to view the other as another and develop the ability to withstand multiple perspectives that depends on a self-reflective capacity.

(sublimated) manner. This process may go on unconsciously and may only be apparent to the person when others comment on his or her new disposition. There obviously can be a variety of traits like this that the patient can have altered during an analysis. I believe that the process of internalizing these traits is in part a function of recognition and a discriminatory function that is similar to, and a precursor of, verbal insight.

Whatever one's view of insight, Fonagy has presented us with an important version of what I would term the *growth of analytic trust*. His evocative presentation leads me to the growing realization that with some patients the beginning of the treatment is not only the longest phase of the treatment but also the most important aspect of the treatment. In addition, for me he has raised the question of how we are to conceive of the question of insight in the psychoanalytic situation.

Leonard Shengold, in sharing his wealth of experience with soul murder victims (1989), brings us to a new understanding of the analytic attitude. His even-handed stance with respect to trauma is an updated version of how analytic neutrality can be rethought as a type of respect for the patient's psychic reality. He outlines a path of following the patient's reality and not having the therapist impose his or her version of trauma. He reminds us that "even when the trauma is clearly re-membered or unequivocally established, uncovering the accompanying and obfuscating minimization and distortion is a large part of the work of the therapy" (p. 216). He cites that above all the therapist must have the "knowledge of the need to be nonjudgmental and empathic" (p. 216). He is attempting to help the patient tolerate states of hate and love "rather than feel the unbearable primal intensity of *either* hating *or* loving" (p. 220) that cannot be tolerated for long. He takes us further into the transference cycles (since he is not writing about a specific case) and sees as a crucial step in a treatment the access to loving feelings that have been obscured by conflict induced by trauma. In his words, the patient's "gradual acquisition of the ability to tolerate caring about the analyst as a separate and predominantly benevolent person different from the internalized traumatizing parent" (p. 220) is a crucial step in overcoming the devastating effects of trauma. That would involve the acquisition of a considerable feeling of trust in the analyst, and he quotes McLaughlin, who says, "When [the patient] could trust me enough to feel I loved and believed him, he found in himself capacities to trust and claim his own positive as well as negative feelings toward himself and others" (p. 222). Here in the development of analytic trust the patient has to experience (to paraphrase Steingart [1995]) that the analyst has mature love for the analysand's solitude. In a similar vein, Shengold quotes McLaughlin, seeing his patient "fighting to own his feelings—good as well as bad" (p. 220). Here we have the paradox of this position, for at some point in the unfolding of the transference, the analyst's love of the patient's mind and struggle (developing analytic trust in the therapeutic relationship) allows the patient to experience his or her solitude and own feelings good and bad, consciously and unconsciously derived. It is a contemporary Freudian position that acknowledges the relationship (Ellman and Moskowitz, 1998) while striving to allow the patient to experience how they uniquely have internalized their self and object world.[6]

These comments are not meant as serious clinical comments but rather to frame a discussion on the importance of the capacity to be alone. Winnicott's ideas about ego relatedness (Winnicott, 1958, 1962, 1963a) are important in this regard, for the capacity to be alone is dependent on the internalization of a good object. This internalization (or in Freud's terms the predominance of libidinal over destructive cathexes in cathecting the object) allows the child to enjoy exciting experiences without feeling overwhelmed. At some point, for the child to be alone it must see the supporting object as apart from itself, not always related and having different and separate aims (Winnicott, 1958, 1963b). The question to be asked is when, or do we have to provide the space for the patient to be alone with his thoughts? For me this is a crucial element of analytic trust. The traumatized patient feels that we trust him to be alone, and he senses that we believe that he can tolerate this state and that we can also tolerate his separateness. It may be that many analysts find it difficult to allow the patient to be fully separate and alone.

---

[6] None of the panelists soars, or perhaps more accurately descends, to spending much of their allotted time on the theory that guides their interventions.

PAPERS BY JACOB ARLOW, SCOTT DOWLING, MARYLOU LIONELLS, AND ANNA ORNSTEIN

Jacob Arlow's paper brings us back to some of the essentials of psychoanalytic discourse. He certainly agrees that what happened matters, but he characteristically asks the crucial question: What happens matters, but who it happens to also matters. In his clinical vignettes he illustrates the variability of response to external circumstances. Perhaps more importantly, he states that we don't really know what in early development leads to traumatic consequences. He then suggests Brenner's (1986) formulation where he states that "One can define trauma only with reference to its effects on the psyche" (p. 121). This definition does not take us very far, but it should be a subject of discussion about whether we can be content with a tautological definition.

Scott Dowling, building on work by Person and Klar (1994), takes us a step further in looking at the dissociated quality of traumatic memories. In this view splitting is seen as providing a key to locating traumatic memories as distinct from repressed fantasies. Vertical splitting is seen as a "wholly different regulatory device from the horizontal splitting that occurs with repression" (p. 131). Despite these statements, Dowling is close to Arlow's position when he says that psychological trauma is not automatic injury from an external source; rather it is the name we give to the state of helplessness and hopelessness which accompanies a psychological event whose meaning is felt as overwhelming.

In Lionell's and Ornstein's papers we are reminded of the important contribution self-psychological and interpersonal–relational perspectives have provided in widening the scope of, and bringing important reflections to, the analytic situation. I have written in another context (Ellman and Moskowitz, 1998) that the manner in which the question of analyzability was handled in the United States was defensive at best, shameful at worst. I use the word *shame* because it is my view that standard or classical analysts attempted to put their shame and discomfort into analysands whom they could not help or who were challenging to the analyst. Frequently these were traumatized patients.[7]

---

[7] The restricted sellers' market allowed the analyst relative freedom in serving out the declaration of unanalyzability.

It is my view that clinicians like Sullivan, Stone, Kohut, and Kronold[8] in some ways kept alive the field during these repressive times. But enough about my rant. Instead, let me go to Anna Ornstein's sensitive portrayal of Mr. S. I share her belief that her acceptance of the intensity of his affects in the transference and her "relatively sparse . . . interpretive comments facilitated" his treatment and allowed for a "genuine mourning for his mother" (p. 166). In this quotation I have left out the word *reality* because, as I will try to show later, this is an assumption of Anna Ornstein's and in some ways is an unnecessary assumption.

It is my view that Kohut and the Ornsteins (Ornstein and Ornstein, 1995) help open the door to a systematic view of the treatment of narcissistic and borderline disorders. They described what I have called *entering the patient's world* (Ellman, 1991, 1997a,b) and have made a large contribution to the development of the concept of analytic trust. At one point I was tempted to write an article on the two analyses of Mr. Z (Kohut, 1979) where I tried to show that, while the Kohutian approach builds analytic trust in early phases of the treatment, this type of treatment does not trust the patient to enter into and remain for a period of time in either active positive or negative transference states. I would join Brian Bird (1972) when he emphasized the importance of the exploration of negative transference states and the frequent inability of analysts to allow this exploration. Kohut's emphasis on selfobject compensatory structures in termination (Kohut, 1977) is another example of what from another perspective I would consider to be a lack of appreciation of the need for respecting and providing trust in the patient's solitude.

Going from the general to the specific, it seems to me that there is a false dichotomy presented when the patient's "need to idealize the analyst . . . " is presented as either a "defense against oedipal rivalry" or as a "legitimate developmental need" that has been "traumatically interfered with" (Ornstein, p. 170). My developmental assumptions, and Freud's in a number of papers (1911, 1913, 1914b), are that idealizations are normal developmental phenomena that serve many functions. One function is a legitimate developmental need to idealize a figure that eventually will provide an impetus for both identifications and partial identifications over a prolonged period of development (certainly through the oedipal stage and superego development and beyond). Another legitimate need is the defensive function of such

---

[8] Ed. note: Edward Kronold, M. D. (Eduard Kronengold) (1899–1993) was a New York psychoanalyst, known by some as the "analyst's analyst."

an idealization that helps the child handle anxieties that are perceived as coming from both external and internal sources. In my view there is a strong relationship between "traumatic disillusionment," "poorly sublimated aggressive drive" (Ornstein, p. 170), and the lack of ability to be appropriately and usefully assertive or aggressive. As a last point, Anna Ornstein quotes Arlow (p. 167) where he says that "it is most important to be able to uncover the unconscious instinctual wish which is given form in the fantasy" (Arlow, 1963, p. 21). I would amend this and say that the full development of analytic trust is dependent on analyzing the unconscious phantasy that is always present, whether or not we consider the patient to be traumatized. We at times do not fully reach this point with patients who have been severely traumatized, even if we are able to be helpful to these patients. Still, I would maintain that the analysis of unconscious phantasy allows the patient, in Loewald's terms (1960), to increasingly become an associate in the analytic process. To the extent that we have analyzed unconscious phantasy, then to that extent the patient can be more of a full partner in the analytic process.

One of the questions that has been raised here is whether the full development of an analytic process always involves the analysis of unconscious phantasy. Insight in some senses of the term does not seem to be the main goal of many approaches that have been presented here. Let me rejoin Scott Dowling and turn to Person and Klar (1994), who have tried to distinguish the effects of trauma by maintaining that trauma leads to disassociated states similar but not identical to vertical splitting that is present in other conditions. Their position differentiates traumatic memories from unconscious phantasy and highlights the separation (dissociation) of traumatic memories from other mental activities. They see this splitting as different from splitting that involves "the separation of good from bad." Here I would say that, while they have produced a useful article that highlights a number of key elements of trauma, their view of splitting is too dichotomized. Splitting is a defense that in severe cases leads to fragmentation, depersonalization, at times fuguelike states, and frequently oscillation of such states. In addition the key elements that they cite in trauma are present in many narcissistic and borderline patients. When they say traumas may be reenacted, in my experience, almost all narcissistic, borderline, and psychotic patients reenact elements of their past. What characterizes many borderline transferences in the beginning of a treatment, is seeing the transference as real and the rapid oscillations of the transference states (what Person and Klar have called a sudden break in the transferential flow). Thus, either all or most patients in this category are trauma victims, or perhaps we should realize that we are setting up this category as a response to the analyst becoming unexpectedly overwhelmed by a sudden break in the transference. I would suggest that it is difficult to enter the patient's world and then allow an extremely intense transference reaction to develop. Starting to question the patient about his traumatic past, as they suggest, helps attenuate the transference and shifts us back to the sins of the parent(s). It is seductive to follow this path and leave the frequently not so pleasant playground of the transference.

Let me now end with a whimper: Analyzing the here and now transference is logically equivalent to reconstructing the past.[9] *Transference* is a theoretical term that implies storage and memory systems (either encoded as fantasy or memories), and they are assumed to be unconscious. Interpreting unconscious motivation is an inference that cannot be directly supported by experience. Almost all of our interventions are based on a theory that can only derive from indirect support. We cannot know the unconscious any better than we can know the patient's past. We can often get some reports on the patient's past, but this is truly besides the point as are some of the historical arguments about Freud. A theory is defended by a convergence of evidence from a number of sources, and few if any serious theories have received only direct empirical support. This is not to say that my theory, whatever it may be, has received a great deal of converging evidence. I do believe that many of Freud's theoretical suppositions have received more empirical validation than has been appreciated. That having been said, psychoanalysis still does not have any system of thought that truly approaches a unified theory. We need more conferences like

---

[9] When I say logically equivalent, I mean that one is making a theoretical inference in either case. It is an illusion to think that analyzing the transference is somehow free from theory or more experience near.

this one so that we can at least commiserate with each other while we
are developing more complete theoretical structures.

CONCLUDING POINTS

Bob Michels, in discussing several papers, commented that Marylou
Lionells and Anna Ornstein were reconstructing as if they knew the
patient's past when ''in fact'' they could not know the patient's past.
All one could know is the patient's responses in the treatment room.
I would argue that it depends on what one means by *know*. I would
further argue that Robert Michels is implicitly using epistemological
assumptions that no self-respecting psychoanalyst would want to be
caught associating with, or in less sarcastic terms, for Michels's point
to be relevant he would have to invoke positions that were similar to
or the same as the logical positivists'. In a similar vein, although I
greatly appreciated George Makari's contextualization of Freud's
struggle with the seduction hypothesis, his questioning Harry Smith's
data was, it seems to me, an intervention on the wrong level. Smith
was putting forth a hypothesis about the status of Freud's mind, and
the data for this were Freud's subsequent theorizing. In a vein similar
to Smith's, I have put forth a view that to understand Freud's concept
of the seduction hypothesis, one must understand Freud's struggles
with the issue of transference. In more general terms we have to more
fully grasp the seductive possibilities in transference–countertransference issues that are present in virtually every psychotherapeutic encounter.

As the reader may already surmise, there were a number of pivotal questions raised during the conference, and most of these questions centered on clinical conceptualizations that emanated from issues
surrounding trauma. I try to summarize and respond to these issues
in my discussion, since these were papers that I received before the
conference. I did not, however, receive the discussion(s) of each panel
before the conference, so I add here brief comments on two points:
One point by George Makari was brought up in the informal discussion
session, and the other by Bob Michels was raised in his written discussion. Michels questions what an analyst can know; that is, what inferences can an analyst draw based on experiences from an analytic

session? When he raises this issue, he brings up something that is central to the epistemology of psychoanalysis and the clinical situation. Moreover, he presents a variant of criticism that has become popular at least since the early 1980s by maintaining that we cannot know the patient's past; rather, we can only know the narrative the patient presents to us. Thus, he tells us that Marylou Lionells's historical remarks (or reconstructions in general) are beyond the knowledge base of an analyst. She knew only the patient's view of his history, and her historical comments can be seen only in terms of the patient's psychic reality. I would maintain that what the analyst "knows" depends on the type of epistemological assumptions that we either explicitly or more usually implicitly make. If all statements that an analyst or a scientist makes are required to have direct verification, then certainly reconstructions are statements that are in principle beyond the knowledge base of an analyst. From my perspective this is a strange requirement for an analyst. Certainly, one would not make a similar requirement of archaeologists, cosmologists, or certain types of geologists. More importantly, in my view the only epistemological assumption that would restrict reconstructive statements is a positivist viewpoint similar to one put forth by Ayer (1940) or the Vienna positivists. In a previous publication (Ellman and Moskowitz, 1980), I have tried to indicate that, when criticizing a position, a number of analysts use positivist assumptions in their critiques. This is despite the fact that in their own theoretical conceptualizations they decry positivist assumptions. Moreover, we (Ellman and Moskowitz, 1980) have tried to show that positivist assumptions are not useful in theory construction in psychoanalysis or in other scientific or hermeneutic disciplines. To conclude this brief discussion, I would state that knowing in an analytic situation is a complicated question and that reconstructions can be one form of knowing unless one applies positivist epistemological assumptions. This, of course, does not get at the more important question about whether reconstructions are useful in analysis or, more accurately, the extent to which reconstructions should be utilized in analysis.

My point about Makari is a similar one in a different context. Makari criticized Smith for being historically inaccurate around several points. Although I thought Makari's paper was excellent, his criticism appears to ignore the point that Smith was making an argument about Freud's mind, as opposed to an historical argument. The data that Smith presented involved Freud's theorizing and his later conceptualizations. These data cannot be answered by historical facts but rather by an alternative view of Freud's theoretical attempts. Nevertheless, I reiterate the point that I believe Makari's paper is one of the important papers about this era of Freud's career.

REFERENCES

Arlow, J. (1963), Conflict, regression, and symptom formation. *Internat. J. Psycho-Anal.,* 44:12–22.

Ayer, A. J. (1940), *The Foundations of Empirical Knowledge.* London: Macmillan.

Bach, S. (1985), *Narcissistic States and the Therapeutic Process.* New York: Jason Aronson.

Bird, B. (1972), Notes on transference: Universal phenomenon and hardest part of analysis. *J. Amer. Psychoanal. Assn.,* 20:267–301.

Brenner, C. (1986), Discussion of the various contributions. In: *The Reconstruction of Trauma,* ed. A. Rothstein. Madison, CT: International Universities Press, pp. 195–203.

Ellman, S. J. (1991), *Freud's Technique Papers: A Contemporary Perspective.* Northvale, NJ: Jason Aronson.

——— (1997a), An analyst at work. In: *More Analysts at Work,* ed. J. Reppen. Northvale, NJ: Jason Aronson, pp. 91–115.

——— (1997b), Criteria for termination. *Psychoanal. Psychol.,* 14(2):197–210.

——— Moskowitz, M. B. (1980), An examination of some recent criticisms of psychoanalytic "metapsychology." *Psychoanal. Quart.,* 49:631–662.

——— ——— (1998), *Enactment: Towards a New Approach to the Therapeutic Relationship.* Northvale, NJ: Jason Aronson.

Freedman, N. (1994), More on transformation enactments. In: *The Spectrum of Psychoanalysis: Essays in Honor of Martin S. Bergman,* ed. A. K. Richards & A. D. Richards. Madison, CT: International Universities Press, pp. 93–110.

Freud, S. (1905), Fragment of an analysis of a case of hysteria. *Standard Edition,* 7:1–122. London: Hogarth Press, 1953.

——— (1911), Psycho-analytic notes on an autobiographical account of a case of paranoia (dementia paranoides). *Standard Edition,* 12:1–82. London: Hogarth Press, 1958.

———— (1913), The disposition to obsessional neurosis. *Standard Edition*, 12:311–326. London: Hogarth Press, 1958.

———— (1914a), Remembering, repeating and working-through (Further recommendations on the technique of psycho-analysis III). *Standard Edition*, 12:145–156. London: Hogarth Press, 1958.

———— (1914b), On narcissism: An introduction. *Standard Edition*, 14:67–102. London: Hogarth Press, 1957.

———— (1915), Observations on transference-love (Further recommendations on the technique of psycho-analysis III). *Standard Edition*, 12:157–171. London: Hogarth Press, 1958.

———— (1917), Introductory Lectures on Psycho-Analysis. *Standard Edition*, 15. London: Hogarth Press, 1961.

Gay, P. (1988), *Freud: A Life for Our Time.* New York: W. W. Norton.

Kohut, H. (1977), *The Restoration of the Self.* New York: International Universities Press.

———— (1979), The two analyses of Mr. Z. *Internat. J. Psycho-Anal.*, 60:3–28.

Loewald, H. W. (1960), On the therapeutic action of psychoanalysis. In: *Papers on Psychoanalysis.* New Haven, CT: Yale University Press, pp. 221–256.

Masson, J. (1984), *The Assault on Truth: Freud's Suppression of the Seduction Theory.* New York: Farrar, Straus & Giroux.

Ornstein, P. H., & Ornstein, A. (1995), Some distinguishing features of Heinz Kohut's self psychology. *Psychoanal. Dial.*, 5:385–392.

O'Shaugnessy, E. (1981), A clinical study of a defensive organization. *Internat. J. Psycho-Anal.*, 62:359–369.

Person, E., & Klar, H. (1994), Establishing trauma: The difficulty distinguishing between memories and fantasies. *J. Amer. Psychoanal. Assn.*, 42:1055–1081.

Shengold, L. (1989), *Soul Murder: The Effects of Childhood Abuse and Deprivation.* New Haven, CT: Yale University Press.

Steingart, I. (1995), *A Thing Apart: Love and Reality in the Therapeutic Partnership.* Northvale, NJ: Jason Aronson.

Swales, P. J. (1983), *Freud, Cocaine, and Sexual Chemistry: The Role of Cocaine in Freud's Conception of the Libido.* Privately published.

Winnicott, D. W. (1958), The capacity to be alone. In: *The Maturational Processes and the Facilitating Environment.* New York: International Universities Press, 1965, pp. 29–36.

———— (1962), Ego integration in child development. In: *The Maturational Processes and the Facilitating Environment.* New York: International Universities Press, 1965, pp. 56–63.

———— (1963a), The development of the capacity for concern. In: *The Maturational Processes and the Facilitating Environment.* New York: International Universities Press, 1965, pp. 73–82.

———— (1963b), From dependence to independence in the development of the individual. In: *The Maturational Processes and the Facilitating Environment.* New York: International Universities Press, 1965, pp. 83–92.

———— (1971), *Playing and Reality.* New York: Basic Books.

10

The Seduction Hypothesis Axis: What's External, What's Internal, and What's in Between?

Stephen A. Mitchell, Ph.D.

Why *have* a conference on the seduction theory? Jacob Arlow begins his paper with this most provocative question of all, and implies that there really aren't any *good* reasons. In his view, the seduction hypothesis was a conjecture Freud considered before he had any reliable method for studying psychopathology, before he could make more sophisticated distinctions between fact and fantasies, before he had come to appreciate the role of suggestion in his clinical practice, and, above all, while he was still under the sway of the traditional prepsychoanalytic understanding of sexuality as emerging in adolescence. Arlow argues that the conclusion that an actual experience of seduction is neither essential nor always present in the etiology of hysteria should have long ago been accepted as an incontrovertible principle (p. 118). Arlow wants us to realize that the seduction theory was simply a naive product of Freud's prepsychoanalytic conjectures and, once this is grasped, to assign it to its archival resting place.

But one of the things that has been so dramatically demonstrated here is the manner in which historically important ideas, psychoanalytic and otherwise, change over time, dropping original meanings and picking up new meanings in shifting intellectual and cultural contexts. We have learned a lot not only about what the seduction hypothesis was for Freud, but also what it has become for us. This is why controversies like the one surrounding the seduction hypothesis are really clusters of controversies that have adhered to the original problem Freud was struggling with one hundred years ago. In this sense, I found fascinating and persuasive George Makari's argument that our generally accepted historical understanding of Freud's abandonment of the seduction hypothesis in 1897 was largely a product of Freud's retrospective reconstruction amidst the psychoanalytic politics and polemics of the post-Adler, post-Jung context of 1914. Makari suggests that Freud fashioned an historical parable to serve as an heroic justification for what Freud regarded as a paradigm shift to libido theory by making his prior, and to some extent continuing, belief in the importance of trauma appear to be a dangerous but enticing error.

By recasting the issues surrounding the seduction hypothesis for these rhetorical purposes, Freud was also using the seduction hypothesis controversy to engage a much larger intellectual problem—not just the etiology of a specific neurosis, but also the construction of human experience in general. As Makari demonstrated, Freud's seduction hypothesis was originally part of what he termed the *aetiological equation,* which in 1915 was changed to the *aetiological series.* By 1916 and 1917, in *The Introductory Lectures on Psycho-Analysis,* the wording shifted again from *aetiological series* to *complemental series,* and Freud from there on used the latter phrase to struggle with the enormously complex problems of the relationship between heredity and early experience (1916–1917, p. 362), and also between infantile experiences and adult experiences (1933, p. 126), problems no less complex than the relationships between nature and nurture, and between past and present. Part of the reason we are discussing the seduction hypothesis here, one hundred years later, is that there has been a piggybacking onto the original controversy of later controversies concerning very large issues indeed.

The rhetorical use that George Makari and Jay Greenberg both suggest Freud made of this controversy set in motion a dialectical pendulum. In defending libido and drive theory, Freud often went too far in privileging fantasy over actuality, universalizing mythic themes involving primal (sometimes Lamarckian) phylogenetic fantasies, at the expense of parental character and family dynamics. Then, in turn, there were overcorrections of that overcorrection. Developmentalists sometimes portray developmental arrests as simply the product of "environmental deficiency." And sometimes early interpersonalists, in their abandonment of drive theory, altogether ignored the importance of constitutional and temperamental differences, intrapsychic organization, or childhood sexuality.

Over the course of decades in the development of psychoanalytic ideas, the seduction theory and the notion of trauma, both extraordinary and ordinary, have played a crucial conceptual role. Bob Michels noted that the concept of ordinary trauma seems to be an oxymoron. If trauma is defined in terms of shock, in terms of affects that are extraordinary, affects that cannot be assimilated into ongoing self-organizations, there can be no such thing as trauma of ordinary life. But the concept of ordinary trauma, like the concept of "cumulative trauma," has been historically important because, in the classical literature, the term *trauma* has partly been a code word for acknowledging the impact of actuality. For many decades, instinctually derived fantasies were understood to be the prime pathogenic agent, *except* in cases of trauma, where actuality overloaded the psychic system. The concept of "cumulative trauma," in the work of Masud Khan (1974), for example, became a device for acknowledging the formative and deformative importance of ongoing, nondramatic, early object relations. Michels noted, and I agree, that trauma does not and should not signify "environmental," but it has sometimes come to do just that, in the way psychoanalytic traditions have developed. The problem has been an inadequate attention, until recently, to the profound ways in which interpersonal, social, and cultural relations shape all experience, normal and pathological. Here, medical metaphors have been unfortunate, because, as with physical health and pathology, they suggest a normal way for people to be, as a point of reference for defects and deviations. We do better with a framework that allows for many variations in ways to be human, all shaped within the context of relational and cultural matrices.

One reason to discuss the seduction theory in depth might be to end, once and for all, the needless polarization and the sometimes reckless feuding the theory has generated. This has a certain appeal amidst the tentative ecumenicism in today's psychoanalytic world. Given the troubles besieging psychoanalysis from many quarters, there has been a tendency to want to close ranks and heal old wounds. Besides, it might be argued, the psychoanalytic versions of the Montagues and the Capulets, or, on American soil, the Hatfields and the McCoys, were never all that different anyway. Certainly, the strawmen images that have served as foils for analytic rhetoric were caricatures.

Many of the panelists and discussants have noted that in abandoning the seduction hypothesis as a specific and necessary cause of hysteria, Freud never actually abandoned his belief in the importance of trauma. And he certainly never simply chose nature over nurture, past over present. His concept of a "complemental series" is much more subtle and supple than that. To eliminate experience, traumatic and otherwise, would be to portray the development of human mind as the emergence of an unbridled, solipsistic projection, which would be absurd. Similarly, interpersonal and developmental arrest authors never really subscribed to a theory of total blank-slate environmentalism, or, to use Donald Spence's (1982) phrase, a theory of "immaculate perception," which would be absurd.

So, we might want to end by agreeing that "solipsistic projection" and "immaculate perception" are both preposterous and figments of polemical imagination, thereby finally putting to rest the controversial features of the seduction theory in an atmosphere of congeniality. Freud himself remarked in his *Introductory Lectures* (1916–1917) that this controversy has become a "quite unnecessary dispute" (p. 346). A number of the papers in this volume demonstrate the preferability of an understanding of trauma, and the generation of experience in general, based upon a both–and rather than an either–or strategy: both nature *and* nurture, both body *and* culture, both temperament *and* experience, both event *and* fantasy, and so on.

Henry Smith, in stressing the ubiquity of unconscious fantasy, urged us to keep in mind what he called the natural human tendency to externalize. But the relational literature since the early fifties has explored in many, many different ways the natural human tendency to internalize. The papers in this volume all strive to understand trauma in a complex fashion, with considerations of both external factors—events, parental functioning, and responsiveness—and internal factors—temperament, fantasy elaboration, and meanings laid down prior to the traumatogenic event.

Certainly, we have arrived at a consensus concerning the need for theorizing that embraces both intrapsychic and interpersonal dimensions. But important issues remain. They are joined in the specifics, at the particular points where understandings are generated about *exactly how* specific intrapsychic and interpersonal factors are related to each other. Here, there are interesting differences both in terms of theory and in terms of clinical practice.

There was mention of Arlow's metaphor of the two projectors as an explanatory framework for thinking about the conjunction of internal and external factors, fantasy and reality, in the construction of experience, one projecting on one side of the screen, the other projecting on the other, experience emerging in their mingling. This approach has obviously been useful in many ways, but I find the analogy problematic in several respects. First, like Freud's concept of a complemental series, reality and fantasy are treated here as if they are separable, as if they come from different places. Presumably, if one projector were shut down, the other would keep playing, and each projection is a coherent narrative in its own terms. It is similar in the inverse relationships of Freud's complemental series: this much reality added to this much fantasy, and so on.

From a contemporary constructivist point of view, reality and perception are not separable in that fashion. Reality, including all potentially traumatic events, is fundamentally ambiguous; fantasies, like all perceptions, are constructions of something, past and present. Reality and fantasy are not additive—they bring each other alive, and they also constrain each other. I have always found Loewald's approach to these issues extremely rich and thought provoking, moving us beyond assumptions about the separability of fantasy and actuality and concerns with reality and distortion.

These differences in thinking about the ways in which experience is constructed might sound like subtle and pretty abstract quibbles, but they have enormous consequences. This becomes immediately apparent when we start thinking about something like gender. We would probably all agree that we have material bodies, and that different cultures assign different meanings to what Freud called the "anatomical differences between the sexes." But exactly how much does the physical reality of our bodies, and which features of that reality, constrain the kinds of constructions culture can make of them? Exactly how much *is* anatomy really destiny? Is everyone with a penis, in any culture, going to suffer castration anxiety? And what about womb envy? Is everyone without a penis going to suffer penis envy? And what about the Kleinian notion of the little girl's dread of the retaliatory destruction of her own womb by the mother? Thus, although we can all agree that there is a reality and external events, as well as fantasy and internal dynamics, there are enormous differences between them when it comes down to specifics.

This matter was touched on briefly in relation to Scott Dowling's example of the little boy who thought his father was dead, in which Dowling argued that the event was traumatic because of the boy's prior death wishes in relation to his father. Arnold Cooper asked whether such a perception of an unconscious, spread-eagled father would not be traumatic in all cases. Like most interesting questions, we will never be able to do the research to find out. But in the ways in which these things play out clinically, one's theory of aggression probably would have a lot to do with the kind of analytic inquiry one would conduct and the conclusions reached. A believer in an aggressive drive and universal Oedipus complex, for example, might stop with what would feel like a satisfactory causal account when he had found evidence of aggressive oedipal fantasies. A believer that intense oedipal feelings derive from parental selfobject failures, which Anna Ornstein laid out, would not stop there but would inquire into the more complex interpersonal exchanges between boy and father. We would all agree that both event and perception are important, but not necessarily on which particular events and which particular perceptions are relevant and *how* they came together.

The second problem for me with the projector analogy is the question of where the analyst sits in viewing these movies. There is one screen, the patient's experience, and the two projectors casting images upon it. The implication seems to be that the analyst sits upon some objective platform viewing the proceedings, able to disentangle the contributions from the two projectors. But this seems internally contradictory to me. When it comes to the analyst's experience of the patient's experience, there would have to be a third projector casting images from the analyst's own psychodynamics and fantasies, comingling with the two projectors generating the patient's own experience. More about this third projector in a moment.

At this point I want to return to the seduction hypothesis and suggest that the major reason for the durability of the seduction hypothesis controversy today is that it has contained, embedded within it, not only these complex theoretical issues but also two other dense, thorny problems at the heart of clinical psychoanalysis, issues about which we are not likely to arrive at any clear or simple consensus.

The first embedded clinical issue concerns the very important, very complex question of the ambiguity of cause and effect, accountability and blame, in intimate human relationships. In intense emotional relationships, it is actually very difficult to sort out questions like: What part of it was emotional? What part sensual? What part sexual? This is so because the neatness of these categories that we create in language does not correspond to the interpenetrability of thought and emotion, mind and body, in real life. This is also true of what is often the most difficult question of all: Who started it? Who did what to whom?

But in the clinical psychoanalytic enterprise, the patient is often trying to sort out what happened to them and why. Questions like "Who started it?" and "Who did what to whom?" are of central importance in the kind of compelling self-understanding that patients need. Positions on the seduction hypothesis have served as narrative strategies for answering those questions. The answers are not dichotomous—they are more than just two. The polarized positions on the seduction hypothesis really define a continuum of possible strategies.

On one side of the continuum are answers like: Something terrible happened to you; your pain was never recognized or validated; you have come to omnipotently blame yourself; and your inner world has been deformed through identifications and desperate measures in an effort to survive your experiences.

On the other side of the continuum are narrative strategies like these: You had and still have desires and longings that are simply unbearable for you; you tend to locate these desires in others, or use desires or actions you find in others as a pretext for your own behaviors and experiences; you have used and continue to use unfortunate experiences as rationales for your life choices; you used your dreads to conceal your wishes; your own desires need to be named and owned to make constructive living possible.

From which side of the seduction hypothesis axis do *you* draw your narrative strategies? Most of us would say something like, "Well, it depends on the patient." The question, "What about the patient does it depend on?" might elicit some sort of literal diagnostic distinctions between neurotic and borderline psychopathology. But, more generally, the very process of engaging patients around these issues entails an ongoing quasidiagnostic evaluation: The patients' reactions to their experiences are measured against what we take to have been the experiences themselves, the sequelae to the actual events. As Dowling put it, we strive to "define the nature of the external events to which the trauma state is linked" (p. 138) and take part with the patient "in defining the meaningful interaction of external event" with the patient's personality (p. 138). And Anna Ornstein, while noting the importance of avoiding parent blaming, points to the way in which selfobject transferences are employed to reconstruct childhood states so that "traumatic aspects of the caretakers' personalities become progressively clarified" (p. 162).

Diagnosis in clinical psychoanalysis tends to convey a medical, scientistic tone. I would suggest that this tone conceals the extent to which such judgments are actually made, inevitably at least partially, in the countertransference, in the analyst's necessarily varying identifications with different patients' pain. With some patients, we are likely to feel that what happened to them was much more horrifying than they have ever been able to acknowledge and feel. With other patients, we are likely to feel that they have elaborated what happened to them into a way of life that defensively disclaims their own agency and desire. How do we decide? It seems to me that it must depend heavily on our own life history and dynamics, our own differential identifications with the stories and presentations of different patients. Yet, we tend to conceal from ourselves our own participation in this struggle with patients through a belief that we are arriving at these judgments through a wholly objectivist diagnostic system. I think that diagnosis really begs the question, because it often *follows* the intuitive clinical judgment, and that the intuitive clinical judgment is made, at least in part, in the countertransference. We are back to the missing third projector—there is no way for any of us to have unmediated access to the patient's experience, providing us with grounds for neatly separating its contributory channels. We encounter our patients only in an intersubjective context.

We have heard about patients suffering the traumas of everyday life, and we have heard about severely traumatized patients. In the powerful, poignant clinical work presented by Peter Fonagy, the violence perpetrated against the patient seems unmistakable, and it is difficult to imagine thinking about such patients in any way other than as terrorized people who have spent the rest of their lives struggling both to evade and to come to terms with the horrifying realities that were imposed upon them.

But, thankfully, most patients do not present themselves with these life histories. With most patients, the distinction between ordinary trauma and severely traumatized is more ambiguous. As Leonard Shengold notes, with some patients we never arrive at a confident answer to questions about what really happened, about where resources and handicaps came from. *Sometimes* we have to stand for uncertainty. But that does not stop us—it cannot really stop us—from helping the patient construct a framework for self-understanding. Makari demonstrated the ways in which analysts construct an identity that requires a coherent history of our discipline. So do patients. The clinical process has an urgency to it that overwhelms epistemological ambiguities; patients struggle passionately toward understandings of what happened to them, and, generally, it is crucial to them to know where we stand. In one way or another, each of the papers at this conference made that clear. This is not a problem we can, ourselves, avoid by believing we are neutral or anonymous or invisible or able to float in the air or have any other qualities we might want to attribute to ourselves. We make these judgments, inevitably so, as we go along, and our manner of interacting with the patient reflects those choices.

In this respect, I disagree with the position that Bob Michels took in the discussion. He argued that, based on clinical data in the present, which is the only data we ordinarily have, we cannot really know what happened in the past; we could easily extend this argument to the view that we also cannot really know what is happening currently in the patient's life outside the consulting room. Therefore, he goes on, since we cannot know anything about these things with certainty, we can only maintain good faith with our patients by not pretending that we can, by not taking positions on their own struggles to decide what happened to them and what is happening to them now.

Of course, we can all agree with this on an epistemological level. We cannot know anything for certain. Even so-called "hard" science is now understood, in contemporary philosophy of science, to merely provide provisional falsifiable hypotheses that we cannot really believe are "true," just not yet proven wrong. But this rarefied epistemological level is not where people actually live and is not where clinical psychoanalysis is actually practiced. I think Michels has stranded us in what, in another context, he has called a "postmodern fog." In fact, we cannot operate in the world without constantly making judgments about what is real and what is illusion or fantasy, both in our own experience and in the experience of those we encounter. We would never make it through the day if we did not. I think we get into much worse faith with our patients by pretending we are not making such judgments than by subjecting the judgments we inevitably make to self-reflection and, selectively, to collaborative discussions with the patient.

Michels suggested at one point yesterday, if I grasped his meaning, that perhaps psychoanalysis should not be about pathogenesis and etiology, that perhaps it is a very different sort of discipline than Freud envisioned. I think this is right. In my view, psychoanalysis is fundamentally not about curing pathology but about helping patients enliven and enrich their experience, which includes helping patients sort out their lives.

In this regard I found George Makari's remarks about history making very relevant for our clinical discipline. Contemporary philosophy of history had made it clear that history making is contextual: Accounts of the past are always generated through the lens of the present. We can't ever get it right, Makari said, but it is really important that we keep trying. The conclusion is not, "Oh, well, there is a subjective, constructivist underpinning to history making, so why don't we just all write fiction?'' Historians keep taking positions, committing themselves to beliefs about the past, even though they know such beliefs will be reconsidered and perhaps radically altered as time goes on. This seems to be so true of clinical psychoanalysis. We analysts also need to learn to renounce claims to certainty and still passionately embrace our beliefs, both with patients and in theory making.

Thus, the first key clinical issue embedded in the seduction hypothesis controversy remains and will always remain the problem of the analyst's position vis-à-vis the patient's self-understanding of the relationship between her current pain and the life circumstances she was dealt. We have displaced the problem somewhat in our discussions from the seduction hypothesis, pro or con, to the distinction between ordinary and extraordinary trauma.

In the context of this conference, the ordinary–extraordinary distinction seems to serve as a device for distinguishing the patient who has reacted in an extreme fashion to average expectable stresses from the patient who has reacted in an understandable fashion to unusually terrifying events.

Because Jacob Arlow has presented us with two patients that he assigns to the two different categories, his paper best illustrates the process through which such assignment is accomplished. Arlow argues that what actually happened, in itself, doesn't matter terribly much because it is psychic reality, the impact of the events on the mind of the patient, that counts and, "One person's mouse may be another person's dragon." But his presentation of these two patients strongly suggests that it matters a great deal what the analyst thinks really happened, that it matters a great deal whether the analyst thinks the patient's psychic terrors are, in fact, a response to either a mouse or a dragon.

The housewife that Arlow presents seems to have suffered grave psychic damage consequent to what he describes as "the vicissitudes of toilet training" at the hands of a "peculiar" mother plus a couple of ambiguous, possible "primal scene" exposures. He judges her experiences as "far from rare . . . [representing] the kind of challenges that many, if not most, children growing up have to negotiate. Nothing extraordinary here" (p. 123). As Michels noted, she seems to derive severe difficulties in living from seemingly trivial causes. The brilliant, successful man Arlow presents, by way of contrast, seems to have suffered a more subtle psychic damage consequent to the shock of the revelation that the man he took to be his father was, in fact, his uncle and that his real father had died trying to help him. As Arlow, clearly moved, puts it, "On one day he lost two fathers" (p. 125).

Arlow's theory tells him that the differences in the actual circumstances of these two patients fade in significance because it is only "psychic" reality that counts. But I think that it makes a huge difference clinically whether one regards the patient's traumas as ordinary or extraordinary (our new verbal tags for "fantasy-laden" vs. "realistic"). If one believes the trauma to be "ordinary," one gravitates to the emotional position captured in questions like: "What are you making such a fuss about? Is this really the issue? Is it a displacement from other issues? Is there projection of one's own fantasies and impulses upon the presumably traumatized others?" If one believes the trauma to be "extraordinary," one gravitates to the emotional position captured in statements like: "I can't, I myself don't want to, believe what happened to you. Something terrible happened to you that you've had trouble coming to terms with ever since." The distinction between ordinary and extraordinary trauma rests on the analyst's own judgment about the relationship between the actual events and the patient's psychic registration of them. Arlow is clearly much more admiring of, and identified with, the male patient and his cruel childhood fate, whereas he judges his female patient's mother to have been merely "peculiar."

The latter patient's story reminds me of Kohut's "The Two Analyses of Mr. Z," which we now know, I gather, to have been autobiography. In the first analysis, Kohut understood his mother along lines similar to Arlow's patient, as involved with peculiar toilet-related activities. In the second, self-analysis, Kohut had come to regard his mother as quite mad, and his childhood as having been lived in a reign of psychological terror. These are very different stories, and the patient moves from the category of ordinary trauma of everyday life to extraordinary cumulative trauma. Some readers, positively identified with Kohut, understand him to have finally been able to deal with the reality of his mother's pathology and its impact on him. Other readers, negatively disposed to Kohut, regard the second clinical tale as a disclaiming of his own conflictual fantasies.

What I am suggesting is that, in every analytic dyad, judgments are inevitably fashioned and refashioned about the relationship between actual and psychic reality, about guilt, accountability, and blame—the very issues that were at the center of the seduction hypothesis controversy for Freud all along. I am suggesting that the determination of trauma is an interpersonal negotiation. Arlow poses the choice in an interesting way: mice or dragons? Dragons, of course, do not really exist. They are a product of fantasy. In Arlow's world, there are mice, no *real* dangers, and dragons, fantasied dangers. Other analysts live in worlds populated by different creatures: mice and wolves, hornets, black widow spiders, anthrax. The ways in which each analyst construes his world, the ways he thinks about the prevalence of danger and evil in dramatic and subtle forms has an enormous impact on the ways in which he will hear each patient and participate in coconstructing her understandings of her life.

I would like now to circle back and follow another line of thought stimulated by Jay Greenberg's interesting discussion of the rich ambiguity of Freud's term *seduction*. "Why 'seduction'?" Jay asks. "Why not 'abuse'?" In fact, there are passages where Freud speaks of seduction in terms of the inevitable stimulation of parental body-care of babies, through which they are awakened into life. Greenberg suggests that Freud was actually writing about a lot of different kinds of experiences that got collapsed in the polemics of position taking around the seduction hypothesis.

So, we might want to ask, what is the difference between seduction and abuse? Does it reside solely in the victim's subjectivity? Are they both traumas? Are they traumas of a different sort? The term *seduction* implies at least temporary consent. The action starts with the seducer, but sometimes the seduced is happy to have been seduced. If there is no consent, terms like *abuse* or *rape* are more appropriate. But it is not that simple. We define certain objects of seduction as incapable of meaningful consent. They are under age, or mentally incompetent. Consent is irrelevant in statutory rape. Or the power differential between the two parties is too great to make consent meaningful, as in dyads consisting of doctors and patients, teachers and students, perhaps presidents and White House interns. In such cases, we are claiming that first-person attitude is *not* definitive. Psychic damage might be done whether the consenting object of the seduction knows it or not. I am sure we have all had many patients, like Arlow's second patient, who fall into this category, where a set of circumstances or an event in childhood came to be understood, through the analyst's retelling, as having had profound traumatic impact, unbeknownst to the victim.

Freud, as Greenberg suggests, in his later metaphoric play with the term *seduction*, regarded all of us as seduced through early body care into sensual loving. The relational turn in psychoanalysis over the past several decades might lead us to expand that formulation into the notion that all of us, as children, were seduced, through early significant object relations, into life. Those not seduced wither and die. But how do we distinguish between healthy, constructive, life-enhancing (parental) seductions and abusive, traumatic, crippling (parental) seductions? It is not simple; it is not easy. The issue of betrayal of trust by the "helper" is at the heart of sexual abuse. Abuse and misuse sometimes present themselves as care. These are judgments and discriminations that are made through complex negotiations.

At first, there are the negotiations between the patient and his original significant others. How has the patient come to regard the childhood that they were dealt by their parents? Have they come to regard their life as a precious gift? or an abduction? Have they come to feel gratitude, or do they rail at their parents, like Kierkegaard, with questions about their birth: "Why was I not consulted?" he wanted to know. Have they come to regard the pain of their childhood in terms of the ordinary trauma of everyday life or the extraordinary traumas of the failure of average expectable parental care?

One way to define the analytic process, as Marylou Lionells suggested, is as the reopening of those earlier negotiations in the context of new, transference–countertransference negotiations between patient and analyst. The analytic situation is a new interactive field in which are revisited all the issues of blame and responsibility, activity and passivity. But, it is not just a question of a remembering and reevaluation of the old determinations around the seduction–abuse axis. In Greenberg's sense, a new seduction is going on. As Fonagy noted, "[T]he mere remembering of experience, however horrific, could only have therapeutic value if the experience was lived in the here and now" (p. 208). Despite the traditional analytic mythology of "abstinence," we cure through establishing, developing, often fighting passionately for, a complex, specifically analytic form of caring, in which we are "good enough" and also, as Glen Gabbard noted, "bad enough."

Many authors over the past several decades have suggested that the analyst becomes, and necessarily so, a new object, and that the new, analytic object relationship plays a key role in making it possible for the patient to renounce and transform old object relationships, old patterns of seduction and abuse. And a key element in the new seduction of the analytic relationship is the renegotiation of patients' understanding of their own past, including their own prior negotiations with their caregivers. Will they come to see past, apparent care as abusive? Will they come to see what had been felt as abusive as more ordinary? Can the analyst find a way not to seduce the patient or to be seduced by the patient into collusion, parent blaming, and glorification of victimization that, in the long run, truncates patients' experience of their own powers and resources? Can the analyst find a way not to reenact earlier abuses by blaming the patient for complicitous desires or hypersensitivity?

I believe that a second deep reason for the tenacity of the seduction hypothesis controversy over the years is that it has served as a somewhat displaced arena for our struggle to come to terms with the ambiguities of seduction in the analytic relationship. Peter Fonagy confesses his inevitable enactments to us so as to draw us complicitously into the toxic affects he shared with his patient. He found ways to turn transference–countertransference situations of coercion-seduction-abuse into opportunities for growth. He found ways of providing creative seductions. It is an awesome responsibility to come to terms with the centrality of our personal influence in the analytic situation. And it is important that we keep struggling with it (Mitchell, 1997). One thing that helps a lot is to return again and again to central psychoanalytic controversies like the one this conference has helped us explore in a search for new understandings.

REFERENCES

Freud, S. (1916–1917), Introductory Lectures on Psycho-Analysis. *Standard Edition,* 16:241–464. London: Hogarth Press, 1961.

———— (1933), New Introductory Lecture on Psycho-Analysis. *Standard Edition,* 22:15–182. London: Hogarth Press, 1964.

Khan, M. M. R. (1974), *The Privacy of the Self.* New York: International Universities Press.

Kohut, H. (1979), The two analyses of Mr. Z. *Internat. J. Psycho-Anal.,* 60:3–28.

Loewald, H. (1960), On the therapeutic action of psychoanalysis. *Internat. J. Psycho-Anal.,* 41:16–33.

Mitchell, S. (1997), *Influence and Autonomy in Psychoanalysis.* Hillsdale, NJ: Analytic Press.

Spence, D. P. (1982), *Narrative Truth and Historical Truth: Meaning and Interpretation in Psychoanalysis.* New York: W. W. Norton.

Postscript

The Seduction Theory: A Leitmotif in the Evolution of Psychoanalytic Theory, But Is It a Testable Hypothesis?

Michael I. Good, M.D.

Psychoanalytic theory has evolved by fits and starts. Although increasingly informed by investigations in related fields, our theory has developed within a social and historical context in which theoretical advances have been based more on informed individual perceptions, insights, and inspirations than on unwieldy systematic studies or experiments (Kuhn, 1962; Polányi, 1974; Grünbaum, 1984; Edelson, 1984; Spencer, 1987, 1994; Gedo, 1999; Makari, 2000; Fonagy, 2003a).

The course of the seduction theory can be viewed as a paradigm of this evolutionary pattern. It has been a leitmotif in the unfolding of considerable theory, recurring with variations but without solution or resolution. The introduction to this volume described social–historical precursors to the entrance of the seduction hypothesis onto the scientific scene. Although this theory did not endure for long in its original form, it did not disappear either. Rather, it reemerged episodically during the twentieth century and served as a counterpoint that awaited fuller integration into the main corpus of psychoanalytic theory. In the past two decades, the seduction theory has had a renaissance that has further influenced our understanding of psychic trauma and the roles of reality and fantasy in human experience. These wide-ranging and enriching developments in psychoanalytic thinking have been explored within the body of this book. Nevertheless, fundamental questions remain about the scientific correctness or incorrectness of the seduction hypothesis as originally formulated in 1896. These questions bear upon current controversies regarding trauma, fantasy, and reality.

This postscript has three related aims. The first is to highlight recurring themes and conflicts regarding the theoretical standing of the seduction theory since 1897, when Freud saw the need for a fuller explanation of neurosogenesis. Although Freud began his scientific career following inductivist principles, when he moved away from the seduction theory he also relied more on "rhetorical persuasion" than on an appeal to data (Spence, 1994, p. 77).[1] The second is to underscore the fact that Freud did not utilize clinical examples to demonstrate that cases of putative seduction believed to play a role in causing hysteria were based instead on fantasy. In fact, exceedingly few illustrative cases on this specific issue have been published at all. Controversy over the role of seduction in causing neurosis has waxed and waned, but it is an issue around which the need for scientific clarification remains. The seduction theory entails reconstruction of sexual experience from early childhood. In a scientific sense, it requires postdictive confirmation or disconfirmation (Rubinstein, 1980; Edelson, 1984; Good, 1994a,b, 1998; Brenneis, 2000). Consequently, and third, it is proposed that attention to gathering a series of clinical cases in which it is possible from extraclinical sources to confirm or refute the

---

[1] In Freud's letter of December 17, 1911, to Jung, for example, regarding his study of totemism and other work, he wrote, "[M]y interest is diminished by the conviction that I am already in possession of the truths I am trying to prove. . . . I can see from the difficulties I encounter in this work that I was not cut out for inductive investigation, that my whole make-up is intuitive, and that in setting out to establish the purely empirical science of [psychoanalysis] I subjected myself to an extraordinary discipline" (McGuire, 1974, p. 472; cited in Spence, 1994, p. 77).

likelihood of reconstructed seduction in early childhood be among the goals of future psychoanalytic research. Using the case study method (Edelson, 1984) together with open dialog about the significance of clinical and extraclinical findings, we may be able to place the seduction theory on firmer scientific ground. The following discussion elaborates on these points.

THE GAP BETWEEN THEORY AND EVIDENCE

Psychoanalytic thinking has had a tendency to decouple theory from clinical evidence and in that respect has not met its scientific potential (Spence, 1994). As a result, competing theories persist, without sufficient access to the kind of clinical data that would make one theory more probable than another (as by means of eliminative induction or falsification [Edelson, 1984]). The seduction theory has been a case in point. Although it has evolved over the past 100 years, fundamental questions and issues remain unsolved. One conundrum involves the veridicality of psychoanalytic reconstructions of seduction or abuse. A related issue involves the complementary roles of fantasy and external reality (including historical reality) in determining psychic reality. Disagreement about the place of external reality in psychoanalytic theory and practice (Oliner, 1996), in turn, has affected the gathering of data regarding what is factual and the role such facts play in clinical theory and practice. In the analytic situation, extraclinical reality tends to be remote, evanescent, indeterminate, and may be used defensively. Consequently, psychic reality, which already has a central place in psychoanalytic theory, receives preponderant attention. Psychoanalysis has a "problem with external reality" (Fonagy and Target, 2003), and the seduction theory reflects this problem (see also Blum, 2003a,b; Fonagy, 2003b).

In a similar vein, Rangell opined that "controversy in psychoanalysis is based on a repetitive series of fallacies and flawed thinking . . . in which a preexisting set of observations or piece of explanatory theory is entirely replaced by another when both the old and the new apply" (2002, pp. 1114–1115). This replacement fallacy is related to the error of *pars pro toto,* in which a partial explanation is taken as an entire explanatory system. In particular, the replacement fallacy arose early in psychoanalytic thinking, when Freud shifted from the seduction theory to posit the role of unconscious fantasy in the etiology of the neuroses (p. 1115). Although Freud vacillated between the theories and ostensibly settled into the belief that both theories applied, his main occupation was with developing theory based on fantasy and childhood sexuality. While invested in the new theoretical paradigm, neither Freud nor his followers published cases illustrating the distinction between fantasy and material reality (Simon, 1992; Good, 1994a).

KARL ABRAHAM AND THE SEDUCTION THEORY

Despite the major theoretical shift in Freud's thinking, in 1907 Karl Abraham (1877–1925) attempted to develop the seduction theory further with two of the first published articles specifically on psychoanalytic aspects of sexual trauma (K. Abraham, 1907a,b). Abraham saw himself as a psychoanalytic pupil and sought Freud's approval for his ideas, which included the notion of a "traumatophilic diathesis," a precursor of Freud's concept of the repetition compulsion. Although Freud appreciated having followers and was generally encouraging of Abraham, his reaction to these 1907 papers was mixed in that he was critical of a number of Abraham's assumptions (H. C. Abraham and Freud, 1965, pp. 1–4; Falzeder, 2002, pp. 1–4; Good, 1995).

Freud wrote to Abraham on July 5, 1907, that the complication of distinguishing real from fantasied sexual trauma and the issue of forgetting and remembering was a chief reason he did not undertake a "conclusive account" or "definitive presentation" of the issue (H. C. Abraham and Freud, 1965, p. 2; Falzeder, 2002, p. 2). What is remarkable, however, is that Freud never did publish clinical material that detailed the issues, and neither did his followers, apart from Abraham's initial, brief attempt in 1907 and Ferenczi's efforts extending into the early 1930s (Ferenczi, 1912, 1919, 1924, 1932a, 1933).

Abraham subsequently did not actively continue his investigations of the seduction theory, except for an unpublished paper entitled "Incest and Incest Phantasies in Neurotic Families: Case Contributions

Concerning Actual Sexual Relations within Neurotic Families and Symptoms of Illness Based on Incest Phantasies." This paper was delivered in Berlin in 1910 and apparently was later lost (Simon, 1992). One might speculate whether the fate of this paper resulted from reactions similar to the adverse reactions to Ferenczi's "Confusion of Tongues" paper delivered in 1932 (discussed below). Thereafter, Abraham loyally advanced Freud's new theory of neurosogenesis (Good, 1995).

Freud had acknowledged that "[p]hantasies of being seduced . . . so often are not phantasies but real memories" (e.g., 1916–1917, p. 370), but he partially exonerated fathers from the real memories when he asserted that "if in the case of girls who produce such an event in the story of their childhood their father figures fairly regularly as the seducer, there can be no doubt either of the imaginary nature of the accusation or of the motive that has led to it" (p. 370). This conclusion he related to the tendency of a child to screen the autoerotic period of sexual activity and to project responsibility by imagining seduction by a desired figure in those earliest times so as to avoid masturbatory shame (p. 370). Regarding fathers, or "male relatives," yet again he noted that "[m]ost analysts will have treated cases in which such events were real and could be unimpeachably established"—but these real cases he believed pertained to later years of childhood that had been transposed into earlier times (p. 370). The time element is a crucial variable in the original seduction hypothesis and is often overlooked in controversy regarding its applicability. Yet, in any event, interesting as Freud's theoretical developments and clarifications regarding the seduction issue might be, detailed clinical cases to bolster his arguments were remarkably lacking.

"SEDUCTION" BY THE MOTHER

By 1905 Freud made it clear that seductive excitation and even neurosis could occur in connection with an infant or child's mothering figure: "A child's intercourse with anyone responsible for his care affords him an unending source of sexual excitation and satisfaction from his erotogenic zones. . . . [A]s a rule his mother, [she] regards him with feelings that are derived from her own sexual life . . . and quite clearly treats him as a substitute for a complete sexual object" (1905, p. 223). Furthermore, "[N]europathic parents, who are inclined as a rule to display excessive affection, are precisely those who are most likely by their caresses to arouse the child's disposition to neurotic illness. Incidentally, this example shows that there are ways more direct than inheritance by which neurotic parents can hand their disorder on to their children" (pp. 223–224).

In another permutation of the seduction theory, in 1931 Freud posited an alternative explanation for seduction fantasies, also rooted in the early mother–child relationship. He reported that "girls regularly accuse their mother of seducing them" (p. 238) because they necessarily received their first or strongest genital sensations while being cleaned and diapered by the mother or mother figure. But later, with the onset of the genital phase and oedipal stage, the girl begins to turn away from the mother and toward the father and in this process makes the father into the sexual seducer. Although an interesting and plausible explanation for certain cases, Freud presented no illustrative case material.

In 1933 he reiterated that the seducer is regularly the mother and that here the fantasy "touches the ground of reality" because of the mother's normal contact with the preoedipal child's genitals (p. 120). In his paper on narcissism (1914), Freud had already introduced the related ground of reality that exists in early object relations and the impact of the nurturing environment on self-esteem. Later these developmental considerations came to be studied further under the headings of object relations theory and self psychology (Izenberg, 1991).

Before the current reinvigorated reconsideration of the seduction theory, Krohn (1978) asserted that hysteria[2] is the outcome of a hysterogenic situation in which incestuous acts, and even fantasies of such acts, are both conspicuously forbidden and unconsciously promoted

---

[2] Although the term *hysteria* has fallen into some disuse nosologically and has gone partially "underground" in clinical discourse, it appears instead in "splintered" form under different names and still retains significance in contemporary psychoanalytic thinking (e.g., Brenman, 1985; Micale, 1995; Bollas, 2000; Borossa, 2001). In fact, the DSM-IV (American Psychiatric Association, 1994) includes such diagnoses as conversion disorder, dissociative disorder, and histrionic personality but simply no longer applies the adjective *hysterical,* as it did up to and including the DSM-III (1980). Likewise, some would view current terms like "PTSD/borderline" (e.g., Kroll, 1993) as deriving directly from persisting questions involving hysteria, trauma, fantasy, and reality.

by the close, sometimes seductive, ties with parents. The conflict resulting from the contradictions in the parents' libidinal behavior is resolved by dissociating the conflicting perceptions of, and reactions to, the parents (p. 134). Among other theories, Laplanche's (1989, 1997) ideas on primal seduction stemming from unconscious communication of the mother's enigmatic sexuality, which I referred to in the Introduction, can again be noted (see also Haynal, 1993, pp. 20–24). In a related manner, Bollas (2000) looked at hysteria not in terms of an echo of Freud and Breuer's innovative studies but again from the perspective of more modern developmental views of early mother–infant relations—in addition to the role of the father. He went on to differentiate the effects of early seduction and sexual abuse, hypothesizing that the original trauma might ironically be a failed seduction in which the mother does not put into words the infant's sexuality expressed through physical displays and movements (analogous to the hysterical attack). Only by resorting to fantasy can the infant then rescue itself from this absence of sensorial confirmation and verbal transformation. Thus, in Bollas's view, the abuse conundrum (did it really happen or is it imagined?) is actually a dual memory: It links a happening that did not occur except in fantasy that was essential to repair the damage of the nonevent (p. 115).

PSYCHIC REALITY AS FANTASY, AND INHERITED MEMORY TRACES AS REALITY

Seeking to address and perhaps unify the theoretical duality involving external and internal realities, Freud (1916–1917) asserted that both ''indisputably false and sometimes equally certainly correct'' analytic constructions or memories of sexual scenes from infancy occur, sometimes combining truth and falsehood. But, he argued, the difference between the etiologic theories did not really matter, that it is ''psychical reality'' which is determinative, and that ''we should equate phantasy and reality and not bother to begin with whether the childhood experiences under examination are the one or the other'' (pp. 367–368). Here Freud was equating psychic reality with the patient's fantasy [and belief influenced by fantasy], even though actuality influences fantasy and is included in how psychic reality is generally understood today (Laplanche and Pontalis, 1967; Arlow, 1969). In this broader view of its determinants, psychic reality can be modified by new experience and by direct or indirect influence of the analyst, which is part and parcel of how the transference is used to facilitate insight and therapeutic progress. As an external reality, even the analytic situation itself can influence the analysand's psychic reality (Oliner, 1996).[3] But in 1917 Freud was attempting to underscore the role of patients' fantasies in contrast to their "low valuation of reality" in the path to symptom formation. He repeated this clarification in 1923: "[I]t became possible to appreciate the extraordinarily large part played in the mental life of neurotics by the activities of *phantasy*, which clearly carried more weight in neurosis than did external reality" (p. 244). With such statements, his authority evidently furthered a group conclusion and belief among many psychoanalysts that reports of seduction were based on *fantasies alone*. Yet what Freud evidently was explaining is that, in the neurotic patient's mind, fantasy dominates over external reality insofar as *both* are elements of psychic reality.

Freud had not yet resolved the problem of external reality in the historical or material sense, an issue he returned to most notably in the case of the Wolf Man (1918) and again in "Constructions in Analysis" (1937). On the one hand, as pointed out by Laplanche and Pontalis (1968), the passionate conviction with which Freud sought to establish the reality of scenes down to their smallest details in the case of the Wolf Man is convincing evidence that "Freud had never entirely resigned himself to considering such scenes as purely imaginary creations" (p. 8). But, on the other hand, regarding whether a scene was "a phantasy or a real experience," Freud demurred: "I must admit that the answer to this question is not in fact a matter of very great importance. These scenes of observing parental intercourse, of being seduced in childhood, and of being threatened with castration are unquestionably an inherited endowment, a phylogenetic heritage, but they may just as easily be acquired by personal experience" (1918, p. 97).

Here Freud gave fantasy *a new kind of reality*, that of an inherited basis as "precipitates from the history of human civilization" (p. 119).

---

[3] On the other hand, impediments to changing psychopathologic aspects of psychic reality require a process of working through during analysis.

He wanted to show that *real occurrences* were at the base of unconscious fantasies (Perron, 2001, p. 589). But if he could not find events in the individual's past to account for the neurosis, he inferred that primal fantasies derived from the history of the human species, the "phylogenetic hypothesis" (Freud, 1987). Although evidence for unconscious fantasies suggested the explanatory need to postulate inherited schemata, his speculative psycho–Lamarckian theory of biological inheritance of experience met with little support. Perhaps another reason for the theory is clearer: Psychologically it displaced incest far back into human prehistory. Seduction was acknowledged, but it was imbued with temporal remoteness. Similarly, Grubrich-Simitis (1988) proposed that Freud's phylogenetic fantasy was an effort to integrate theoretically traumatic etiologic factors into drive theory—a task that still confronts us today. She also observed that Freud had a latent fear that the trauma model might endanger the drive model, and so the phylogenetic fantasy set up a buffer of hundreds of thousands of years (p. 17).

In *Moses and Monotheism*, Freud returned again to this theme of the historically real basis of primal fantasy and the "inheritance of memory-traces" (1939, pp. 98–102). The issue of the interplay of heredity and experience had long been a concern of Freud, but the idea of the inheritance of actual ancestral experience was relatively new. In the *Outline of Psycho-Analysis* (1940) he mentioned both the mother as the child's "first seducer" and how the "phylogenetic foundation" has much the upper hand over personal accidental experience (p. 188).

Regarding what was the patient's actual neurosogenic experience, Freud at times vacillated in his theorizing and at other times was supremely confident. In the absence of relevant memories during analysis, he offered constructions. The patient's direct responses to a construction, he asserted, "afford very little evidence upon the question whether we have been right or wrong" since there are "indirect forms of confirmation which are in every respect trustworthy" (1937, p. 263). While acknowledging that a particular reconstruction could contain both true and false elements, he sanguinely claimed that this posed no problem because it was the "kernel of truth" that made all the difference (1937, pp. 267–269). Yet how the "kernel of truth" can be distinguished from myths comprising the patient's autobiography remains obscure. As Spence (1982) points out, if we have no sure way of identifying historical truth, we are seriously handicapped in our attempt to frame psychoanalytic theories (p. 51).

TRAUMA LINKED WITH NONTRAUMATIC ETIOLOGIES

In 1939 Freud incorporated trauma theory even further into an intrapsychic point of view. He observed that the genesis of a neurosis invariably derives from very early childhood impressions, some of which may be traumatic in the sense of a complemental series that includes constitutional predisposition. Because of the potential quantitative variability of the traumatic factor in causing neurosis and the fact that traumatic factors work in concert with constitutional ones, he stated that we can disregard the distinction between traumatic and nontraumatic etiologies as at times irrelevant (1939, p. 73). As with his assertion in 1916–1917 that the distinction between fantasy and reality is not germane to the question of childhood seduction, now certain traumatic consequences were dovetailed into neurotic "fixations" and the "compulsion to repeat." Thus, a girl who was seduced in early childhood may in later life provoke similar attacks, with implications for our understanding of character formation in general (pp. 75–76). The compulsion to repeat serves to recall the forgotten traumatic experience or to make it real in the present, "even if it was only an early emotional relationship, to revive it in an analogous relationship with someone else" (p. 75). Alternatively, a forgotten trauma may not be repeated but instead cause "avoidances" in the form of "inhibitions" and "phobias" that also powerfully contribute to the stamping of character traits (p. 76).

In these instances, the seduction theory had metamorphosed into a theory of neurotic character formation. Here Freud focused more on what could be observed in the present within the consulting room. Character traits could be witnessed in the here and now. Memory about the past was inherently unreliable. Epistemologically, writing about the psychical apparatus and the external world, he believed that reality ultimately remains "unknowable" (1940, p. 196), even if he felt sure of when his constructions were correct.

THE SEDUCTION THEORY AND
PSYCHOANALYTIC GROUP PROCESSES

While it is beyond the scope of this postscript to describe the various group psychological factors that appear to have been in effect during the shift from the seduction theory to the oedipal theory and beyond, historically many psychoanalysts apparently could identify with Freud regarding the inventive aspects of the new theoretical developments, not only intellectually but also as a way to deal with countertransference feelings involving the seduction theme. These countertransference pressures likely resembled those that Freud had been addressing by means of his creative theoretical insights (Blass and Simon, 1994). Today we refer to these pressures in terms of the potential for boundary violations. Sándor Ferenczi (1873–1933) was a striking counterexample with his boundary experiments in technique, which were worrisome and even alarming to Freud (Hoffer, 1991; Good, 1995). Blum (1994) underscored the dramatic effect on the wider psychoanalytic community of the dispute between Freud and Ferenczi, some analysts fearing that any threat to the status of psychic reality could undermine the psychoanalytic movement itself. Too often problems of loyalty, idealization, authority, dependency, and rivalry clouded scientific pursuits.

FERENCZI'S EMPHASIS ON SEDUCTION AND
TRAUMA

Ferenczi's work on trauma, and especially his impassioned 1933 paper, "Confusion of Tongues between Adults and the Child,"[4] highlighted both technical and theoretical differences and confusions in psychoanalysis. A major difference and confusion concerned the roles of fantasy and trauma in causing neurosis. Ferenczi bemoaned the "unjustly neglected" matter of trauma in the pathogenesis of neuroses, leading to "the danger of resorting prematurely to explanations—often

---

[4] Originally titled "The Passion of Adults and Their Influence on the Sexual and Character Development of Children," the paper was not published in its English version until 1948. For various reasons, there was opposition to Ferenczi's presentation of the paper at the 1932 International Psychoanalytical Association Conference at Wiesbaden and to its later publication (Simon, 1992; Blum, 1994; Rachman, 1997).

too facile explanations—in terms of 'disposition' and 'constitution' "
(p. 225). In this claim, Ferenczi seems to have anticipated Freud's
1939 assertion that the distinction between traumatic and nontraumatic
etiologies be considered irrelevant. There is some irony in Freud's
and Ferenczi's differences, given Freud's struggle against innate disposition in the 1890s in favor of trauma as a cause of hysteria. But the
later question concerned not so much heredity as early developmental
experience, which Freud considered to be on the constitutional side
of the complemental equation.

Ferenczi's "Confusion of Tongues" paper touched upon many
issues germane to psychoanalysis today (Hoffer, 1991; Blum, 1994),
including the real relationship, countertransference, splitting, dissociation, enactment, parameters, intersubjectivity, empathy, and corrective
emotional experience—but unsettled questions regarding the seduction
theory in particular were reactivated. Ferenczi wrote, for example, "I
obtained above all new corroborative evidence for my supposition that
the trauma, especially the sexual trauma, as the pathogenic factor cannot be valued highly enough." In addition, "*It is* [the confidence in
the analyst] *that establishes the contrast between the present and the
unbearable traumatogenic past,* the contrast which is absolutely necessary for the patient in order to enable him to re-experience the past
no longer as hallucinatory reproduction but as an objective memory"
(Ferenczi, 1933, p. 160; 1949, p. 227).

Yet how Ferenczi claimed the memories as objective is question-
able, since he had advocated for suggestively influencing the patient's
recollections and "forcing" fantasies. Regarding patients with few or
no fantasies, Ferenczi (1924) explained, "Supported by the precon-
ceived notion that in these cases such conduct is due to repression of
psychical material and suppression of affect, I now have no hesitation
in forcing the patients to recover the adequate reactions, and if they
still persist in saying that they have no ideas, I commission them to
discover such reactions in phantasy" (p. 70). Ferenczi then illustrated
this method with a "case . . . in which the patient brought me an experience of being seduced (which in all probability really happened), but
with innumerable variations in order at the same time to confuse both
me and herself and to obscure the reality. I had again and again to
constrain her to 'fabricate' such a scene, and thus new details were

established with certainty'' (p. 73). Even when the patient objected, he would not accept her skepticism.

As pointed out by Bacon and Gedo (1993), Ferenczi's patients were unable to gain conviction about putative historical events precisely because such a predominant focus on childhood stood in the way of reexperiencing the relevant transactions in the present. Even though he was ostensibly attentive to the transference–countertransference complex, it appears that screen reconstructions proliferated as a result of his countertransference and suggestive influence (Good, 1998). Regarding suggestive influence, as late as 1932, the same year in which Ferenczi delivered the "Confusion of Tongues" paper, he wrote that "[h]ysteria is regression to the state of complete *lack of will* and to acceptance of another's will as in childhood" (1932a, p. 255) and that "analysis is preparation for suggestion" (1932b, p. 270). "The truth," Ferenczi asserted, "cannot be discovered quite spontaneously, it must be 'insinuated', 'suggested,' '' a method he considered necessary in order to help the patient "to acquire convictions" (1932b, p. 269; Good, 1996, 1998). His description caricatures Freud's (1937, pp. 265–266) arguable view about producing conviction in the absence of actual memory. Just as Freud's theoretical elaborations regarding the seduction issue following 1897 suffer from a lack of clinical illustrations, so Ferenczi's writings on the topic point to technical errors predestined to reconstruct sexual abuse, whether or not it had actually occurred.

THE SEDUCTION THEORY AS A "DEVELOPMENTAL STAGE" IN THEORIZATION

Following the death of Abraham and then Ferenczi, controversy regarding unresolved issues in the seduction theory was virtually nonexistent for almost half a century. Group processes working against attention to the seduction theory are reflected in Anna Freud's statement in a letter to Masson on September 10, 1981: "Keeping up the seduction theory would mean to abandon the Oedipus complex, and with it the whole importance of phantasy life, conscious or unconscious phantasy. In fact, I think there would have been no psychoanalysis afterwards" (Masson, 1984, p. 113).

Even so, Anna Freud, in her work with children, and like her father, certainly acknowledged the occurrence of incest. We might ask why there could not have been further scientific study of the seduction theory without sacrificing the intrapsychic point of view—unless study of the seduction theory was tantamount to a developmental regression. As with the shift from oedipal to latency stages, the seduction theory (Freud's "error") became taboo. Just as his initial conflict about the seduction theory related in part to personal oedipal conflicts, so the "renunciation" of it had to do not only with a scientific reevaluation of data but also from a working through and "dissolution" of oedipal residuals in his own makeup by means of cognitive advances (Mahon, 1991).

Thus, from a developmental perspective, Freud moved on from the problematic idea of seduction as *the* cause of neurosis to a theory of fantasy that *represented* incest. *Impulses* were transformed by intellectual means into a *theory* of oedipal fantasy. Although seduction as a theoretical construct was not "repressed" entirely, as in latency there was a shift from it to a theoretical emphasis on psychic reality (Good, 1995). Following this "latency" of the seduction theory, the current resurgence of interest in it can be seen as an "adolescent" phase in its theoretical development. As with adolescent development and the coming to grips with external reality, psychoanalysis has yet to develop a more complete theory integrating internal with external reality (Oliner, 1996; Fonagy and Target, 2003). To do so is a current developmental task.

SEDUCTION FANTASY VERSUS REALITY IN THEORIZATION: THE NEED FOR SPECIMEN CLINICAL CASE STUDIES

A widespread version of the seduction theory and its revision are based on Freud's wording in 1933:

> In the period in which the main interest was directed to discovering infantile sexual traumas, almost all my women patients told me that they had been seduced by their father. I was driven to recognize in the end that these reports were untrue and so came to understand that hysterical symptoms are derived from phantasies and not from real occurrences [p. 120].

Freud's statement appears to indicate that he had to change his initial seduction hypothesis because he became aware that he had been misled by patients presenting fantasies as true memories. Schimek, however, clarified that what Freud rejected was not necessarily patients' reports of incest and seduction but rather his *reconstruction* of fragments of the patient's memories that he initially inferred to indicate an earlier seduction. If so, this clarification could help explain why Freud did not publish cases in which a patient's memory of an early seduction could be shown to be a fantasy or screen memory that was untrue. If he subsequently considered reconstructions he had made to be erroneous, he probably would have been disinclined to detail them in writing early in the development of psychoanalysis. Even so, given his interest in screen memories (1899), it is surprising that he did not describe specific cases in which he considered explicit reports of early seduction to represent screen phenomena.

In a panel on the seduction hypothesis (Furman and Marans, 1988) (originally with the fuller title, "The Seduction Hypothesis: The Interaction between Psychic Reality and Objective Reality"), Wallerstein addressed the question whether it really matters how certain we can be around questions of historical fact. He answered by noting: "[M]uch of life is built around distinguishing the thought from the deed. One perspective within which we can conceptualize the essence of the psychoanalytic enterprise is in its insistent dedication to the constant elucidation between fantasy and reality" (p. 768).

In general, however, case-specific reconstructions in the psychoanalytic literature have given sparse attention to the issues of whether an event was "real or fantasied, actual or plausible, specific or generic, a past reaction or a current derivative" (Wetzler, 1985, p. 194). In terms of the seduction question, attention to such issues has come largely from critiques of published cases (e.g., Klumpner and Frank, 1991; Spence, 1994; Good, 1992, 1996, 1998, 1999; Brenneis, 1997, 2000).

While warning of the perils of relying on coherence alone, Spence (1994) also noted the difficulties of deconstructing patients' composites of real and make-believe regarding figures in their psychic reality. He pessimistically claimed that "the truth of the stories about these figures can never be checked against the outside world." Yet he then immediately tempered this assertion slightly but still claimed, "Hence, it seems pointless to rely on a correspondence theory when there is often nothing to check against, nothing for the clinical material to correspond to" (p. 71). However, "never anything" and "often nothing" are not equivalent. If psychoanalysis is open to the serendipitous occurrence of cases that might clarify fantasy and reality through external data as they apply to the seduction theory, a series of specimen cases might come to light.

There can be instances in which elucidating the distinction between fantasy and historical fact ultimately requires comparison of intra-analytic and extra-analytic historical data (when available), provided that doing so furthers (at least does not hinder) analytic process (Shevrin, 1995, p. 972; Good, 1998; Good, Day, and Rowell, 1999). Psychoanalytic truth requires not only coherent narrative but ideally also includes correspondence to actuality, such as whether a reconstruction parallels historical facts insofar as such facts might be determined (Hanly, 1990). Expressed in terms of the tally argument, coherence alone is bolstered by methods that assess correctness of interpretations or reconstructions independent of treatment outcome. As Spence (1987) put the issue, if clinical arguments remain at a metaphorical or narrative level, no proposition will ever be disconfirmed because metaphors are not falsifiable. Moreover, if the data supporting a theory are not available for public scrutiny and discussion, there is no opportunity for clarification and elaboration of theory analogous to what happens with the gradual process of refining principles in legal case law. Although I concur with Spence's call for a series of specimen cases to illustrate (or falsify) psychoanalytic arguments, as well as his view (1987, pp. 179–188) that parallels exist between psychoanalysis and law, I do not agree that legal metaphors are necessarily *more* apt than natural science analogies in psychoanalysis. Yet it is ironic that more cases involving the question of seduction have been detailed in court proceedings than in published clinical cases (see also Strenger's [1991] view of psychoanalysis as situated between hermeneutics and science). In terms of the seduction theory, it is entirely possible that *both* scientific principles *and* a series of cases open to public scrutiny will provide a means of testing the seduction theory in a range of clinical circumstances. While psychoanalysis and its tenets as a whole have become so broad and complex as to be difficult to test, a return to examining the crucial hypothesis of psychoanalysis at its origin appears not only to be possible but also could clarify the nature of its foundation.

So far, the investigation of cases with question of seduction remains a largely untapped portal by which to clarify the roles of fantasy and external reality. Brenneis (1997, 2000) surveyed reports of recovered memories in which there is either authentication or inadequate corroboration. Altogether, the authenticated cases (e.g., Schooler, Bendiksen, and Ambadar, 1997) are remarkably limited in number, usually involved traumatic experiences from middle childhood and beyond, and tended to be nonclinical cases differing in context and content from what is reported in the clinical literature.

There are even fewer cases in which recollection or belief regarding early sexual trauma can be verified not to have happened (Good, 1994a). To establish that an event did not happen may be more difficult than to demonstrate that it did; however, at times it is possible to confirm that certain events could not have occurred as remembered. Extraclinical information may lead to surprises in our understanding of an analytic case. Yet it does not mean that we must forego considering the meaning of outside information for the treatment process nor fail to analyze the intrapsychic significance of having obtained it. Patients who eventually seek out extra-analytic data do not necessarily do so as a resistance but rather to address fundamental questions about fantasy and reality. At times the analyst may be inclined to focus on understanding the meaning of the enactment at the expense of considering the information or insights that might be gleaned from the actual material uncovered (Castelnuovo-Tedesco, 1997, p. 662). Indeed, it is the meaning of actuality, if actuality is determinable, that is often pivotal (Galatzer-Levy, 1994). Yet even when extra-clinical data are available to the treater, they may not be stated in any detail in published clinical cases (e.g., Sinason, 1997; Fonagy and Target, 2003). The reader is left either to accept the author's conclusion or to wonder (Klumpner and Frank, 1991). In contrast, Spence (1986) has advocated for "clinical reporting that would allow the reader to participate in the argument, allow him to evaluate the proposed links between evidence and conclusion (instead of relying on the authority of the analyst-author), and open up the clinical report to the possibilities of refutation, disconfirmation, and falsification" (p. 3). Only then can the seduction theory be clarified and our theories revised (Lehmann, 2003).

In brief, we need a body of published clinical material (a series of specimen cases) on the question of early seduction, with ample intra-analytic and extra-analytic detail for readers to draw their own conclusions. Perhaps in this manner, over time, the original seduction hypothesis can be tested and integrated with the rest of the body of psychoanalytic theory.

REFERENCES

Abraham, H. C., & Freud, E. L. (1965), *A Psychoanalytic Dialogue: The Letters of Sigmund Freud and Karl Abraham, 1907–1926.* New York: Basic Books.

Abraham, K. (1907a), On the significance of sexual trauma in childhood for the symptomatology of dementia praecox. In: *Clinical Papers and Essays on Psycho-Analysis.* New York: Basic Books, 1955, pp. 13–20.

———(1907b), The experiencing of sexual traumas as a form of sexual activity. In: *Selected Papers of Karl Abraham.* New York: Brunner/Mazel, 1979, pp. 47–63.

American Psychiatric Association (1980), *Diagnostic and Statistical Manual of Mental Disorders,* 3rd ed. (DSM-III). Washington, DC: American Psychiatric Press.

———(1994), *Diagnostic and Statistical Manual of Mental Disorders,* 4th ed. (DSM-IV). Washington, DC: American Psychiatric Press.

Arlow, J. A. (1969), Fantasy, memory, and reality testing. *Psychoanal. Quart.,* 38:28–51.

Bacon, K., & Gedo, J. E. (1993), Ferenczi's contributions to psychoanalysis: Essays in dialogue. In: *The Legacy of Sándor Ferenczi,* ed. L. Aron & A. Harris. Hillsdale, NJ: Analytic Press, pp. 121–139.

Blass, R. B., & Simon, B. (1994), The value of the historical perspective to contemporary psychoanalysis: Freud's 'seduction hypothesis.' *Internat. J. Psycho-Anal.,* 75:677–694.

Blum, H. P. (1994), The confusion of tongues and psychic trauma. *Internat. J. Psycho-Anal.,* 75:871–882.

———(2003a), Repression, transference and reconstruction. *Internat. J. Psycho-Anal.,* 84:497–503.

—————— (2003b), Response to Peter Fonagy. *Internat. J. Psycho-Anal.,* 84:509–513.

Bollas, C. (2000), *Hysteria.* London: Routledge.

Borossa, J. (2001), *Hysteria.* Cambridge, U.K.: Icon Books.

Brenman, E. (1985), Hysteria. *Internat. J. Psycho-Anal.,* 66:423–432.

Brenneis, C. B. (1997), *Recovered Memories of Trauma: Transferring the Present to the Past.* Madison, CT: International Universities Press.

—————— (2000), Evaluating the evidence: Can we find authenticated recovered memory? *Psychoanal. Psychother.,* 17:61–77.

Castelnuovo-Tedesco, P. (1997), Photographs, reconstructions, and the psychoanalytic task: A clinical note. *J. Amer. Acad. Psychoanal.,* 24:661–673.

Edelson, M. (1984), *Hypothesis and Evidence in Psychoanalysis.* Chicago: University of Chicago Press.

Falzeder, E., Ed. (2002), *The Complete Correspondence of Sigmund Freud and Karl Abraham: 1907–1925. Completed Edition.* London: Karnac.

Ferenczi, S. (1912), Suggestion and psycho-analysis. In: *Further Contributions to the Theory and Technique of Psycho-Analysis.* London: Hogarth Press, 1950, pp. 55–68.

—————— (1919), On influencing of the patient in psycho-analysis. In: *Further Contributions to the Theory and Technique of Psycho-Analysis.* London: Hogarth Press, 1950, pp. 235–237.

—————— (1924), On forced phantasies: Activity in the association-technique. In: *Further Contributions to the Theory and Technique of Psycho-Analysis.* London: Hogarth Press, 1950, pp. 68–77.

—————— (1932a), Notes and fragments. Suggestion=action without one's own will. In: *Final Contributions to the Problems & Methods of Psycho-Analysis,* ed. M. Balint. New York: Basic Books, 1955, pp. 254–255.

—————— (1932b), Notes and fragments. Suggestion in (after) analysis. In: *Final Contributions to the Problems & Methods of Psycho-Analysis,* ed. M. Balint. New York: Basic Books, 1955, pp. 269–270.

—————— (1933), Confusion of tongues between adults and the child: The language of tenderness and of passion. In: *Final Contributions to the Problems & Methods of Psycho-Analysis,* ed. M. Balint. New York: Basic Books, 1955, pp. 156–167.

—————— (1949), Confusion of tongues between the adult and the child—(The language of tenderness and of passion). *Internat. J. Psycho-Anal.,* 30:225–230.

Fonagy, P. (2003a), Genetics, developmental psychopathology, and psychoanalytic theory: The case for ending our (not so) splendid isolation. *Psychoanal. Inq.,* 23:218–247.

—— (2003b), Rejoinder to Harold Blum. *Internat. J. Psycho-Anal.,* 84:503–509.

—— Target, M. (2003), A psychoanalytic theory of external reality. Paper presented at the Boston Psychoanalytic Society and Institute, February.

Freud, S. (1899), Screen memories. *Standard Edition,* 3:299–322. London: Hogarth Press, 1962.

—— (1905), Three Essays on the Theory of Sexuality. *Standard Edition,* 7:123–243. London: Hogarth Press, 1953.

—— (1906), My views on the part played by sexuality in the aetiology of the neuroses. *Standard Edition,* 7:269–279. London: Hogarth Press, 1953.

—— (1914), On narcissism: An introduction. *Standard Edition,* 14:67–102. London: Hogarth Press, 1957.

—— (1916–1917), Introductory Lectures on Psycho-Analysis. *Standard Edition,* 16:241–496. London: Hogarth Press, 1961.

—— (1918), From the history of an infantile neurosis. *Standard Edition,* 17:1–122. London: Hogarth Press, 1955.

—— (1923), Two encyclopedia articles. *Standard Edition,* 18:235–259. London: Hogarth Press, 1955.

—— (1933), New Introductory Lectures on Psycho-Analysis. *Standard Edition,* 22:1–182. London: Hogarth Press, 1964.

—— (1937), Constructions in analysis. *Standard Edition,* 23:255–269. London: Hogarth Press, 1964.

—— (1939), Moses and Monotheism: Three Essays. *Standard Edition,* 23:1–137. London: Hogarth Press, 1964.

—— (1940), An Outline of Psycho-Analysis. *Standard Edition,* 23:139–207. London: Hogarth Press, 1964.

—— (1987), *A Phylogenetic Fantasy: Overview of the Transference Neuroses,* ed. I. Grubrich-Simitis; tr. A. Hoffer & P. T. Hoffer. Cambridge, MA: Belknap Press of Harvard University Press.

Furman, R. A., & Marans, A. E. (1988), The seduction hypothesis. *J. Amer. Psychoanal. Assn.,* 36:759–771.

Galatzer-Levy, R. M. (1994), Children, bad happenings, and meanings. *J. Amer. Psychoanal. Assn.,* 42:997–1000.

Gedo, J. (1999), *The Evolution of Psychoanalysis: Contemporary Theory and Practice.* New York: Other Press.

Good, M. I. (1992), Witnessing pornography and the reconstruction of suspected child sexual molestation [letter]. *J. Amer. Psychoanal. Assn.,* 40:630–633.

—— (1994a), The reconstruction of early childhood trauma: Fantasy, reality, and verification. *J. Amer. Psychoanal. Assn.,* 42:79–101.

—— (1994b), Differential constructions of trauma in cases of suspected child sexual molestation. *The Psychoanalytic Study of the Child,* 49:434–464. New Haven, CT: Yale University Press.

—— (1995), Karl Abraham, Sigmund Freud, and the fate of the seduction theory. *J. Amer. Psychoanal. Assn.,* 48:1137–1167.

—— (1996), Suggestion and veridicality in the reconstruction of sexual trauma, or can a bait of suggestion catch a carp of falsehood? *J. Amer. Psychoanal. Assn.,* 44:1189–1224.

—— (1998), Screen reconstructions: Traumatic memory, conviction, and the problem of verification. *J. Amer. Psychoanal. Assn.,* 46:149–183.

—— (1999), Book review of *Recovered Memories of Abuse: True or False,* ed. J. Sandler & P. Fonagy. *J. Amer. Psychoanal. Assn.,* 47:237–240.

—— Day, M., & Rowell, E. (1999), False memories, negative affects, and psychic reality: The role of extra-clinical data in psychoanalysis. Paper presented at the 41st Congress of the International Psychoanalytical Association, Santiago, Chile, July 27.

Grubrich-Simitis, I. (1988), Trauma or drive—drive and trauma: A reading of Sigmund Freud's phylogenetic fantasy of 1915. In: *The Psychoanalytic Study of the Child,* 43:3–32. Hew Haven, CT: Yale University Press.

Grünbaum, A. (1984), *The Foundations of Psychoanalysis: A Philosophical Critique.* Berkeley: University of California Press.

Hanly, C. (1990), The concept of truth in psychoanalysis. *Internat. Rev. Psychoanal.,* 71:375–383.

Haynal, A. (1993), *Psychoanalysis and the Sciences: Epistemology—History,* tr. E. Holder. Berkeley: University of California Press.

Hoffer, A. (1991), The Freud–Ferenczi controversy—a living legacy. *Internat. Rev. Psychoanal.,* 18:465–472.

Izenberg, G. N. (1991), Seduced and abandoned: The rise and fall of Freud's seduction theory. In: *The Cambridge Companion to Freud,* ed. J. Neu. Cambridge, U.K.: Cambridge University Press, pp. 25–43.

Klumpner, G. H., & Frank, A. (1991), On methods of reporting clinical material. *J. Amer. Psychoanal. Assn.,* 39:537–551.

Krohn, A. (1978), Hysteria: The Elusive Neurosis. *Psychological Issues,* Monogr. 45/46. New York: International Universities Press.

Kroll, J. (1993), *PTSD/Borderlines in Therapy: Finding the Balance.* New York: W. W. Norton.

Kuhn, T. S. (1962), *The Structure of Scientific Revolutions.* Chicago: University of Chicago Press.

Laplanche, J. (1989), *New Foundations for Psychoanalysis.* Cambridge, MA: Basil Blackwell.

────── (1997), The theory of seduction and the problem of the other. *Internat. J. Psycho-Anal.,* 78:653–666.

────── Pontalis, J.-B. (1967), *The Language of Psycho-Analysis.* New York: W. W. Norton, 1973.

────── ────── (1968), Fantasy and the origins of sexuality. *Internat. J. Psycho-Anal.,* 49:1–18.

Lehmann, C. (2003), False sex abuse accusations lead to revision of theories. *Psychiatric News,* 38 (June 20), p. 14.

Makari, G. J. (2000), Change in psychoanalysis: Science, practice, and the sociology of knowledge. In: *Changing Ideas in a Changing World: The Revolution in Psychoanalysis, Essays in Honour of Arnold Cooper,* ed. J. Sandler, R. Michels, & P. Fonagy. London: Karnac, pp. 255–262.

Mahon, E. J. (1991). The ''dissolution'' of the Oedipus complex: A neglected cognitive factor. *Psychoanal. Quart.,* 60:628–634.

Masson, J. M. (1984), *The Assault on Truth: Freud's Suppression of the Seduction Theory.* New York: Farrar, Straus, and Giroux.

Micale, M. (1995), *Approaching Hysteria: Disease and Its Interpretation.* Princeton, NJ: Princeton University Press.

Oliner, M. M. (1996), External reality: The elusive dimension of psychoanalysis. *Psychoanal. Quart.,* 65:267–300.

Perron, R. (2001), The unconscious and primal phantasies. *Internat. J. Psycho-Anal.* 82:583–596.

Polányi, M. (1974), Scientific Thought and Social Reality. *Psychological Issues,* Monograph 32, ed. F. Schwartz. New York: International Universities Press.

Rachman, A. W. (1997), The suppression and censorship of Ferenczi's Confusion of Tongues paper. *Psychoanal. Inq.,* 17:459–485.

Rangell, L. (2002), The theory of psychoanalysis: Vicissitudes of its evolution. *J. Amer. Psychoanal. Assn.,* 50:1109–1137.

Rubinstein, B. B. (1980), The problem of confirmation in clinical psychoanalysis. *J. Amer. Psychoanal. Assn.,* 28:397–417.

Schooler, J. W., Bendiksen, M., & Ambadar, Z. (1997), Can we accommodate both fabricated and recovered memories of sexual abuse? In: *Recovered Memories and False Memories,* ed. M. Conway. Oxford: Oxford University Press, pp. 251–292.

Shevrin, H. (1995), Is psychoanalysis one science, two sciences, or no science at all? A discourse among friendly antagonists. *J. Amer. Psychoanal. Assn.,* 43:963–986.

Simon, B. (1992), ''Incest—see under oedipus complex'': The history of an error in psychoanalysis. *J. Amer. Psychoanal. Assn.,,* 40:955–988.

Sinason, V. (1997), Remembering in therapy. In: *Recovered Memories of Abuse: True or False?* ed. J. Sandler & P. Fonagy. Madison, CT: International Universities Press, pp. 81–99.

Spence, D. P. (1982), Narrative truth and theoretical truth. *Psychoanal. Quart.,* 51:43–69.

———— (1986), When interpretation masquerades as explanation. *J. Amer. Psychoanal. Assn.,* 34:3–22.

———— (1987), *The Freudian Metaphor: Toward Paradigm Change in Psychoanalysis.* New York: W. W. Norton.

———— (1994), *The Rhetorical Voice of Psychoanalysis: Displacement of Evidence by Theory.* Cambridge, MA: Harvard University Press.

Strenger, C. (1991), *Between Hermeneutics and Science: An Essay on the Epistemology of Psychoanalysis.* Madison, CT: International Universities Press.

Wetzler, S. (1985), The historical truth of psychoanalytic reconstructions. *Internat. Rev. Psychoanal.,* 12:187–197.

Name Index

Abraham, H., 60, 284, 298
Abraham, K., 5, 32, 54, 56n, 284, 285, 293, 298
Adler, A., ix, 57, 58, 264
Agrippa, H., 9
Aichorn, A., 137, 138
Ambadar, Z., 297, 302
Andersson, O., 4, 30, 33
Andreas–Salomé, L., ix
Anthony, E., 160, 171
Appelbaum, A., 210, 211
Aretaeus, 7
Aristotle, 27, 30
Arlow, J., xi, xvii, 90, 94, 95, 101, 104, 105, 111, 117–127, 167, 171, 175, 179, 181, 186, 188, 237, 248, 254, 256, 260, 263, 264, 267, 273, 274, 275, 276, 287, 298
Armstrong, K., 5, 33
Arnold, M., 51
Auden, W., 218, 225
Ayer, J., 259, 260

Bach, S., 251, 260
Bacon, K., 293, 298
Baginsky, A., 13, 24, 49
Bailly, J., 11
Barnes, J., 30, 33
Barron, J., 13, 33
Bauer, I., 55
Beard, G., 25, 33
Beharriell, F., 23, 33
Bendiksen, M., 297, 302
Benedikt, M., 13–14, 17, 26
Beres, D., 121, 127
Bergman, I., 118
Bernays, M., 5
Bernheim, H., 11–12
Bettelheim, B., 22, 33
Binet, A., 50, 60
Bion, W., 234
Bird, B., 255, 260
Black, M., xx
Blass, R., 3, 26, 27, 30, 33, 54, 55, 57, 60, 291, 298

Blechner, M., 71n
Bloom, H., 86, 95
Blum, A., 137, 139
Blum, H., 5, 31, 33, 120, 127, 283, 291, 292, 298
Boer, D., 46, 63
Bollas, C., 286n, 287, 299
Bonaparte, M., 87, 91, 95
Bond, D., 135, 136, 138
Bonner, T., 49, 60
Bonomi, C., 19, 24, 33, 49, 60
Borossa, J., 286n, 299
Bose, J., 71n
Brenman, E., 286n, 299
Brenneis, C., 282, 295, 297, 299
Brenner, C., 121, 127, 254, 260
Brentano, F., 27
Breuer, J., 7, 12–13, 16, 17, 19, 20, 21, 22, 25, 27, 33, 47, 60, 66, 67, 69, 72, 75, 103, 108, 119, 127, 287
Briquet, P., 6, 15, 17, 33
Bromberg, P., 228, 229, 235
Brouardel, P., 24
Bynum, W., 48n, 60

Carr, A., 210, 211
Carter, K., 25, 33, 48, 49, 60
Castelnuovo–Tedesco, P., 297, 299
Chagall, M., xv
Charcot, J., 7, 8, 11, 13, 14, 15, 16, 17, 18, 19, 21, 23, 24, 26, 31, 33, 47, 61
Chertok, L., 13, 34
Cohen, A., 27, 34
Collyer, brothers, 43
Cooper, A., x, xi, xii, xvii, 111, 115, 137, 182, 183, 186, 187, 188, 268
Copi, I., 30, 34
Crabtree, A., 9, 11, 34
Crocq, L., 15, 34

da Vinci, L., 65, 74
Dallemagne, J., 26
Darnton, R., 9–10, 34

Darwin, C., 27
Day, M., xix, 296, 301
de Chastenet, A., see de Puységur, M.
de Lavoisier, A., 11
de Puységur, M., 10, 15
Debreyne, Father, 25
Deleuze, J., 11
Descartes, R., 7, 20, 34
DeVerbizier, J., 15, 34
Dowling, S., xi, xvii, 111, 129–139, 175, 176, 180, 181, 182, 183, 188, 248, 254, 256, 268, 270
Drinka, G., 7, 8, 15, 16, 23, 34
Dupanloup, Bishop, 25
Dupont, J., 231, 235

Edelheit, H., 121, 127
Edelson, M., 281, 282, 283, 299
Eisold, K., 153, 156
Eissler, K., 7, 14, 19, 24, 25, 26, 29, 30, 34, 46, 53, 61
Ellenberger, H., 4, 6, 8, 9, 10–11, 12, 14, 15–16, 17, 21, 23, 25, 26, 34
Ellman, C., xii
Ellman, S., xi, xviii, 243, 245–262
Esman, A., 120, 127
Esquirol, J., 24
Esterson, A., 29n, 34

Fairbairn, W., 228, 235
Falzeder, E., 284, 299
Fenichel, O., 121, 127
Féré, C., 26, 35
Ferenczi, S., 156, 231, 232, 284, 285, 291, 292, 293, 299
Fine, R., 4, 5, 35
Fiscalini, J., 152, 156
Fliess, W., 3, 7, 16, 20, 25, 29, 30, 45, 47, 48, 50, 51, 53, 56, 58, 72, 79, 80, 87, 91, 92, 94, 107, 118, 119
Fonagy, P., xi, xv, xviii, 191, 194, 195, 196, 199–211, 215, 220, 227, 229, 231, 232, 233, 234, 237, 238, 239, 247, 248, 249, 250–251, 252,

271, 276, 277, 281, 283, 294, 297, 299
Forbes, M., 99
Foulcault, M., 23, 35
Frampton, M., 27n, 35
Frank, A., 295, 297, 301
Franklin, Benjamin, 11
Freedman, N., 249, 260
Freud, A., 114, 115, 137, 138, 160, 163n, 171, 172, 293, 294
Friedman, L., xii, 1
Friel, B., 235
Fromm, E., ix–x
Furman, R., 295, 300

Gabbard, G., xi, xii, xviii, 191, 227–236, 238, 239, 277
Galatzer–Levy, R., 297, 300
Galen, C., 6, 7
Garcia, E., 27, 36
Gardiner, M., 137, 139
Gattel, F., 29, 36, 52, 55, 62
Gauld, A., 16, 36
Gay, P., 5, 24, 31, 36, 53, 62, 245n, 246n, 261
Gedo, J., 281, 293, 298, 300
Gelfand, T., 4, 36
Geyskens, T., 4, 28, 36
Gill, M., 94, 95
Gilman, S., 18, 37, 47, 62
Ginsberg, A., 214
Ginsburg, L., 5, 6, 37
Ginsburg, S., 5, 6, 37
Good, M.I., xiii–xvi, xviii, 3–40, 10, 29, 30, 37, 281–303
Greenacre, P., 157, 158, 172, 193, 194, 195, 197
Greenberg, J., x, xi, xii, xv, xix, xx, 43, 65–75, 77, 78, 79, 81, 82, 86, 87, 88, 89, 90, 91, 94, 97, 98, 99, 101, 102, 104, 105, 246, 265, 275, 276
Greenson, R., 224
Grossman, W., 215, 225
Grubrich–Simitis, I., 289, 301

Grünbaum, A., 281, 301
Guillotin, J., 11

Hacker, F., 5, 37
Hale, N., ix–x, xii
Hanly, C., 296, 301
Hansen, "The Magnetist", 12
Havens, L., 18, 37
Haynal, A., 287, 301
Healy, D., 47, 62
Heidegger, M., 229
Herbart, J., 21, 27
Hippocrates, 6
Hoffer, A., 291, 292, 301
Hoffman, L., xi, xii, xix, 191, 238, 239
Horney, K., ix–x, xi, 156
Horwitz, L., 234, 235
Hughes, C., 48, 62

Imber, R., xii
Isräels, H., 46, 62
Izenberg, G., 46, 62, 286, 301

Janet, P., 7, 8, 14, 16, 17, 18, 21, 22, 37, 66
Jones, E., 4, 21, 22, 31, 37, 45, 56, 59, 62
Jung, C., 5, 57, 58, 230, 264, 282n

Kardiner, A., 112, 116
Kennedy, J. F., 215
Kernberg, O., 210, 211
Kerr, J., 4, 36, 58, 62
Khan, M., 265, 278
Kierkegaard, S., 276
Killingmo, B., 232, 236
King, H., 6, 37
Kirshner, L., 232, 236
Klar, H., 131, 139
Klein, M., 91, 206, 233, 268
Klumpner, G., 295, 297, 301
Koenigsberg, H., 210, 211
Kohut, H., 114, 115, 116, 162, 163, 171, 172, 177, 255, 261, 274, 278
Krafft–Ebing, R. von, 23, 37, 48, 49, 50, 51, 52, 62, 86

Kris, E., 3, 27n, 37–38, 45, 62, 87, 90, 96, 160, 161, 172, 185
Krohn, A., 286, 301
Kroll, J., 286n, 301
Kronold, E., 255
Kuhn, T., 281, 301

Lamarck, J., 265, 289
Laplanche, J., 4, 26, 32, 37–38, 73, 74, 75, 81, 105, 116, 287, 288, 301
Laskin, M., xii
Laufer, M., 137, 139
Laurence, J., 7, 39
Leach, E., 5, 38
Lehmann, C., 298, 302
Lehmann, H., 6, 38
Lepois, C., 7
Lesky, E., 14, 38
Levi, P., xv, 218, 225
Levin, K., 4, 7, 14, 17, 23, 38
Levinson, L., xii
Levinson, N., xii
Lévi–Strauss, C., 5
Liébault, A., 13
Lindner, G., 21
Linehan, M., 209, 211
Lionells, M., xi, xii, xix, 111, 141–156, 176, 177, 178, 180, 183, 184, 187, 248, 254, 259, 258, 276
Loewald, H., 232, 236, 256, 261, 278
Lombard, A., 11
López Piñero, J., 7, 38
Louis, XVI (King), 11
Löwenfeld, L., 49, 56n, 57, 62

Macmillan, M., 18, 25, 29n, 38
Magnan, V., 23
Mahon, E., 294, 302
Makari, G., xi, xii, xv, xix, 25, 28, 38, 43, 45–63, 77, 78, 79, 80, 82, 86, 87, 89, 90, 91, 92, 93, 96, 97, 98, 100, 101, 103, 104, 105, 106, 107, 258, 259, 260, 264, 265, 271, 272, 281, 302

Mandl, E., 17, 38
Mann, C., 152, 156
Marans, A., 295, 300
Masson, J., 3–4, 16, 20, 23, 24, 25, 26, 28, 29, 31, 38, 46, 47, 48, 49, 50, 51, 52, 53, 54, 59, 63, 71, 72, 75, 78, 79, 87, 96, 98, 118, 119, 127, 245, 246n, 261, 293, 302
May, U., 4, 28, 29, 38
Mayer, F., 137, 139
McDermott, W., xx
McDonald, M., 137, 139
McFarlane, A., 15, 39
McGrath, W., 5, 18, 38
McGuire, W., 5, 38, 230, 236, 282n
McLaughlin, J., xv, 220, 221, 222, 223, 225, 253
Meers, D., 137, 139
Meissner, W.W., xiv, xvi
Mesmer, F., 8, 9, 10, 11
Meyers, H., xi, xix, 43, 77, 98, 99, 100, 101, 102, 104, 105, 107
Meynert, T., 12
Micale, M., 14, 38, 286n, 302
Michels, R., xi, xx, 111, 173, 181, 183, 184, 185, 187, 258, 265, 271, 272, 273
Mill, J.S., 21
Miller, J.A., 38
Milton, John, 5, 224
Mitchell, S., xi, xx, 152, 156, 263–278
Moll, A., 29, 39
Moran, G., 210, 211
Mosher, P.W., x, xii
Moskowitz, M., 247n, 253, 254, 259, 260
Muroff, M., 13, 39

O' Shaugnessy, E., 249, 261
Oliner, M., 283, 288, 294, 302
Oppenheim, H., 13, 16
Ornstein, A., xi, xx, 111, 121, 127, 157–172, 176, 177–178, 179, 180, 184, 185, 186, 188, 248, 254, 255, 256, 258, 268, 270

Ornstein, P., 255, 256, 261

Pacella, B., xix
Pacernick, G., 215, 225
Perron, R., 289, 302
Perry, C., 7, 39
Person, E., 131, 139, 254, 256, 257, 261
Pfeiffer, E., ix, xii
Phillips, A., 223, 225
Piso, C., 7
Plato, 22, 129
Polányi, M., 281, 302
Pontalis, J., 4, 26, 38, 287, 288, 302
Powell, R., 46, 63

Rachman, A., 291n, 302
Radó, S., xi
Ramzy, I., 21, 22, 27n, 29, 39
Rand, N., 54n, 63
Rangell, L., 283, 302
Redl, F., 137, 139
Renik, O., x, xi, xii, xxi, 43–44, 97, 100,
    101, 102, 103, 104, 105, 106,
    107, 108
Richards, A., ix–xii, xiii, xv, xxi
Richer, P., 16
Richet, C., 15
Rieff, P., 58, 63
Ritvo, L., 27, 39
Robinson, M., 229, 236,
Rosen, I., 231, 236
Rosenbaum, M., 13, 39
Rosenthal, R., xv
Rothstein, A., xi, xii, xiii, xxi, 116, 159,
    172, 243, 248
Rowell, E., xix, 296, 301
Rubinstein, B., 282, 302

Sacerdoti, C., xix
Sand, R., 21, 39
Santayana, G., 43
Schachter, J., xii
Schafer, R., 126, 127, 172
Schatzman, M., 46, 62

Schimek, J., 50, 63, 295
Schlessinger, N., 13, 39
Schnitzler, A., 23
Schooler, J., 297, 302
Schopenhauer, A., 8
Schrenck–Notzing, A. von, 50, 63
Schröter, M., 53, 63
Seltzer, M., 210, 211
Shakespeare, W., 85, 86, 94, 96
Shapiro, R., 154, 156
Shengold, L., xi, xv–xvi, xxi, 5, 39, 191,
    194, 195, 196, 213–225, 227, 228,
    230, 233, 237, 238, 240, 247, 248,
    249, 252–253, 261
Shevrin, H., 296, 302
Simon, B., 3, 26, 27, 29, 30, 33, 39, 54n,
    55, 57, 60, 284, 285, 291, 298,
    302
Sinason, V., 297, 303
Smith, Harry, xi, 97, 98, 99, 101, 104,
    258, 259, 260
Smith, Henry, xii, xxi, 43, 59n, 85–95,
    101, 104, 105, 107, 267
Socrates, 105
Solnit, A., x, xii
Spence, D., 266, 278, 281, 282, 283, 290,
    295–296, 297, 303
Steingart, I., 253, 261
Stekel, W., 26, 39
Stepansky, P., 58, 63
Stern, D., 152, 156
Stern, D. B., 152, 156
Stewart, W., 4, 12, 29n, 39
Stimmel, B., xii
Strachey, J., 22, 39, 45, 59, 63
Strenger, C., 296, 303
Sullivan, H., 142, 143, 149, 152, 156, 255
Sulloway, F., 14, 15, 16, 21, 22, 23, 27n,
    28n, 29, 31, 39, 52, 53, 63
Swales, P., 245n, 261
Sydenham, T., 7
Symington, N., 234, 236

Target, M., xv, 199n, 209, 210, 211, 283,
    294, 297, 300

Tarnowsky, B., 50, 63
Tatar, M., 9–11, 39
Thompson, C., ix–x, xi
Torok, M., 54n, 63
Trimble, M., 47, 63
Tyson, P., xii

van der Kolk, B., 15, 39
Veith, I., 6, 7, 39
von N., Frau Emmy, 19
von Paradies, M., 9

Waelder, R., 4, 39
Wallerstein, R., 295

Weil, S., 218, 219, 225, 240
Weisaeth, L., 15, 39
Wetzler, S., 295, 303
Whitman, W., 224, 225
Wilde, O., 148
Wilkinson, S., 234, 235
Willis, T., 7, 17
Wilson, E., 23, 39
Wineman, D., 137, 139
Winnicott, D., 204, 211, 223, 246, 248,
    249, 253, 261
Wittels, F., 59n, 63
Wolff, L., 24, 40
Wolstein, B., 155, 156
Wozniak, R., 7, 15, 16, 21, 40

Subject Index

Abuse, xiv, 15, 40, 63, 71, 86, 113, 178, 195, 201, 204, 205, 207, 209, 215, 216, 217, 219, 220, 224, 229, 230, 231, 233, 235, 237, 239, 261, 275, 276, 277, 283, 301, 303
  abuse conundrum, 287
  sexual, 23, 24, 29, 31, 49–52, 54, 59, 72, 77, 82, 112, 276, 287, 293, 302; *see also* Seduction
"Aetiology of Hysteria" (Freud), 49, 70
Alien other, 205, 209, 250
Alienist and Neurologist, 48
American Psychiatric Association, 107
American Psychoanalytic Association, 111
Analytic love, 232
Analytic trust, 248, 249, 250, 251, 252, 255, 256
Angstneurose, 48, 49, 52
Animal Magnetism, *see* Mesmerism
Anna O, case of, 12, 13, 39, 66
Anxiety avoidance, 149

Assault on Truth (Masson), 79
Auschwitz, 222

Bad enough object, 231
Bad internalized objects, 228
Bisexuality, 50
Borderline personality disorder, 112, 204, 208, 209, 215, 234, 255, 256–257
Boundary violations, 291

Capacity to be alone, 253
Caritas, 217
Castration, 67, 68, 72, 161, 166, 268, 288
Chains of memory, 21, 22, 67
Childhood
  emotional states, 162
  hysteria, *see* Hysteria
  onanism and, 24
  sexual behavior and, 25, 52–56, 71
  sexual disturbances and, 26
  sexuality and etiology of neurosis, 19, 56; *see also* Perversion, Seduction

311

"Coitus in Childhood" (Stekel and Freud), 26
Complemental series, 113, 160, 264, 266, 267, 290
Compromise formation, 186, 187
"Confusion of Tongues" (Ferenczi), 285, 291, 293
Constitutional state, 239
"Constructions in Analysis" (Freud), 119, 288
Constructivist point of view, 267
Containment, 233, 251
Correspondence theory, 296
Cumulative trauma, see Trauma

Dancing at Lughnasa (Friel), 235
Darwin's influence on Freud, 27n.7
Degeneration theory, 100
    perversion and, 26,
    vs. trauma theory, 47–48, 51–53
Diagnosis in clinical psychoanalysis, 270
Diagnostic and Statistical Manual, 112, 239, 286n.
Disidentification with the aggressor, 231
Dissociation, 70, 247, 248, 254, 256, 292
Dissociative disorder, 112
Dora, case of, 55
Drive theory, 55, 68, 289
Drowned and the Saved (Levi), 218
Dual therapeutic context, 209, 210
Dynamic psychiatry, 8

Empathic failure, 178
Enactments, 204, 210, 239, 248, 249, 250, 251, 277, 292, 297
Enlightenment (The)
    animal magnetism and, 8; see also Mesmerism
    development of dynamic psychiatry and, 8
    hypnosis and, 8
    hysteria and, 8
    ideas of seduction & psychopathology, 8

Entering the patient's world, 255
Eroticism, cult of, 22–23
Etiological equation, 27–28, 264
Études Cliniques sur l'Hystéro–épilepsie ou Grand Hystérie (Richer),16

Fantasy
    as a new kind of reality, 288
    as compromise, 94, 105
    biological ground for, 57, 101
    forcing, 292–293
    historical truth and; see Historical truth
    libido theory and, 55, 57–58
    masturbation and, 100
    primal, 289
    seduction theory and, 55–58, 66, 72, 73, 78, 94
    unconscious; see Unconscious
    undischarged impulses and, 44, 101
    vs. internal reality, 44, 101–102
    vs. external reality, 44, 45, 59, 85–95, 101–102, 104, 137–138, 159, 175, 178–179, 224, 235, 254, 264, 283, 284, 295–296, 297
"Female Sexuality" (Freud), 73
Fetishism, 192, 193–194
"Further Remarks on the Neuro–Psychoses of Defense" (Freud), 70

Gender, 268
Genesis
    etiology of neurosis and, 5
    Freud's self–analysis and, 6
    mother incest and, 6
Germ theory, 48, 51, 57

Historical truth, 55–60, 81, 82–83, 86, 92, 99, 143, 259–260, 272–273, 290
Holding, 233
Homosexuality, 50
Hypnoid states, 66
Hypnosis
    Breuer's use with Anna O., 12

development of dynamic psychiatry
    and, 8
emergence of, 8
erotic attachment and, 11–12
Freud's early use of, 12–13, 230; *see
    also* Mesmerism
hysteria and, 8
Mesmer and, 8; *see also* Mesmerism
traumatic hysteria and, 16
Hypnotismus und Suggestion (Benedikt),
    17
"Hypothesis of Infantile Sexuality"
    (Freud), 58
Hysteria
    as "nervous disease," 7
    as regression to complete lack of will,
       293
    Benedikt's role in theory of, 13–14
    Briquet's study of, 15
    Charcot and, 14–17
    childhood, 24
    contemporary significance of, 286n,
       287
    early sexual trauma and, 26, 47–50,
       67, 117
    external vs. psychic causes of, 69, 100
    fantasy and, 282, 286
    first identified, 6
    Galenic tradition and, 6–7
    hereditary vs. traumatic, 25, 55, 292
    humoral theory and, 7
    masturbation as cause of, 53
    paralytic symptoms and, 15
    paternal sexual abuse and, 52, 54
    prototype of disturbance in body &
       mind, 6
    role of uterus and, 5
    seduction and, 48–49, 72, 77, 118,
       263–264, 282
    sexuality and etiology of, 17–25, 67,
       117

"Incest and Incest Phantasies in Neurotic
    Families . . . " (Abraham), 284

Ich, 82
Idées fixes as Charcot's core of
    neuroses, 16
Immaculate perception, 266
Infantile Sexuality, 53, 58, 59, 88, 90,
    118, 179, 246n
Inhibitions, Symptoms and Anxiety
    (Freud), 73
Insight, definition of, 251–252
Internalization of good object, 253
Interpersonal field, 183
Interpersonal matrix, 155
Intrapsychic point of view, 290, 294, 297
*Introductory Lectures on
    Psycho–Analysis* (Freud), 103,
    266

King Lear, 85
Koch's postulates, 25, 48, 52

"Laying–on of the hands," 10
Les Passions de l'Âme (Descartes), 7
Libido
    as chemical substance, 68
    Benedikt's early use of, 14
    discovery of, 53
    dissenters to theory of, 58
    fantasy, seduction and, 55–58, 80; *see
       also* Fantasy
    functional disorder of and hysteria, 14
    theory, 55, 57–58, 68, 80, 264, 265
Library of Congress, 98
Little Hans, case of, 73, 163
Logic and seduction hypothesis, 28–31.
    See also Proton Pseudos
Logical positivists, 258, 259
Love and Fear of Flying (Bond), 135
Love as cure, 217, 219, 220–222,
    230–231, 232, 238, 240, 252

Magnetism. *See* Mesmerism
Masturbation
    as cause of neurosis, 48, 80, 92–93; *see
       also* Neurasthenia

as pathogenic act, 100–101
childhood sexuality and, 49, 54–55
defensive attempt to avoid memeory
    of, 54, 72
fantasy and, 100–101
Fliess and, 92
hysteria and, 53
traumatic sexual overstimulation and,
    53, 55, 80
Maternal nonresponsiveness, 204
Maturational process, 211
Medical community, Freud's relation to,
    46, 51–52, 56–60, 80–81, 98, 100,
    245, 246n
Memory
    falseness concerning, 54–57, 59, 78,
        83, 93
    objective, 292
    reconstructed, 126, 259, 289, 290,
        295, 296
    recovered, 78, 119, 131, 162, 178, 297
    repressed vs. unconscious fantasy, 131
    screen, 295
    traces, 289
Menninger Clinic, 233
Mesmerism
    as first treatment of neurosis, 8–9
    exorcism and, 11
    hypnosis, seduction and, 8
    magnetism (animal & sexual) and,
        8–11
    rapport and, 9–10
    sexual theories and, 10–11
    technique of fascination and, 9
    transference/countertransference and,
        11
Moses and Monotheism, 5, 289
Myth
    origins of neurosis and, 5
    origins of psychoanalysis and, 32, 265

Nachträglichkeit, 113
Nancy school of psychotherapeutics, 12,
    13

Narcissistic disequilibrium, 247, 248, 249
"Negation" (Freud), 73
Nervous disease, see Hysteria
Nervous shock, 47
Neurasthenia
    Gattel's testing for, 52
    Masturbation and, 24–25, 48, 80
    Sexuality and, 24–25, 48
Neurosciences, 94
Neurosis
    Charcot and theoretical development
        of, 16
    childhood seduction and, 26, 45–60,
        67, 287
    etiology of and The Bible, 5, 32
    fantasy as cause of, 55, 158, 284,
        287–288, 291
    hereditary disposition to, 52, 289
    mesmerism and treatment of, 9
    multiple etiologies of, 114
    negative of perversion, 50–51
    psychic reality and development of, 93,
        283, 287
    psychic shock and, 8, 47
    seduction as cause of, 282
    specific cause of, 161
    sexuality and development of, 18–22,
        92
    sexual toxins and, 7
    traumatic precipitants to, 26, 70, 290,
        291–292; see also Trauma
Neurosogenesis, 159, 160, 161, 163, 282,
    285, 289
Neurotica, 71, 72, 79, 91

Object relations, 73, 88, 90, 277, 286
Oedipal fantasies, 160
Oedipal phase, 163, 286
Oedipus complex, 53, 67, 74, 88, 105,
    158, 159, 161, 163, 166, 167, 223,
    238, 255, 268, 291, 293, 294
"On Hysteria" (Freud), 103
"On the History of the Psycho–Analytic
    Movement" (Freud), 58

Outline of Psycho–Analysis (Freud), 192, 289
Owning, 220–221, 223, 228, 270
Oxford English Dictionary, 111

Paradise Lost (Milton), 5
Paradoxia, 23
Parameters, 292
Parent blaming, 178, 270
Pediatric training, Freud and early psychoanalysis, 24
Pedophilia, 48, 50
Perception as creation, 94
Perversion
  childhood seduction and, 28, 50
  degeneration theory and, 26; *see also* Degeneration theory
  negative of neurosis, 50–51
  neurosis and, 28, 51
  polymorphous sexuality and, 28
Phylogenetic hypothesis, 289
Plato's theory of reminiscence and Freud, 22
Positivism, 69
Postdictive confirmation, 282
Postmodern, 55, 60, 107, 272
Posttraumatic paralysis, 15
Posttraumatic stress disorder, 107, 112, 286n.
Primal affects, 213
Primal fantasy; *see* Fantasy
Primal scene, 67, 120, 123
Primal seduction, 31–32
Prior Analyticus (Aristotle), 30
Projective identification, 81
Projective–introjective oscillations, 251
Project of 1895, 90
Proton Pseudos
  Aristotle and, 30
  as "false connection" or transference, 30
  seduction hypothesis and, 28–31
Protosymbol, 249
Psychic determinism and Freud, 27

Psychic pruning, 176, 182
Psychic reality, 82, 83, 93, 94, 102, 250, 252, 259, 273, 275, 283, 287–288, 291, 294, 295
Psychic shock; *see* Neurosis
Psychoanalysis
  as lacking a unified theory, 257
  contract therapy in, 209, 210
  interpretation in, 210, 223, 234, 248
  methodology of, 66, 184–185, 191–192, 208–211, 222–223, 233–234, 248–249, 270–272
  problem with external reality and, 283
  scientific potential of, 283
  situated between hermeneutics and science, 296
  vs. natural science, 182, 272, 296
Psychoanalytic playground, 246, 249, 257
Psycho–Lamarckian theory of biological inheritance, 289
Psychological deficit (Kohut), 114–115
Psychopathia Sexualis (Krafft–Ebing), 23
Psychopharmacology, 177, 209
Psychotherapeutics, 12; *see also* Nancy school

Rape, 15, 24, 31, 81, 275
Rapport
  mesmerism and, 9–10
  sexual magnetism and, 10; *see also* Mesmerism
  transference and, 10–11
Reality as holistic activity, 44, 101, 102; *see also* Fantasy vs. internal reality, vs. external reality. Psychic reality
Reconstructed truth, 92, *see also* Memory
Reconstruction of Trauma (Rothstein), 111
Reflected appraisals, 152
Reflective function, 204, 205, 210, 211, 233, 234, 250
Relatedness, 74, 75

Relational expectations, 148
Relational matrix, 183
Relational point of view, 88, 187, 254, 276
Repetition compulsion, 154, 284, 290
Replacement fallacy, 283–284
Rorschach test, 122

Scientia sexualis, 23
Scotomized, 192
Seduction
    ambiguity in concept of, 70–71, 74, 77, 79, 80, 81, 275
    as cause of hysteria, 28–29, 46–50, 67; see also Hysteria
    as contemporary umbrella concept, 31
    as screen phenomena, 295
    childhood and, 23–28, 48
    contrasted with trauma, 173–174
    earliest representation of, 4
    fantasy, and, 55–58, 73, 94, 285, 290; see also Fantasy
    Freud's earliest allusions to, 26
    Genesis and, 5, 32
    germ theory and, 48
    in psychoanalytic treatment, 43, 97, 102–103, 105, 203, 209, 230, 231, 245–246, 258, 277, 291
    Laplanche's generalized theory of, 32, 73, 81, 287
    mother's role in, 285–287, 289
    other terms to describe, 31
    paternal, 54, 78, 83, 98; see also Hysteria
    pathogenic sexual experiences and, 70–71
    perversion and, 50
    primal, 31–32
    psychosis, memory and, 52
    reconstructions of, 282, 283; see also Memory
    relatedness to caretakers and, 74, 79, 81, 275, 276; see also Relatedness

repression and, 50
    role of myth and, 5
    vs. abuse, 31, 275, 276, 287
    what Freud meant by, 31, 67
Seduction hypothesis
    as clinical hypothesis and evidence for, 28–29, 282–283, 284, 285, 293, 296–298
    as developmental stage, 293
    as metaphor, 68, 79, 88–89
    as screen memory in psychoanalysis, 179
    childhood hysteria, and, 24–25; see also Hysteria
    cultural context, and, 51–52, 245–246, 281
    etiological theories of, 3–4, 26–27, 51, 70
    fantasy and, 55–58, 66; see also Fantasy
    father's role and, 51, 59, 71–72, 78, 80, 86–88, 92, 98, 285, 294, 295
    first communicated by Freud, 3–4, 246
    first revision of, 53
    Freud's doubt/repudiation of, 29–31, 45, 52–53, 54, 56–57, 59, 72, 78, 79, 80, 106, 118, 159, 266, 294
    Freud's self–analysis and, 31, 87–88
    historical truth and, 55–57, 59; see also Historical truth
    key clinical issue embedded in, 273
    logical considerations and, 28–31
    mother's role and, 73
    notion of specific causes and, 53, 79, 87, 91, 104, 119, 126, 179
    origins of and repression, 3n, 50
    otherness of objects and, 73
    passivity and, 31
    prehistory of, 3–32
    repression and, 80
    role of transference in, 258
    scientific clarification of, 282–283
    sexological theories and, 50

subjective factors influencing, 30–31
vs. degeneration theory, 47; *see also*
    Degeneration
Sehnsucht (longing), 100
Self–analyzing function, 251
Selfobject transferences, 163, 169, 170,
    248, 255
Self psychology, 179, 184, 185, 254, 286
Sexology, 23, 50, 51, 52, 57, 79, 100
Sexual effects, delay of and trauma,
    26–28
Sexual magnetism; *see* Mesmerism
Sexual shock, 47
Sexual theory of trauma; *see* Trauma
Sexual toxins, 7; *see also* Neurosis
Shakespeare as Freud's model, 86, 94
Solipsistic projection, 266
Soul murder, 215, 217, 218, 222, 223,
    224, 225, 237, 252
Spellbound (Hitchcock), 118
Strain trauma, 181
Studies on Hysteria (Breuer & Freud), 72,
    106, 119
    Benedikt's relation to, 14
    seduction in psychoanalytic situation
        and, 103
    trauma theory and, 19, 47, 69
Suggestion
    Bernheim's book on, 12
    Ferenczi's use of, 292–293
    Freud's method of treatment and,
        117, 263
    psychotherapeutics and, 12
    rapport and, 10; *see also* Rapport

Tally argument, 296
Three Essays on the Theory of Sexuality,
    56n, 57, 68
*Traité Clinique et Thérapeutique de
    l'Hystérie* (Briquet), 15
Transference
    as "royal road," 184
    cycles, 249, 252, 257
    love, 89

metaphor and, 90
seduction hypothesis and, 30, 246–247
split the, 209
storage and memory systems, 257
Transitional space, 249
Transmuting internalization, 170–171
Trauma
    as crystallization of relational patterns,
        145, 153
    as explanation for nervous ills, 47
    as extreme regulatory measure, 131
    as incommensurate with precipitating
        event, 115
    as symbolically encoded memories,
        180, 181
    capacity for self–reflection and, 251
    childhood sexuality and, 23–28, 47–60
    cultural variance and, 121
    cumulative, 265
    definitions of, 111–112, 114, 121,
        130–132
    delayed effects of, 28, 74, 126; *see also*
        Sexual effects
    Descartes and, 7
    developmental phase and, 120, 159
    doing away with the language of, 188
    environment and, 174–175, 266
    external vs. fantasy, 79, 81, 82, 93,
        133, 137–138, 159–160, 224,
        266, 284; *see also* Fantasy
    growth enhancing and, 188, 277
    hypnosis, psychopathology and, 16
    hysteria and, 15–18, 69; *see also*
        Hysteria
    impact on total psychic functioning,
        126
    "is as trauma does," 121
    memory and, 131; *see also* Memory
    nineteenth century medicine and, 47
    of everyday life, 113–114, 121,
        125–126, 136–137, 158, 171,
        174–175, 180, 214, 237, 265,
        271, 276

ordinary vs. extraordinary, 273–274, 276
organismic, 182
pathogenesis and, 117–127, 179
preexisting psychic conflicts and, 122, 126
primal scene and, 120–121
psychological, definition of, 129, 132
repression and, 80, 119, 193
seduction as only one version of, 111
sensory stimulation and, 132
severe, 192, 193, 195–196, 200, 213–225, 229, 230, 231, 233, 234, 237, 271
sexual theory of, 53–54, 56, 80
stress vs., 188
subsequent life course and, 113
unconscious conflicts rising from, 126, 135
unconscious fantasies and, 131, 180; *see also* Unconscious
vertical splitting and, 131
World War I & II and, 107
Traumatogenic, 135, 136, 292
Traumatophilic diathesis, 284

"Two Analyses of Mr. Z" (Kohut), 274
Two projectors (Arlow's), 94, 101, 104, 267

Unconscious
fantasy, 94, 102, 180, 186, 215, 256, 267, 284, 289
indistinguishability of truth and fiction in, 52
instinctual, 102, 167
seduction and, 73, 81
theory of, 66

Validation, 177, 179, 183, 187, 232, 234, 269
Verführung (seduction), 71, 81
Vienna Medical School, 59
Vienna Polyclinic, 14
Vienna Society for Psychiatry and Neurology, 48
Vienna, University of, 93

Winnicott (Phillips), 223
Wolf Man, case of, 120, 288